MOUNT WHITNEY

THE COMPLETE TRAILHEAD-TO-SUMMIT GUIDE

MOUNT WHITNEY

SECOND EDITION

PAUL RICHINS, JR.

THE MOUNTAINEERS BOOKS

THE MOUNTAINEERS BOOKS
is the nonprofit publishing arm of The Mountaineers Club, an organization founded in 1906 and dedicated to the exploration, preservation, and enjoyment of outdoor and wilderness areas.

1001 SW Klickitat Way, Suite 201, Seattle, WA 98134

© 2008 by Paul Richins, Jr.

All rights reserved
First edition, 2001. Second edition, 2008.

Every reasonable attempt was made to secure permission for use of all quoted material in this book. Any publisher whose quoted material appears here without permission is invited to contact The Mountaineers Books.

No part of this book may be reproduced in any form, or by any electronic, mechanical, or other means, without permission in writing from the publisher.

Manufactured in the United States of America

Copy Editor: Joan Gregory
Cover, Book Design, and Layout: Mayumi Thompson
Cartographer: Ben Pease
Photographer: All photographs by Paul Richins, Jr., except where noted
Information on pages 57–59 and 61, Colin Fuller, M.D.; information on pages 73–74, Gene Leach; information on pages 77–80, John Moynier.

Cover photograph: *Sunrise reflection of Mount Whitney in a beautiful tarn below Iceberg Lake*
Page 1: *The east face of Mount Whitney and the Mountaineers Route as seen from the Whitney Portal Road*
Page 2: *The east buttress and the Mountaineers Route (Route 6)*

Library of Congress Cataloging-in-Publication Data
Richins, Paul, 1949-
  Mount Whitney : the complete trailhead to summit guide / Paul Richins. — 2nd ed.
      p. cm.
  Includes bibliographical references and index.
  ISBN 978-1-59485-042-4 (ppb)
  1. Hiking—California—Whitney, Mount—Guidebooks. 2. Whitney, Mount (Calif.)—Guidebooks. I. Title.
GV199.42.C22W455 2008
917.94'86—dc22
                                    2007041251

♻ Printed on recycled paper

In memory of my good friend Gene Leach, who at ages 65, 68, and 71 hiked Routes 10, 5, and 7, climbing Mounts Langley, Whitney, Tyndall, Williamson, Russell, and Muir. And, at age 73, four months after quadruple heart bypass surgery, completed the Circumnavigation Route of Whitney (Route 7), ascending Mount Russell and Mount Whitney en route. And, at age 76, rode his mountain bike and hiked to the top of White Mountain (third highest peak in California) as a tune-up for Route 11, in which he carried a full pack to Trail Crest (13,600 feet) before scampering to the summit of Whitney. Gene has been a lifelong friend and inspiration to all of us.

He will be forever missed.

CONTENTS

Opposite: Mount Whitney, the Mountaineers Route, and camp at Iceberg Lake in April

FOREWORD

In 1954 I approached the top of Mount Whitney as a pilgrim might approach Mecca. Having dreamed of this moment for several years, I raced up that final level path with my heart thumping—and not just from the altitude.

I had been lucky enough to attend the first-ever Sierra Club Wilderness Base Camp, and one of the lures of this ten-day outing was the possibility of climbing Whitney at the end, if the weather cooperated. It did, and that stifling August day still sparks my memory. How thrilled I was to stand on the highest spot in the Lower 48! Far below, to the east, the dull Owens Valley quivered in the haze. In the other three directions rose uncountable peaks, nameless and unclimbed as far as I knew. This wasn't true, but the mystery seized me. My mountaineering career began at this very moment. I was thirteen.

I've been back to those sere summit rocks three times since, by various routes. Much of the attraction, of course, is that the highest spot of the contiguous forty-eight states is a desirable goal simply because of its preeminent position. Yet Whitney's human history also draws me in. The striplings King and Cotter named the mountain for their boss but ended up on the wrong peak, and Josiah Whitney must have been both pleased and pained. King's later failures even now make us cringe. John Muir's shunning of the easy way up makes us aware of challenges then and now. The Smithsonian experiments cause us to ponder the heavens. The pioneering ascent of the formidable east face alerts us to the "impossible." All these stories, so well related by Paul Richins in this book, add spice to the ascent, no matter which route you take.

Although the summit of Whitney is the end result of each hike described herein, it's the chase rather than the conquest that will appeal to many readers. Days might go by before you reach the summit, and these might well be the best days of your life. The interior of the High Sierra, invisible from any road and visited by few people, is one of the magical spots on our planet. Elegant lakes occupy grand cirques. Streams of diamond clarity dart toward the canyons below. Marmots whistle from the talus, and mountain bluebirds hawk for insects near their nests in golden snags. Wildflowers. Meadows. Paradise.

Many of the routes Richins has chosen lie in timberline country, the narrow zone lying between the lowland forests and the naked crags above. Traveling through this region usually is easy, and the vistas are endless. On a clear day—which is the rule during the summer and early fall—you can reach out and touch peaks a dozen miles away, or so it seems. Sometimes thunderstorms disturb the calm, and shadows race each other across the landscape. The mountains tremble and the wind howls. What a time to be setting up camp and gazing out into a true wilderness!

Paul Richins knows this region as few do. His love for the Range of Light shines on every page, and I hope that more books from him are in the offing. I'll look forward to them.

—*Steve Roper*

PREFACE TO THE SECOND EDITION

Each year more than 30,000 outdoor enthusiasts secure a wilderness permit to climb Mount Whitney, while many others are less fortunate and fail to obtain the required permit. Of those who attempt the peak, only one in three actually reach the lofty summit. The advice in this second edition of *Mount Whitney: The Complete Trailhead-to-Summit Guide* is designed to help you succeed where so many others may have failed. The information will increase your chances not only of standing on the top of the highest peak in the Lower 48, but also of reaching the summit safely.

What distinguishes this guidebook is that it not only features the popular Mount Whitney Trail but also details fourteen other trails and cross-country hiking routes from 12 to 96 miles long. Each route passes through some of the finest mountain scenery and most exhilarating terrain in America, ending atop the coveted granite-block summit.

The first edition was published in 2001. Second, third, fourth, and fifth printings quickly followed, demonstrating the book's value and popularity. This second edition has been updated and expanded. Three new routes, nine route variations, numerous side trips, daily itineraries, camping recommendations, a detailed discussion of going light, a new chapter on climbing Whitney in the winter, and an appendix that lists the routes by difficulty have been added.

Additionally, over the past couple of years I have received numerous suggestions and route description refinements from readers. Thank you for the feedback—I appreciate your excellent ideas and observations. Many of these suggestions have been included and will prove to be valuable additions.

With the late Walt Wheelock's booklet *Climbing Mount Whitney* in hand, I first ascended the Whitney Trail over the Thanksgiving holiday break from college more than 35 years ago. It was a brisk Thanksgiving morning. The temperature had dipped to twelve degrees Fahrenheit at my tent at Trail Camp. Fresh snow covered the ground and ice encrusted the nearby tarn. Despite the cold, I was up at dawn ready to climb. I ascended toward Trail Crest with great anticipation. With each step, I broke through the fresh snow to my knees. The climbing was arduous but the adrenaline was flowing and I pressed on, excited to be on the mountain for the first time. I finally reached Trail Crest and then the summit that glorious morning, a solitary climber alone on the mountain, inspired by the solitude and energized by the mountain's rugged beauty.

Over the years I have returned often to share the mountain's glory with friends and explore the uniqueness of each season. Two more recent adventures were particularly memorable. In the winter of 1998, in blowing snow and poor visibility, I ascended and then skied from near the summit via the Mountaineers couloir (Route 6). Again, I was alone on the mountain that day with Prince, my American Eskimo dog. On the summit we huddled on the lee side of the stone hut to escape the howling wind, relax and eat lunch, and to absorb the glorious moment. After spending an hour, we headed back to the safety of the tent at Iceberg Lake. My ski descent was not elegant, but I survived without mishap.

In the winter of 2003, in a classic adventure, Prince and I spent six days circling this magnificent mountain via the Mountaineers Route, Whitney–Russell Col, Arctic Lake, Guitar Lake, Crabtree Lakes, Sky-Blue Lake, and out to Whitney Portal via Meysan Lake. This is one of my most prized winter experiences. Chapter 4, "Whitney in Winter," has been added for those desiring to explore the mountain when it is blanketed with snow and ice.

This guidebook will help hikers and backpackers of all ages and abilities experience the splendor and rugged beauty of the mountain and its surrounding wilderness. Ascending this great peak is not technically difficult but requires thoughtful planning, superior physical stamina, perseverance, and, ideally, a lightly loaded pack. Whether you are planning your first ascent, have climbed the mountain many times before, or are considering a winter climb, this primer will equip you with the knowledge for a safe and successful adventure.

No one is too young or too old to aspire to the lofty summit of this, the highest peak in the land. In so doing, you too may be inspired to new personal heights. With an excellent trail to the summit and a variety of approaches, Mount Whitney has something for everyone. The array of hiking routes and trailheads described herein should broaden even the most accomplished climber's wilderness horizons. Regardless of the route you ascend, the experience will return immeasurable memories for years to come.

Your questions and feedback are encouraged (prichins@jps.net).

Happy Climbing!!!

—*Paul Richins, Jr.*

A NOTE ABOUT SAFETY

There are inherent risks in hiking, backpacking, and winter climbing: rockfall, avalanches, snowstorms, rain, high winds, lightning, hypothermia, mountain sickness, and the unexpected emergency. All pose varying hazards for the backcountry traveler. Although the author and publisher have done their best to provide accurate information, conditions change from day to day and from year to year. It is presumed that the users of this guidebook possess the requisite hiking, backpacking, and winter climbing skills for safe travel in the mountains and are proficient in using compass and map for navigation. The author and publisher disclaim any liability for injury or other damage by anyone hiking, backpacking, climbing, or camping in areas described in this guidebook or traveling to and from these outings.

Safety is an important concern in all outdoor activities. No guidebook can alert you to every hazard or anticipate the limitations of every reader. Therefore, the descriptions of roads, trails, routes, and natural features are not representations that a particular place or excursion will be safe for your party. When you follow any of the routes described in this book, you assume responsibility for your own safety. Under normal conditions, such excursions require the usual attention to traffic, road and trail conditions, weather, terrain, the capabilities of your party, and other factors. Keeping informed on current conditions and exercising common sense are the keys to a safe, enjoyable outing.

—*Paul Richins, Jr. and The Mountaineers Books*

AUTHOR'S NOTE OF CAUTION

This guidebook includes detailed descriptions of fifteen hiking routes of which ten follow well-maintained trails over their entire distance to the summit of Whitney. The remaining five routes (Routes 4, 6, 7, 9, and 10) and several route variations combine cross-country travel over seldom-trodden trail-less terrain with trial hiking. The cross-country segments of these routes are difficult and strenuous, and should not be attempted unless you are proficient with map and compass, have extensive route-finding experience, are in superior physical condition, and can scramble across rugged terrain (cliffs, boulders, granite slabs, and unstable talus) with a heavy pack.

—*Paul Richins, Jr.*

1 THE MOUNTAIN

*On the very edge of the world of man, standing upon the
summit which had been the magic focus of his dreams,
the young mountaineer lifted up his body, his heart, his
soul and his secret longings. As far as the eye could see
a realm of snow and rock lay stretched out before him,
wrapped in the silence and mystery of the infinite. It was
like being in another world; the mountains seemed less a
part of this planet than an entirely independent kingdom,
unique and mysterious, where, to venture forth, all that
was needed was the will and the love.*
—Gaston Rébuffat, *from* On Snow and Rock, *1963*

FROM THE SMALL TOWN OF LONE PINE along US 395, the rugged east face
escarpment of the Sierra Nevada rises precipitously from the semi-arid
desert floor of Owens Valley to the lofty 14,491-foot summit of Mount
Whitney. This defiant and nearly impenetrable monolithic wall of granite blocks the way to Whitney's grand summit, adding to the challenges
faced by hikers and rock climbers seeking to scale the highest peak in
the contiguous 48 states.

The 13-mile drive from Lone Pine to the Whitney Portal trailhead re-
veals dramatic views of the mountain's east face and provides glimpses of
hidden scenic treasures lying beyond the end of the road. The beauty and
splendor of Mount Whitney and the Sierra Nevada wilderness are beyond
compare, encompassing the most diverse and extraordinary topography
imaginable. This is a land of high adventure, uninterrupted by roads and
civilization. This unbroken chain of mountains offers an endless variety
of outdoor opportunities stretching nearly the length of California.

The Sierra Nevada is a unique and unforgettable region of extremes—a
land of perpetual sunshine and semi-perpetual snow. It is home to the
deepest canyon in North America (Kings River Canyon), the largest living thing on earth (the giant sequoia), and of course, the highest peak
in the Lower 48 (Mount Whitney). Just across the Owens Valley in the
White Mountains is the world's oldest living thing (the bristlecone pine),
and not far away is Death Valley, the hottest, driest, and lowest spot in
North America.

The satisfaction that comes from exploring the Sierra Nevada backcountry and climbing Mount Whitney is the opportunity to go beyond
the relatively insignificant outer edge of the wilderness and immerse

oneself in its grandeur. To fully appreciate all that the mountains have to offer, experience the wilderness firsthand. Hike backcountry trails, explore cross-country routes, walk alongside cascading mountain streams, enjoy lush meadows and colorful wildflowers, before scrambling up Whitney's rugged slopes. It is this opportunity to personally experience nature that is so rewarding.

There is no finer wilderness experience than to cross a high-mountain pass and view the vast pristine wilderness, ascend a nearby summit, camp next to a secluded alpine lake nestled in an ancient glacial cirque, or watch the brilliant alpenglow of a sunrise/sunset splash across the sheer granite walls of a nearby summit. From these magnificent high places, the grandeur of the Sierra Nevada stretches as far as the eye can see, miles. and miles of rock on rock, mountain on mountain. One returns from such experiences refreshed and invigorated. To paraphrase Steve Roper, author of *The Climber's Guide to the High Sierra*, it may be days before you reach Whitney's celebrated summit but it is the chase rather than the conquest

The east face of Whitney with Mount Muir in the background (Routes 6 and 7); the Whitney Trail (Route 8) traverses the snow on the far left.

that is so appealing. And those days exploring the Sierra Nevada back-country may well be the best of your life.

Sir Francis Younghusband, in *Mount Everest: The Reconnaissance* (1921), made the following observation: " . . . to those who have struggled with them, the mountains reveal beauties they will not disclose to those who make little effort. That is the reward the wilderness bestows on those who exert themselves. And, it is because they have so much to give and grant it lavishly, that men [and women] go back again and again to the mountains they love. . . . the mountains reserve their choicest gifts for those who stand upon their lofty summits."

The beauty and sheer size of the Sierra Nevada are remarkable. Its crown jewels—Lake Tahoe and three fabulous national parks (Yosemite, Sequoia, and Kings Canyon)—are world-renowned for their splendor. The borders of the Sierra Nevada encompass a region larger than the entire European Alps—the French, Swiss, Austrian, and Italian Alps combined.

This unique mountain range was formed over many millions of years through a series of uplifts that pushed the great Sierra Block upward and tilted it toward the west. From a geologic perspective, the range is essentially a gigantic granite block 350 miles long and 40 to 80 miles wide that has been tilted on its side. While the Sierra Block was being pushed upward, the land to the east began to drop thousands of feet, creating the impressive east face of the range that is readily seen from US 395. This explains why the east side of the range is so precipitous while the slopes on the west gradually rise to the crest over many miles.

The Sierra Nevada begins near Lassen Volcanic National Park and continues south to Mount Whitney, ending at Tehachapi Pass. The range runs generally north and south along the eastern side of the state, forming the geographic backbone of California. The Sierra Nevada gradually increases in elevation from north to south in a surprisingly orderly manner. The highest peaks in the north, near Lake Tahoe, barely reach 10,000 feet. Moving south along the crest, one encounters progressively higher and higher peaks: 11,000-foot peaks appear for the first time near Sonora Pass (Highway 108), 12,000-footers begin east of Bridgeport in the Sawtooth area, and 13,000-foot summits initially emerge in the Yosemite high country. The first 14,000-foot peak does not appear until the Palisades region (south of Bishop), 250 miles south of the start of the range.

Five of the Sierra Nevada's eleven 14,000-foot peaks tower above the magical 14,000-foot level, jutting skyward in the Palisades region. These peaks are some of the most rugged in California and the glaciers that cling to the escarpment are the largest in the Sierra Nevada. The north-facing couloirs, filled with snow and ice, are challenging ice climbs for experienced mountaineers and comprise the most alpine region of the state.

These magnificent peaks are soon followed by the remaining six 14,000-foot peaks of the Whitney region. The Sierra Nevada culminates atop Mount Whitney's towering summit. Mount Langley, 6 miles to the south, is the last 14,000-foot peak in the range. From this point the mountains rapidly decrease in elevation, ending near Mojave. Appendix 1 contains a list of California's 14,000-foot peaks.

HISTORY—A SHORT RECORD OF THE PAST

The Sierra Nevada received its name from Fray Pedro Font, who, in April 1776, spotted the range from a hill east of the contemporary town of Antioch. *Sierra Nevada* is Spanish for "snowy mountain range." *Sierra* is the word for "saw" and when used in this context means "jagged range of mountains"—the teeth of the saw being similar to a row of mountain peaks. In describing what he saw, Font wrote:

"If we looked to the east we saw on the other side of the plain at a distance of some thirty leagues a great Sierra Nevada, white from the sum- mit to the skirts, and running diagonally almost from south-southeast to north-northeast."

Unlike Mount Shasta, Mount Rainer, and Mount Hood, which are clearly visible for miles in all directions, Mount Whitney is discernible from only a few select locations. From the north, south, and west, Whit- ney cannot be seen from any road, only from remote backcountry loca- tions in Sequoia and Kings Canyon National Parks. From the east, the peak can be observed only from a limited number of points in Owens Valley and only briefly along Highway 395. When viewed from the east near Lone Pine, the mountain does not dominate the view, nor is it read- ily apparent that it is the highest peak in the range.

Mount Shasta was identified as early as 1788, Mount Rainier and Mount Hood in 1792, but Mount Whitney was not discovered until July 2, 1864, nearly ninety years after the Sierra Nevada was named by Font. William Brewer and Charles Hoffman of the California State Geological Survey field party first sighted Whitney from the remote and rugged slopes of Mount Brewer, nearly 15 miles to the north. Clar- ence King and Richard Cotter were also a part of the survey party and were anxious to climb the distant peak, as it was obviously the highest in the region.

Clarence King's passion to be the first to climb Whitney resulted in

Twin Lakes along the JMT and Mount Clarence King (right of center) and Mount Brewer (left of center)

three failed attempts in the 1860s and early 1870s. His two most notable attempts were in 1864 and 1871. On July 2, 1864, after spotting the peak from Mount Brewer, King and Cotter set out to hike across 15 miles of unexplored terrain. On July 6, 1864, after several days of arduous cross-country travel, they made the first ascent of Mount Tyndall (14,019 feet) and spotted the mountain of their desires still 6 miles away. Lacking adequate provisions to continue, they returned to their base camp below Mount Brewer.

On seeing Mount Whitney from Mount Tyndall, Clarence King wrote, "Mt. Whitney, as we afterwards called it in honor of our chief, is probably the highest land within the United States. Its summit looked glorious, but inaccessible." (Their boss, Josiah Dwight Whitney, was a professor of geology at Harvard and chief of the California State Geological Survey from 1860 to 1874.)

In 1871 King again attempted to climb Mount Whitney but failed. Proclaiming to the world that he had climbed Whitney, he had actually climbed Mount Langley (6 miles south of his goal). It was an overcast day and he could not see Mount Whitney a short distance to the north.

Two years later, on August 18, 1873, Whitney was finally climbed by three local fishermen from Lone Pine: Charley Begole, Johnny Lucas, and Al Johnson. They named the peak Fishermans Peak, but the name did not stick. Clarence King at last climbed the peak on September 19, 1873. When he reached the summit, he was disappointed to learn that he was not the first but rather the tenth one up (see Appendix 6).

On October 21 of that same year, John Muir made the first ascent via what is today called the Mountaineers Route (Route 6). Muir's climb was unique because all the previous climbs were made from Crabtree Meadow and Guitar Lake on the west side. His climb was a direct ascent from the east.

Hope Broughton, Mary Martin, Anna Mills, and Mrs. Redd (her first name was not recorded) were the first women to reach the summit, climbing the peak in 1878. They approached the peak from the west, coming all the way from Visalia on horseback. At the base of the mountain, possibly near Crabtree Meadow or Guitar Lake, they left their horses and ascended the peak's west slopes.

Other women of the nineteenth century ventured into the high Sierra, and at least one inadvertently left evidence of her presence. While climbing Mount Hitchcock in September 1999, I found a woman's high-heeled shoe on the sandy slopes due south of Discover Pinnacle. The shoe dated back to the 1800s and dozens of square nails were holding it together.

The other major peaks in the region were soon climbed, with the exception of Mount Russell, which because of its difficult rock faces and exposed ridges was not climbed until 1926 by Norman Clyde.

In 1904, the people of Lone Pine raised the necessary funds to build a horse trail to the summit of Mount Whitney, which they rebuilt and repaired in 1909. This trail allowed the Smithsonian Institution to erect a stone shelter near the top for use by their astronomers and other scientists. Mount Whitney became the site of many scientific experiments in the late 1800s and early 1900s. The U.S. Weather Service conducted experiments and observations on the summit for twenty years. The hut is still used today as an emergency shelter but was the site of at least one lightning strike death of a hiker who took refuge there during a thunderstorm. The shelter has since been grounded but is not considered safe during a thunder and lightning storm.

The Mount Whitney Trail was again rebuilt and realigned in 1928–30. After World War II, the U.S. Forest Service realigned the trail one last time. With the aid of a large compressor, an excellent trail with ninety-seven switchbacks was blasted from the rocky buttress between Trail Camp and Trail Crest. This new trail, the one used today, bypassed dangerous rock slides and snowfields that often blocked the old trail until late summer.

During the time the Whitney Trail was being built and rebuilt, the residents of the area formed the "Inyo Better Roads Club." It was the group's goal to improve US 395, as the journey from Los Angeles took two days. As the roads improved in the early years of the century, the eastern Sierra became a Hollywood playground. Actor Lon Chaney built a cabin on Pine Creek under the Palisades, and Rock Creek Lodge became known as "Little Switzerland." Many Western movies were filmed east of Lone Pine just off the Whitney Portal Road on Movie Road A and B, and automobile and truck commercials are still filmed in the area.

The popularity of the peak has grown over the past forty years, as evidenced by those recording their names in the summit register. In 1957, 2658 signed the summit register. By 2004 this number had grown to approximately 13,200. Appendix 6 includes detailed data on the number of hikers and climbers reaching the summit each year and an interesting list of Mount Whitney firsts.

JUST HOW HIGH IS MOUNT WHITNEY?

The height of the mountain has been the subject of much speculation and debate over the years. Even today you will see incorrect elevations in books, on maps, and embossed on hats and shirts. The most common incorrect elevations are 14,494 feet, 14,495 feet, and 14,497 feet.

Using the best barometer technology of the 1870s, John Muir noted in his writings that the elevation of Whitney approached 14,700 feet. Later measurements and publications reported elevations of 14,501 feet, 14,497 feet, 14,496 feet, and 14,494 feet. The summit sign placed on September 5, 1930, commemorating the completion of the John Muir Trail (JMT), "the highest trail in the United States," fixed the elevation at 14,496.811 feet. However, the most recent U.S. Geological Survey (USGS) 7.5-minute map establishes the height of the summit at 4416.9 meters (3.2808 feet per meter x 4416.9 meters = 14,490.97 feet).

At 14,491 feet, Mount Whitney is the highest peak in California as well as in the 48 contiguous states. Hikers from throughout California, the United States, and the world covet the privilege of standing on its prestigious summit block. All this attention makes Whitney the most frequently climbed peak in the Sierra Nevada (excluding Half Dome in Yosemite National Park).

HOW TO USE THIS GUIDEBOOK

HIKING VS. CLIMBING

The word "climbing" is used throughout this guide and is employed interchangeably with the words "hiking," "backpacking," and "trekking." No technical rock-climbing skills involving rope management and hardware are necessary for the trails and hiking routes featured in this guidebook.

Route titles containing the word "trail," as in "Bishop Pass Trail," involve trail hiking only. Those with the word "route," as in "University Pass Route," require cross-country travel to link one trail with another.

Each year 30,000 hikers with diverse skills and various levels of preparedness attempt to reach the magnificent summit of Whitney. I have observed an unsteady eighty-year-old woman with tattered tennis shoes and no socks inching her way up the trail above Trail Crest without even a walking stick for assistance; joggers wearing only shorts and windbreakers with water bottles in hand; backpackers with all types of unnecessary gear strapped to the outside of their overburdened packs; discouraged hikers at Trail Crest, blue around the gills, looking and

Opposite: The east face escarpment of the Sierra Nevada with Mount Whitney in the background

feeling as if they were going to die from the effects of the altitude; and fathers with young children starting out at Whitney Portal with high hopes of reaching the top. In just three days hiking along the John Muir Trail, I met two couples from Wisconsin with their five children ages seven to eleven years, a couple from England, two chaps from Australia, three fellows from Minnesota, and another from Germany, all hiking from Yosemite to Whitney. Whatever route you travel, you are likely to meet some of the nicest people in the world.

Whether you are planning your first ascent of Mount Whitney, have climbed the peak before, or are contemplating a winter attempt, this guidebook will help you avoid the mistakes of others and will equip you with the necessary information for a safe and successful trip. Critical information on planning, preparation, gear, food, mountain medicine, and wilderness permit requirements is detailed in Chapters 2 and 3. Advice for climbing Whitney in the winter is covered in Chapter 4.

Fifteen terrific hiking routes culminating on the summit are described in Chapters 5 and 6. Eleven routes begin on the east side of the Sierra Nevada crest and four begin on the west side in Sequoia and Kings Canyon National Parks. Of the fifteen trails/hiking routes, ten (Routes 1–3, 5, 8, and 11–15) follow well-maintained trails over their entire length. Five others (Routes 4, 6, 7, 9, and 10) require some cross-country travel over seldom-trodden trail-less terrain in combination with trail hiking.

All the hikes are challenging, demanding a good measure of stamina and perseverance. The cross-country routes are considerably more difficult than the hikes that follow trails over their entire course. The routes requiring cross-country travel should not be attempted by hikers with little or no previous routefinding experience. Inexperienced hikers lacking proficiency in the use of a compass and map may find themselves off route and on dangerously steep terrain. The cross-country routes should be attempted only by the most experienced and well-conditioned backcountry hikers.

Routefinding on cross-country routes can be simplified with the use of a Global Positioning System (GPS) receiver. These instruments, if used correctly, can be invaluable in all types of weather conditions. The GPS receiver can point the way, informing you of the direction and distance to a critical point, and can be particularly useful in a storm when visibility is limited. On an east–west ski traverse of the Sierra Nevada, a GPS receiver was instrumental in guiding us over a 12,000-foot pass in a blizzard with zero visibility. With only a map and compass, we would not have found the small notch in the ridge that we had to traverse.

Iceberg Lake as viewed from atop Mount Whitney

The Mountaineers Route (Route 6 and the first day of Route 7) includes universal transverse mercator (UTM) coordinates at eleven critical points along the route. These were taken in the field. UTM coordinates can also be taken directly from a map and stored in your GPS receiver before you leave on your trip. Since most maps are based on North American Datum 1927, that is what was used in this book. The North American Datum 1927 UTM grid coordinates for the summit of Whitney are 384490mE and 4048710mN. The first UTM grid value represents the easterly coordinate in meters (mE) and the second value the northerly coordinate in meters (mN). For a more detailed discussion of UTM coordinates and GPS, refer to the glossary (Appendix 7).

The table on pages 28 and 29 summarizes the fifteen routes described in this guidebook. You will notice that several routes have major variations or detours. These are indicated with an alpha and numeric designation, such as V1.1. These route variations provide you with additional options when planning your excursion. Some may avoid difficult cross-county terrain, others may add strenuous travel, while others provide a convenient shortcut. In Appendix 2 the routes and route variations are arranged according to their difficulty and distance.

The Route Descriptions—The Headings Explained

Each route description begins with the following information, presented in list form and providing a quick overview of the hike/climb:

- starting point
- ending point
- difficulty rating
- distance
- elevation gain/loss
- trip duration
- necessary maps
- major access road(s) and nearest town
- car shuttle requirements

After the above list of key information, each route description includes the following tables, graphs, and narrative descriptions. Each route is also clearly charted on one or more maps (see Maps).

- a trail profile graph illustrating the ups and downs of the route
- "In a Nutshell" summary providing an informative narrative overview of the route
- "How to Get There" driving directions to the trailhead
- identification of the trailhead facilities, such as campgrounds, resorts, and nearby stores
- location of wilderness bear-proof food storage boxes placed by the National Park Service
- trail profile table summarizing the distance between mileposts, the cumulative total, and the elevation gain/loss between each milepost
- detailed, day-by-day narrative description of the route
- discussion of route variations, side trips, peak scrambles

Most of the above categories require no further explanation. For those that would benefit from a discussion of how to use the information, an explanation is provided below.

The Ratings Explained

When a route includes both trail hiking and cross-country travel, the number of miles for each is provided. Off-trail travel (designated "x-c" for "cross-country) may be over well-defined climbers trails or "use trails," or over rugged, trail-less terrain requiring excellent routefinding skills. When routes ascend one or more passes, that information is also provided in the "Rating Class" section.

Each hiking route has been given one or more ratings to describe its overall level of difficulty. The standard system for rating mountain climbs is called the Yosemite System. It was first introduced by the Sierra Club in 1937. The system is a general guide to assist in determining the difficulty of a climb. It is geared to technical rock climbing, but the lower end of the scale is used to describe trail hiking, cross-country travel, and rock scrambling over uneven, difficult terrain. The system is as follows:

Class 1 (C-1): Trail walking. This includes all the maintained trails covered in this guidebook: Routes 1–3, 5, 8, and 11–15.

Class 2 (C-2): Includes hiking and scrambling over uneven terrain, through brush, and up and around rock bluffs, steep gullies, scree, and talus, where hands may be needed for balance. Routes 4, 7, and 10 are Class 2. Route 9 is Class 2+, which denotes slightly more difficult terrain than Class 2.

Class 3 (C-3): Terrain becomes steeper and the exposure increases. Arms and hands are used for balance and leverage. Handholds are easily identified but there is an increased risk of falling and being injured. Some inexperienced hikers may desire a roped belay over certain Class 3 terrain. Route 6 and the east ridge of Mount Russell (PS6.1) are predominately Class 2 and 2+ but some may consider certain portions of these climbs Class 3.

Class 4: Terrain is steep and exposed. Most climbers need a rope for protection. Skill and a thorough knowledge of climbing procedure and rope techniques are necessary. Handholds are smaller and less defined. There is a greater risk of falling and injury. Falling could result in a broken leg or arm or even more serious injury. No Class 4 routes are described in this guide.

Class 5: This begins the ratings for technical rock climbing, using rope and hardware. It demands experience and knowledge of climbing techniques and rope management. A fall could result in death. Class 5 climbing is broken into a decimal system of ratings from 5.0 through 5.14. The east face of Whitney contains a number of classic 5.4 through 5.8 climbing routes. No Class 5 routes are included in this guidebook.

Route Number and Name	Rating/Class
Eastside Trails	
1. Bishop Pass Trail	Trail hiking (C-1)
V1.1. Palisades Basin	7.9 miles x-c, w/3 passes (C-2/2 +)
2. Taboose Pass Trail	Trail hiking (C-1)
3. Kearsarge Pass Trail	Trail hiking (C-1)
4. University Pass Route	3.6 miles x-c w/1 pass (C-2)
5. Shepherd Pass Trail	Trail hiking (C-1)
6. Mountaineers Route	10.8 miles x-c (C-2/2 + /3)
7. Circumnavigation Route of Whitney	7.4 miles x-c w/1 pass (C-2)
8. Mount Whitney Trail	Trail hiking (C-1)
9. Meysan Lake Route	14.6 miles x-c w/6 passes x-c (C-2/2 +)
V9.1. LeConte–Mallory Pass	13.6 miles x-c w/6 passes (C-2/2 +)
10. New Army Pass Route	7.5 miles x-c w/1 pass (C-2)
V10.1. Lower Solider Lake	5.7 miles x-c w/1 passes (C-2)
11. Cottonwood Pass Trail	Trail hiking (C-1)
V11.1. Return to Horseshoe Meadow	Trail hiking (C-1)
Westside Trails	
12. Bubbs Creek Trail	Trail hiking (C-1)
V12.1. Woods Creek	Trail hiking (C-1)
V12.2. Thunder Pass	7.4 miles x-c w/1 passes (C-2)
13. Avalanche Pass Trail	Trail hiking (C-1)
V13.1. Sugarloaf Trail	Trail hiking (C-1)
V13.2. Silliman Pass Trail	Trail hiking (C-1)
14. High Sierra Trail	Trail hiking (C-1)
V14.1. Whitney Creek cutoff	3.0 miles x-c/no passes (C-2)
15. Farewell Gap Trail	Trail hiking (C-1)

Distance (miles)	Elevation Gain (feet)	Trip Duration (days)	Car Shuttle	Nearest Town
96.4	20,911	7–10	Yes	Bishop
92.2	19,938	7–10	Yes	Bishop
75.4	20,279	5–8	Yes	Big Pine
50.6	11,651	4–7	Yes	Independence
43.0	11,631	4–6	Yes	Independence
41.8	11,711	4–6	Yes	Independence
12.4	6,126	1–3	No	Lone Pine
24.6	7,866	3–5	No	Lone Pine
22.0	6,486	1–3	No	Lone Pine
28.8	11,961	4–6	No	Lone Pine
27.8	11,866	4–6	No	Lone Pine
36.9	9,051	4–7	Yes	Lone Pine
38.4	8,451	4–7	Yes	Lone Pine
42.4	8,323	5–7	Yes	Lone Pine
62.8	11,715	6–8	No	Lone Pine
53.9	13,656	5–8	Yes	Fresno
68.5	16,034	6–8	Yes	Fresno
53.9	13,256	5–8	Yess	Fresno
65.0	16,969	5–8	Yes	Fresno
63.4	13,391	5–8	Yes	Fresno
73.7	16,091	5–8	Yes	Fresno
73.5	15,531	6–8	Yes	Three Rivers
66.7	15,091	5–8	Yes	Three Rivers
72.2	16,268	6–9	Yes	Three Rivers

Distance

The mileage for "Distance" is for the *entire* trip, from the trailhead to the summit and out. Routes 6, 8, and 9 are round-trip hikes, following their approach route to the summit and back out. All other routes are one way, beginning at an eastside or westside trailhead, ascending the Whitney summit, and then descending to Trail Camp to exit via the Mount Whitney Trail to Whitney Portal.

To ensure an acceptable level of accuracy regarding the distance of each route, many sources were checked, including Tom Harrison Maps, USGS 7.5-minute and 15-minute maps, U.S. Forest Service data, previously printed guidebooks, and trail signs. Unfortunately, discrepancies abound and no two sources seem to agree on many of the basics of elevation and distance. Therefore, the distances should be considered educated approximations.

Some hikers have expressed a frustration that some of the distances between destination points, as provided in the first edition of this book and used on various maps, seem too short. This may be a fair observation but one must remember that hiking over steep terrain with a heavy backpack at these high elevations requires considerably more effort than hiking at lower elevations and distances may seem longer than expected.

Elevation Gain/Loss

Where exact elevations are not marked on a map, the elevations of lakes, passes, trail junctions, and peaks are estimated using USGS maps and Tom Harrison Maps. For each trail segment and for the overall distance of the route, I estimated the amount of elevation gained and lost. This was not a simple comparison of the elevation at the start and end points of each trail segment but includes an estimate of the ups and downs along the way. Because of the limited accuracy of the maps, only large undulations in the trail—those greater than 80 feet—have been captured. Consequently, the actual elevation gain/loss will be greater than what has been identified in the tables and narrative.

Elevations are reported in feet. When a map or information source uses metric measurements, they have been converted to feet. The conversion factor used is meters times 3.2808 (39.37 inches/12 inches). For example, the USGS 7.5-minute map indicates that Mount Whitney is 4416.9 meters. To convert meters to feet, multiply 4416.9 meters by 3.2808 for a height of 14,490.97 feet, rounded to 14,491 feet.

Trip Duration

Each route includes a suggested day-by-day itinerary. These travel plans take into consideration mileage, elevation gain/loss, and desirable campsites. I attempted to keep the daily distance to about 9 to 12 miles but sometimes the distance is a little longer or shorter depending on the camping opportunities. The itineraries reflect my preference to camp at lakes or alongside streams with exceptional panoramic views, not in heavily timbered areas with little opportunities for open vistas. This is the primary reason for the longer or shorter daily distances in a given itinerary.

The trip duration information is a range of days, such as five to seven days. A strong hiker who can average 12 to 14 miles per day and who does not take a rest day could complete such a route in five days, whereas someone who feels more comfortable averaging 9 to 10 miles per day should plan for a seven-day trip.

Maps

The maps provided in this guidebook are for general reference only. They highlight the various trails and hiking routes and include many geographic features such as prominent lakes, streams, meadows, ridges, and peaks. Established trails are distinguished from cross-country travel: dashed lines represent existing trails and dotted lines represent cross-country segments of a route. (See the "Key to Map and Graph Symbols" legend in Chapter 7.) These maps may be adequate for routes that follow a trail but if you plan on doing cross-country travel over trail-less terrain, take a detailed topographic map.

In the list of information at the beginning of each route description, the appropriate Tom Harrison topographic map is listed. Where these excellent maps do not completely cover a specific route, the appropriate USGS map is identified.

In addition to Tom Harrison and USGS maps, there are other excellent map sources, including the U.S. National Park Service and Forest Service. Maps in an electronic format are also available and allow you to view and print out a specific area at various map scales. Additionally, you can trace your route, calculate mileage and elevation gain/loss, and enter coordinates into a GPS receiver with electronic maps.

Trail Profile Graphs and Tables

The trail profile graphs depict the ups and downs of the route in an illustrative format and are handy references for what lies ahead. As with the maps, the graphs use dashed lines to represent existing trails and dotted lines to indicate those portions of the route that require cross-country travel.

For the trail profile tables, each trail and cross-country hiking route has been broken into short segments with suggested daily itineraries. These tables include the milepost, distance, a running total, and the elevation gain/loss for each trail segment and day. The notation "x-c" indicates segments requiring cross-country travel.

Variations, Side Trips, Peak Scrambles

In the text, charts, and on the maps, route variations (V), side trips (ST), and peak scrambles (PS) are designated with an alpha and numeric designation such as V1.1, ST1.3, and PS5.1. The first number to the right of the letter is the route where the write-up can be found. The number to the right of the decimal point indicates whether it is the first, second, or third descriptor for that particular route. For example ST1.3 would be the third side trip described in Route 1.

Variations are major detours or shortcuts that leave the featured trail and rejoin it later. They may either avoid or add difficult terrain to the route. Side trips are just that—places you can visit for part of a day without necessarily carrying your backpack. There are some exceptional side excursions that you will enjoy immensely. Peak scrambles provide route descriptions of six 14,000-foot peaks that you could consider climbing in addition to Whitney. Each of the six peaks is accessible from at least one of the featured routes (see table below), affording an excellent opportunity for an enjoyable climb.

Peak Name	Where Described	Identifying Number	Peak Can Be Climbed From
Mount Sill (14,153 feet)	Route 1, V1.1	PS1.1	Route 1, V1.1
Split Mountain (14,058 feet)	Route 1	PS1.2	Route 1
Mount Muir (14,015 feet)	Route 1	PS1.3	Routes 1–5, 7–15
Mount Tyndall (14,019 feet)	Route 5	PS5.1	Routes 1–5, 12
Mount Russell (14,088 feet)	Route 6	PS6.1	Routes 6–7
Mount Langley (14,027 feet)	Route 10	PS10.1	Route 10

2 PLANNING YOUR SUCCESSFUL ASCENT

Freedom of the hills is a concept that combines the simple joy of being in the mountains with the skill, equipment, and strength to travel without harm to ourselves, others, and the environment. The hills do not offer this freedom inherently—only in trade. What must you offer in this trade? Training, preparation, and desire.

— Mountaineering: The Freedom of the Hills, 7th Edition, *2003*

COMPLETING ANY OF THE FIFTEEN ROUTES described in this guide will require thoughtful planning, excellent physical stamina, a generous dose of mental perseverance, and, ideally, a lightly loaded pack. Each of these principles is discussed below. If you effectively execute these fundamentals, you will experience an increased likelihood of a safe, successful, and enjoyable climb.

THOUGHTFUL PLANNING

An essential part of responsible planning is to select a route that does not exceed the abilities of the members of your party. Your group will only be as strong as its weakest member, so plan the trip around that individual's strengths and limitations. The steepness of the trail, the amount of elevation to be climbed, the number of miles to be hiked, and the difficulty of the cross-country travel are all critical factors in determining whether the trek is within the capabilities of your party. Shy away from attempting an excursion that may be too challenging for any member of your party; rather, attempt a less arduous trip before embarking on the more difficult journey. The list of critical information provided at the beginning of each route description and in Appendix 2 are useful tools for selecting a route that is right for your group.

A critical factor in the selection process is whether the route follows established trails for its entire length or whether cross-country travel over difficult terrain is necessary to link one trail with another. Of the fifteen routes, ten follow established trails over their entire distance and five require cross-country travel.

Although not technically difficult, all the trails are challenging, demanding a good measure of stamina and perseverance. However, just about any highly motivated hiker in excellent physical condition with some backpacking experience will be capable of completing excursions that stay on

Mirror Lake along the Mount Whitney Trail (Route 8)

well-maintained trails. Some of the less difficult trails are Routes 3, 8, 11, and 12. Appendix 2 rates each route by difficulty and length.

A hiker attempting one of the more physically demanding cross-country routes must be in superior condition; have the ability to scramble over rock, talus, and rugged terrain with a backpack; and be experienced at routefinding with map and compass. The cross-country routes follow creeks and canyons, and traverse obvious mountain passes that are clearly identifiable; nevertheless, an inexperienced traveler could easily become lost on these difficult courses. No matter how thorough the cross-country description, a hiker's routefinding skills are essential ingredients for a successful outing.

Cross-country travel is simplified with the proper use of a GPS receiver. The Mountaineers Route (Route 6 and Day 1 of Route 7) includes UTM grid coordinates (1927 datum) at eleven critical points along the way. Refer to Chapter 1, "How to Use This Guidebook" and the glossary (Appendix 7) for a further explanation. On the cross-country routes you can expect to see spectacular scenery, some of the best in the Sierra Nevada, and significantly fewer people.

In the early season, upper trail segments may be covered with snow. In a heavy snow year it may be well into July before the trails are completely open. Crampons and an ice ax may be necessary. For example, the ninety-seven switchbacks above Trail Camp on the Whitney Trail (Route 8) may become a bit tricky when the steep slopes are covered with snowdrifts. An early season ascent by way of Route 11 may be the best way to avoid most of the snow. Check with the Forest Service and National Park Service for trail conditions.

THOROUGH PREPARATION

Excellent physical conditioning is essential for the success of your climb. To prepare, start at least three months in advance of your trip by developing a personal workout program that focuses on your climbing goals. For instance, if you plan a single-day ascent via the Whitney Trail or the Mountaineers Route, you will be hiking many miles and ascending/descending more than 6400 feet at high altitudes—an undertaking requiring considerable effort and endurance. If you are planning a multi-day backpack excursion, you should be able to carry a backpack containing all your gear for 9 to 12 miles each day while ascending several thousand feet for consecutive days. For each of these climbing goals, your time and energy should be focused on similar but slightly different workouts and muscle groups.

An effective conditioning regimen includes three basic elements: cardiovascular endurance, muscular strength, and flexibility. Improving both your aerobic and anaerobic conditioning is essential. When training for your climb, remember the words of Mark Twight in his book *Extreme Alpinism*: "Strong muscles run out of gas when limited by a sub-par cardiovascular system."

A well-balanced program also recognizes the importance of flexibility training, including stretching before and after workouts. After a strenuous day of hiking and climbing, stretching will help reduce muscle soreness. It may also reduce the potential for injury and stress to the muscles and ligaments.

There are a wide variety of exercises that can be incorporated into an effective conditioning program. However, the best way to train for an activity is to do the activity, gradually increasing the difficulty. Below are some aerobic and anaerobic training suggestions.

■ Leg lifts and stomach crunches to strengthen the lower back and abdominal muscles for carrying a backpack and hiking long distances.

- Squats, lunges, calf raises, dead lifts, and step ups for the lower body. Shrugs and upright rowing for the shoulders. Use a lightly loaded backpack with some of these exercises.
- Climb and descend hills with a loaded backpack. Do not overlook your downhill leg muscles because steep descents with a pack can oftentimes be more demanding on the legs and knees than the ascent.
- On conditioning hikes, carry containers filled with water in your backpack. Before heading down, dump some of the water to lighten your pack, thereby removing some of the stress on your knee joints on the descent.
- Climb flights of stairs in a tall building or a sports stadium with your backpack. Begin by ascending one step at a time, building to two steps at a time.
- Descend stairs slowly, lowering your weight on each step. Begin by descending one step at a time, building slowly to two steps at a time. This will strengthen your downhill leg muscles, which support the knee joint.
- Run a 100-meter windsprint and then walk 100 meters. Repeat until you drop.
- Run uphill then walk down. Repeat this as many times as you can.
- Ride a bike over hilly terrain for two to four hours. During the ride, accelerate to maximum effort for thirty seconds and then coast for thirty seconds, repeating this exercise over and over.
- Alternate between riding a bike in normal (easy) gears and big (hard) gears. This will stress the muscles and shock your cardio-vascular system much quicker than riding predominately in easy gears.
- In the winter, train on snowshoes and skis by traveling a number of miles over hilly terrain with a backpack. In addition, you can simu-late the 100-meter wind sprints, described above. While on your skis or snowshoes, run in short bursts of 25 to 50 meters. Repeat as often as you can.
- Whatever aerobic workout you prefer, it needs to be intense for an hour or more per day, three to four days a week.
- Training at elevation is even more productive.

The training exercises that shock the system by requiring repeated maximum output of effort for short bursts are the quickest and most effective techniques to achieve a strong cardiovascular system. Running wind sprints on level terrain, running up a short hill, thirty-second all-out accelerations on a bike, and riding in big gears are all excellent training techniques, combining aerobic and anaerobic conditioning. Do all you can to be prepared for the challenge of Mount Whitney. The climb is demanding, and the high altitude and lack of oxygen take their toll on the ill-prepared. Mountain sickness and the lack of oxygen at the high elevations are undoubtedly responsible for the large failure rate of would-be Whitney summiters. Those who rush to the mountain and attempt to climb it in a day or two are at the greatest risk for mountain sickness and failure.

A well-conditioned hiker is not immune to mountain sickness. However, ascending the mountain slowly, taking time to acclimatize, is the best formula for avoiding this malady. The more training you can do at elevation, the better your chances for success. Complete training hikes that take you to 10,000 feet, preferably to 12,000 feet, and camp as high as you can for several nights.

If you will be climbing from the east side, the trailheads at Horseshoe Meadow (10,000 feet), Whitney Portal (8365 feet), Onion Valley (9200 feet), and South Lake (9768 feet) have nearby campgrounds that could serve as excellent acclimatization camps before starting your climb. Spend two nights at one of these high-elevation campgrounds and take easy conditioning day hikes before setting out on your ascent of Whitney. On the west side, where the approaches are longer, you should be able to acclimatize slowly as you hike to the mountain.

PERSEVERANCE AND DISCIPLINE

A successful climber is not necessarily the strongest or the fastest but the one with a full measure of mental strength, self-discipline, and persistence. This willpower should be applied during training sessions as well as on the climb itself. When you are tired, sore, or discouraged, continue with a systematic and comprehensive conditioning program. When you are exhausted and feel like dropping your pack to camp early, push on to your planned destination.

Climbing can be as much as 90 percent mental and 10 percent physical. Whatever the ratio of mental to physical, the two are inseparable, and it is clear that the mind controls the body. Understanding the psychological aspects of climbing, both the conscious and subconscious, and our real and perceived limitations, we can reach new heights that were, heretofore, unattainable.

With a large dose of perseverance you can will your way to the top. However, oftentimes a spiritless and discouraged mind can deceive backcountry travelers into believing they are too weak from fatigue to continue. Do not let your mind, with its negative thoughts, mislead you; the body is resilient and much stronger than we realize.

My daughter, Sierra, can attest to the fact that a successful mountaineer need not be the strongest nor the fastest but one that has a full measure of motivation, self-discipline, and mental tenacity. At age ten, she climbed Cirque Peak (by moonlight), Mount Langley, and Mount Whitney on three consecutive days. As she descended the ninety-seven switchbacks on the Mount Whitney Trail, she vowed to climb all of the 14,000-foot peaks in California. By age thirteen she had accomplished her goal. Soon thereafter, she added Mount Rainier and several 14,000 footers in Colorado, including the difficult traverse of the Maroon Bells, to her list of accomplishments. I use this example, not to brag, but rather to illustrate the point that if you are sufficiently motivated to accomplish a goal and add a full measure of self-discipline to the equation, you can accomplish much.

PLANNING TIPS

It is important to have a well-thought-out plan before starting your trip. Below are some valuable tips to consider as you organize your adventure.

- If you have not previously hiked to 14,000 feet, take a preparatory training hike ascending to 12,000 feet while camping above 10,000 feet. If you experience mountain sickness symptoms, descend immediately, and plan several extra days to ascend Whitney.
- Ask your doctor for a prescription for Diamox (125 mg). This will reduce the likelihood of getting altitude sickness.
- If you plan an ascent from an eastside trailhead, camp above 8000 feet for two nights before starting your climb.
- Write down your trip itinerary and leave it with a responsible person. Include a description of where you will park your vehicle; the make, model, year, and color of your car; the license plate number; and your exit date from the mountain and the date you plan to return home. Your itinerary should include a daily accounting of your plans, the name of the starting and ending trailheads, the trails you will use, planned campsite locations, the lakes you will be passing, and the passes and peaks you will be ascending.
- Secure a wilderness permit from the National Park Service or the U.S. Forest Service in advance of your departure.

- Purchase the appropriate topographical maps and study them closely.
- Ensure that all members of your party are familiar with the route, the overall level of difficulty of the trip, and the number of miles and elevation to be gained each day.
- If you take a GPS receiver, be fully versed in its use. Set the UTM coordinates for your route (e.g., starting point and end point, camps, lakes, passes, summits) before starting the trip.
- Follow a personal workout program to improve your physical conditioning; start at least three months in advance of the climb.
- Be mentally tough, persistent, and tenacious about accomplishing your physical conditioning goals as well as your objectives while on the climb.
- Go light, pack light—take only essential items.
- Complete an equipment check before departing. Ensure that all group items (e.g., tent, stove, food) are accounted for and arrive at the trailhead.
- Include extra food in the event of an unexpected emergency or in case the trip takes longer than planned.
- If you take longer to complete the climb than indicated on your itinerary, call the responsible person immediately upon your return or as soon as you can find cellphone reception (you can usually secure reception on the summit of Mount Whitney). Even when you are on schedule, call the responsible person to let them know of your safe return.
- Plan at least one rest day (or easy hiking day) for trips longer than four days.
- Don't hike alone.

GOING LIGHT—WHAT TO TAKE

Freedom in the mountains lies largely in the ability to cope with every problem of wilderness travel and every emergency that arises with the items your party is carrying on its collective shoulders. Because you will have a tent, adequate food supplies, and a stove, there is a feeling of freedom, safety, and self-sufficiency when embarking on a multi-day excursion. If you become exhausted from travel, a sudden storm hits, or an unexpected problem arises, you can stop and camp in relative safety to attend to the situation.

The feeling of freedom is further strengthened when you are able to move briskly through the wilderness. Speed in the mountains equates to safety and enjoyment. It is difficult to move quickly with a burdensome pack, weighing fifty pounds or more, stuffed with the latest gadgets. Only with a light pack will you be able to move freely along the steep trails and over the difficult trail-less terrain. Selecting the correct gear, clothing, footwear, equipment, and food is critical for keeping the weight of your pack in check.

Many hikers, even experienced veterans, take too much with them. I have observed backpackers with all sorts of unnecessary gear tied to the outside of their overburdened packs. You can get by with a lot less than you think without sacrificing safety and comfort. When considering purchasing items, whether hiking boots, parka, backpack, sleeping bag, or tent, consider each item's function and weight. Take a postal scale with you to the store and compare weights. The weight of each item is critical because you will be carrying the cumulative weight of all the items, whether on your person or in your backpack. If a week's worth of supplies do not fit inside a 4200-cubic-inch (70-liter) internal-frame pack, you are taking too much or the wrong type of gear.

The discussion below should assist you in selecting the correct lightweight gear. Appendix 3 contains equipment checklists for a single-day ascent, a multi-day backpack excursion, and a winter expedition to the mountain. Photocopy these lists and use them. They will serve as a convenient reminder and quick reference against accidentally forgetting critical items.

Footwear

If you are planning a single-day hike of the Whitney Trail, select a comfortable pair of trail-hiking shoes or lightweight hiking boots. The most important criteria are comfort and foot-bed support. The 22-mile round-trip journey will be grueling on your feet, legs, knee joints, and hips.

For multi-day trips, select a comfortable, supportive, lightweight or medium-weight hiking boot. Because you will be carrying a pack, additional foot support, ankle support, and traction are desirable. For any of the cross-country routes, select a sturdy, medium-weight boot. Generally, trail-hiking shoes are not adequate for carrying a pack or for cross-country travel because they do not provide the necessary support and ankle protection, and because of their low profile they can fill with loose scree.

When purchasing a pair of trail-hiking shoes or lightweight hiking boots, select one with torsional rigidity. Take the shoe or boot in your hands and attempt to twist the sole as if wringing out a wet washrag. The sole should offer considerable resistance. If you can twist the foot bed easily, do not purchase the shoe or boot. This torsional rigidity provides increased arch support, protection from sharp rocks, and comfort on long hikes; and helps with edging on steep scree slopes and on snow.

Socks

Do not use cotton socks or socks with a high percentage of synthetic fibers. Your feet will sweat profusely and your socks will be soaked by the end of the day. Rather, use medium-weight socks containing a high percentage of wool. One normally thinks of wool for the warmth it provides in the winter, but wool is the best choice, even in summer. Bring a second pair and rotate socks daily.

Clothing

The Sierra Nevada weather is usually stable with cool temperatures at the higher elevations. However, the weather and temperature can change rapidly and thunderstorms are common in July and August. For this reason, plan for the worst by being prepared with the proper clothing for freezing temperatures above 10,000 feet, with the potential for wind, rain, snow, and sleet. In these conditions, synthetic fibers and finely spun wool are the best because they wick the moisture away from your skin. Do not wear cotton clothing—it soaks up moisture, is slow to dry, and provides no warmth when wet.

The following clothing works well for me: Start with a lightweight polyester long-sleeved zippered turtleneck. I like the turtleneck because its high neckline provides sun protection during the day and warmth at night. Over the top of this add a lightweight polyester tee shirt. During the day this can be taken off or put back on depending on the weather. Add a lightweight fleece jacket and a breathable water-resistant parka with a hood.

For the bottom half, two layers are usually adequate. Make the first layer lightweight polyester bottoms/tights. Wear loose-fitting nylon shorts over the tights. When the weather turns cold or the wind picks up, add lightweight wind pants. The beauty of this layering system is that in warm weather you can wear the shorts alone. If the temperature drops suddenly, slip on the nylon wind pants over the shorts. On colder mornings, start with the tights and shorts, followed by the wind pants.

Parka or Poncho

Weather in the Sierra Nevada high country can be unpredictable. Thundershowers accompanied by winds are common on summer afternoons in July and August. Prepare for this eventuality by taking a weatherproof parka or rain poncho. Several large garbage bags can help in an emergency, but they tear easily and are not effective in high winds. Lightweight nylon wind pants also are desirable to protect against rain and strong winds.

Backpacks

If your hiking is limited to trails with no cross-country travel, an external-frame pack is a good choice. However, if you plan on hiking cross-country, an internal-frame pack is preferable. An internal-frame pack holds the load close to the back and is less likely to shift on uneven or steep terrain, thereby throwing you off balance. Also consider an internal-frame pack with a removable back pad. This pad can be used to augment your sleeping pad at night.

Generally speaking, today's internal-frame packs are overbuilt and are too heavy. Packs weighing six, seven, and eight pounds do not merit your use. Find a pack that weighs four pounds or less.

The challenge for backpack designers and manufacturers is to reduce the weight of both men's and women's backpacks. There are a few 4200-cubic-inch packs on the market that weigh around four pounds but additional improvements are welcome.

Tents

Just as it is with backpacks, many tents are too heavy for lightweight backpacking. Two- and three-pole tents are ideal for a multi-day trip. There are many two-person backpacking tents that weigh six to eight pounds. These are much too heavy. A two-person tent should weigh less than five pounds.

Sleeping Bags and Pads

A down sleeping bag weighing two pounds and rated to about 20 degrees Fahrenheit is an excellent choice. A synthetic-filled bag is less expensive and also a good choice but is heavier and bulkier. Use a closed-cell or self-inflating sleeping pad. (A self-inflating sleeping pad is more comfortable but it is also the more expensive choice.) To save weight, use a three-quarter-length pad. To add comfort, use the removable pad from your backpack to augment your sleeping pad.

Crampons and Ice Ax

Crampons and an ice ax usually are not needed to summit Mount Whitney. However, there are three exceptions: You should bring them when climbing the Mountaineers Route (Route 6) in early season, when hiking any of the trails in the early season when snow is on the upper slopes of

From camp, looking across Iceberg Lake toward Mount Russell (Routes 6 and 7)

the mountain, and in the winter. A lightweight ice ax weighs less than a pound and a pair of aluminum crampons a little more than a pound.

Instruction by a qualified individual with practice in the field is important—merely reading about alpine techniques in a book invites a false sense of security. Make sure you know how to use these tools and that the crampons fit snuggly on your boots before you leave home. Getting caught with a loose-fitting crampon on a steep, icy slope is a formula for disaster.

Stoves and Cooking Essentials

There are many excellent, lightweight backpacking stoves on the market today. Some of the lighter burners weigh only a few ounces. All perform adequately with pressurized canister fuel or white gas.

A two-quart cooking pot is all you need to prepare the meals suggested in the "Menu Planner" (Appendix 4). For eating utensils, take a two-cup plastic measuring cup and a plastic spoon and fork.

Water Bottles

You can save weight (about 4 ounces per bottle) by substituting a sports drink (such as Gatorade or Powerade), thin-walled, quart plastic bottle in place of the commercially available thick-walled plastic bottles. Use a thin-walled plastic bottle for one trip and then recycle it. Also, a two-quart water bladder/water bag is extremely light and is useful for supplying water when preparing breakfast and dinner. Take a thin-walled, quart plastic bottle and a two-quart water bag.

Portable Bear-Restraint Food Storage Containers

Bear containers are required on many of the routes. Unfortunately, many of the approved hard-sided canisters are bulky and absurdly heavy, weighing more than three pounds. These containers are the antithesis of going light. However, newer products, such as the bear-proof bags with liners, weigh little more than a pound. These bear bags are superior to the canisters—they are much lighter, fit into your backpack easier, and hold more food. A list of approved containers can be found on the Forest Service and National Park Service websites noted in Appendix 5.

ALPINE CUISINE—WHAT TO EAT

According to the authors of *Mountaineering: The Freedom of the Hills*, good food gives a festive touch to your adventure and lifts the mood of the entire group. Good food improves the scenery and keeps the spirits high even in bad weather. Bad food makes the nights colder and longer, the approaches more difficult, the weather unbearable, and good friends intolerable.

Organizing appetizing meals and tasty snacks that everyone enjoys is an important aspect of planning a successful ascent. Appendix 4 provides a menu planner with suggestions for breakfast, lunch, and dinner. It also contains several tasty gourmet dinners. These meals are easy to prepare, inexpensive, and lightweight, and are far superior to the traditional freeze-dried meals. Most of the ingredients can be purchased at a grocery store and require minimal cooking time.

To keep adequately nourished and to maintain the high level of caloric intake necessary, snack often, eating small portions regularly. Select tasty food, fun food, food that you enjoy. Avoid fatty foods and foods that are difficult to digest. Sweets are easily digested and are craved, even at altitude. Soups are easily prepared, taste good, and slide down smoothly. Eat light, eat right, and eat often.

As a general rule, plan about 1.8 to 2 pounds of food per person per day. Adjust the portions based on the appetites of those in your party. Throw in a couple extra soup packages for emergency rations.

Adequate amounts of food and liquid are critical. Many hikers experience a lack of appetite when going to elevations above 10,000 feet. Others may be too tired at the end of a hard day to eat. Resist the temptation to skip a meal. Eating is essential for the sustained effort needed in the backcountry. Much of the physical fatigue and weakness experienced in the mountains is caused by inadequate food intake, dehydration, and, possibly, potassium loss.

Throughout the day, keep hydrated by drinking water or a sport drink regularly. Again, at dinner, drink plenty of water or a sport drink and soup. Keeping hydrated is important and will help minimize the potential for altitude sickness (see discussion in Chapter 3). To reduce the weight of the sugar-based sports drink, mix the sports drink with an artificially sweetened powdered drink such as Tang or Crystal Light at a ratio of 50/50.

Studies indicate that balancing one's protein and carbohydrate intake can improve performance. However, in the mountains it is difficult to plan an adequately balanced diet of protein and carbohydrates because carbohydrates dominate from bagels to pasta to nutrition bars. Some suggestions for protein sources include turkey and beef jerky; vacuum-sealed packages of salmon, tuna, and chicken; freeze-dried chicken; protein powder added to menu items; cheese; peanut butter; nuts; and nutrition bars that balance protein and carbohydrates at a ratio of 45/55.

WHEN TO GO

Because winter weather conditions and the depth of the snowpack vary considerably from year to year, it is not possible to predict with accuracy when each trail will open each hiking season. Depending on the amount of snowfall that accumulates during the preceding winter, trails usually open in June and July. In the drought years of 1977–79, hikers were able to get into the backcountry in May. On the opposite end of the weather spectrum, there seems to be one or two years each decade with abundant amounts of snowfall that does not melt from the high-elevation trails until well into July or early August. The best advice is to check with the Forest Service or National Park Service and their respective websites for up-to-date trail conditions.

However, that being said, the typical climbing season is mid-June through mid-October. The weather during these months is usually clear and sunny. The weather can be stable for weeks at a time but a slight shift in the high-pressure system can cause conditions in the mountains to change rapidly. Check the weather report before you depart. Cold and stormy conditions with strong winds, hail, sleet, and snow can occur at the higher elevations anytime during the year. Thunderstorms with hail and lightning are most prevalent in July and August.

At the trailhead during the day the temperature can be warm, but at night be prepared for the temperature to drop into the 20s at camps above 10,000 feet. If the weather turns bleak, do not panic. Look for a safe place to camp and sit tight and comfortably in your tent. It is amazing the difference twenty-four hours can make in the mountains. An unexpected summer or fall snowstorm can quickly encompass the mountains but dissipate just as rapidly.

Almost anytime during the climbing season is a good time to plan your outing. Each season has its unique characteristics that make a trip during that particular time of year a rewarding experience. My favorite times are April, late June/July, and late September/October.

Four arbitrary time segments are used to describe the climbing seasons in this guide. Early season includes May 16 to July 15, midseason is July 16 to September 15, late season ranges from September 16 to November 15, and winter covers all of the remaining months, November 16 through May 15.

Early season is a time when the winter snows have not completely melted and the creeks and waterfalls are overflowing with rushing water from snowmelt. Swollen streams can be challenging to ford. Snow may be present in steep gullies and on the colder north slopes. Snow in the morning can be rock hard from the night's freezing temperatures. An ice ax and crampons may be needed to ensure safe travel under these conditions. The hard snow can turn to slush in the warm afternoon, slowing your progress. Ski poles are especially helpful in soft snow.

In a typical year most of the snow should have melted from the trails by mid-July and melted from the cross-country routes by the end of July. Early season is a prime time to view mule deer grazing in the meadows and the wildflowers as they fight their way up through the melting snow. Mosquitoes are becoming a problem in early season and this will continue into midseason.

Midseason is the most popular time for the Sierra Nevada backcountry. The weather is usually stable during this time but expect an occasional thunder and lightning storm in the afternoon. Most of the snow has melted so the streams are lower, making crossing them easier. Mosquitoes are still a problem but this will resolve itself as the season progresses. In areas where bears roam, this seems to be their most active time as they store up food and fat for the coming winter.

By late season the crowds have disappeared; the leaves of the quaking aspen are turning all shades of red, yellow, and gold; the mosquitoes and bugs are gone; the threat of afternoon thunderstorms has passed; and bear activity is on the decline. In the frosty fall mornings, skiffs of ice form on the lakes and streams but quickly melt in the morning sun. The crisp autumn air each evening signals the rapid approach of winter. My annual trips into the backcountry to view the brilliant colors of autumn have been some of the most enjoyable. The fall colors are at their peak from the last week in September to the middle of October.

It is not unusual for a storm to hit during September or October, dusting the higher elevations with an inch or two of snow. If you are caught in one of these storms, wait it out. The weather will clear in twelve to forty-eight hours. If you are planning a late-season climb, do not be fooled into thinking that winter has arrived early. The weather patterns in California are such that after these big storms depart, the weather quickly stabilizes, bringing warm conditions and allowing for many more weeks of backcountry travel.

Late season gives way to the winter season. The days are short, the nights are long, and the temperature drops. Above 8000 feet, the snow accumulates and does not melt until spring. Only experienced climbers, ski mountaineers, snowshoers, and snowboarders should attempt Whitney in the winter. That being said, winter presents untold opportunities for competent adventurers. And, one does not have to reach the summit to have a successful trip during this season. Refer to Chapter 4 for a discussion of climbing Whitney in the winter.

WILDERNESS PERMITS—DO I NEED ONE?

Before setting out for the summit, you must decide when to go and what route to take. Unfortunately, these choices may be determined by your ability to secure a wilderness permit.

A wilderness permit is required year-round on all overnight backpack trips and for single-day hikes on the Mount Whitney Trail (Route 8) and the Mountaineers Route (Routes 6 and 7). All the trails are also subject to wilderness permit quotas that limit the number of hikers allowed to enter the backcountry each day. These quotas are necessary to minimize impacts to the fragile ecology and are in effect for about six months of each year.

The Inyo National Forest has implemented a wilderness permit lottery system for those wishing to ascend the mountain via the Whitney Trail. Thousands apply each year but many are turned away. On average about one-third of the lottery permit applications are rejected because the quotas have been filled.

The good news is that a wilderness permit can be obtained for any of the other trails and cross-country routes described in this guide by applying well in advance, selecting a less-popular trailhead, and planning your departure for the middle of the week. If you are still unsuccessful in securing a permit, plan a late-season excursion. The crowds and demand for permits are greatly reduced at this time of year. For trips occurring outside the quota period, reservations are not necessary and a permit can be secured the day of the trip.

The Forest Service and Sequoia/Kings Canyon National Parks have similar wilderness permit procedures but there are enough differences to keep you guessing. Each permitting organization has a different set of wilderness permit procedures, a different quota season, and a different reservation system that may change from time to time. For Routes 1–11 (eastside trails), look to the Inyo National Forest for your wilderness permit; for Routes 12–15 (westside trails), the permit is issued by Sequoia and Kings Canyon National Parks.

The National Park Service and Forest Service permit systems have evolved over the years. Both agencies are open to suggestions and make changes occasionally. Check with them for current procedures, as some of the information in this guide may have changed since its publication. The following table summarizes key dates and some important differences between the two federal land managers.

Trails	Jurisdiction	Reservation Dates	Quota Season
Whitney Trail (Route 8)	Inyo National Forest	Whitney Lottery Feb 1–29	May 1– Nov 1
Eastside Trailheads (Routes 1–7, 9–11)	Inyo National Forest	6 months in advance and up to 2 days before your departure	May 1– Nov 1
Westside Trailheads (Routes 12–15)	Sequoia and Kings Canyon National Parks	Beginning Mar 1 and up to 3 weeks before your departure	May 27– Sept 24

Mount Whitney Trail (Route 8)

Mount Whitney Trail Lottery applications are accepted during February. For the best results, apply early in February and provide alternative dates. The smaller your group and the more alternative dates you include on your application, the better your chances for securing a permit. Permits are issued through this lottery process for day hikes and multi-day back-pack trips from May 1 through November 1.

Most if not all the quotas are filled through the lottery. However, if some quotas are not allocated, permit applications will be accepted after the lottery has been completed. Cancellations and any unreserved dates are available on a first-come basis the day before or the day of departure.

During February, mail your lottery application to:

Mount Whitney Lottery
Wilderness Permit Office
351 Pacu Lane, Suite 200
Bishop, CA 93514

Mountaineers Route (Routes 6 and 7)

Routes 6 and 7 begin by ascending the Mount Whitney Trail but after 0.8 mile the route leaves the trail to ascend the North Fork Lone Pine Creek via an unmaintained climbers trail. A permit is required for single-day ascents as well as multi-day excursions. To secure a reservation, send your application to the Forest Service up to six months in advance of your departure date. If you plan to ascend the Mountaineers Route and descend the Whitney Trail, review the Trail Crest exit quota discussion below.

All Other Trails Originating in the Inyo National Forest (Routes 1–5 and 9–11)

Wilderness permit reservations can be made up to six months prior to the departure date of your climb. Mail or phone your reservation for non-Whitney Trail permits. The more alternate dates listed on the application, the greater the probability you will receive a wilderness permit. Successful applicants are notified by mail with instructions for picking up the permit. A small number of permits are held from the reservation system for issuance on a walk-in basis the day before and the day of departure.

The permit quota system is in place from May 1 through November 1 for these routes. Make sure you specify on your wilderness permit reservation application if you will be descending the Whitney Trail.

For all Inyo National Forest trails except the Whitney Trail, phone or mail your application to:

Wilderness Reservation Office
351 Pacu Lane, Suite 200
Bishop, CA 93514
Phone: 760-873-2483

Dusy Basin is one of the most picturesque spots in the Sierra Nevada.

Unreserved, walk-up permits for Routes 1–11 can be secured at:
InterAgency Visitor Center
    Lone Pine (at the junction of Highways 395 and 136, about 1 mile
    south of Lone Pine)
    Phone: 760-876-6222

White Mountain Ranger Station
    798 North Main Street
    Bishop, CA 93514
    Phone: 760-873-2500

General Information and Wilderness Permits
    Website: *www.r5.fs.fed.us/inyo*
    Wilderness Information: 760-873-2485
    Wilderness Permits: 760-873-2483

Trail Crest Exit Quotas

Traveling west, the Mount Whitney Trail enters Sequoia National Park at the crest of the Sierra Nevada. This high point in the trail, above Trail Camp and the ninety-seven switchbacks, is called Trail Crest. If you enter the backcountry from another trail, and intend to descend the Whitney Trail, Trail Crest exit quotas will apply. For example, if you start at the Cottonwood Pass Trail or the Kearsarge Pass Trail, and then descend the Whitney Trail, you would be subject to this added restriction. The exit quota will be factored into your permit at the time you apply. If you are denied a wilderness permit because of the exit quota, plan to hike out another route or return the same way you hiked in. Other than the Whitney Trail, the shortest way to hike out over a trail is to follow Route 11 to Horseshoe Meadow.

Trails Originating in the National Parks (Routes 12–15)

For trails originating on the west side of the Sierra Nevada crest (Routes 12–15), a wilderness permit is required from the Sequoia and Kings Canyon National Parks. Their permit quota system is in place from May 27 through September 24. For trips starting during this time and especially over a holiday or weekend, advanced reservations are recommended. For trips starting outside this period, a walk-up or self-registration permit is issued.

Wilderness permit reservations can be made starting on March 1 and can be made up to twenty-one days before the date of departure. The wilderness permit office confirms permit reservations by mail. However, the actual wilderness permit must be picked up in person. To make advance reservations for the routes originating in Sequoia and Kings Canyon National Parks, write or fax:

Wilderness Permit Reservations
   Sequoia and Kings Canyon National Parks
   47050 Generals Highway #60
   Three Rivers, CA 93271
   Phone: 559-565-3766
   Fax: 559-565-4239
   Website: *www.nps.gov/seki*

PROTECT THE FRAGILE ALPINE ECOLOGY

California's mountain wildernesses possess exemplary treasures worthy of preserving for future generations. These unique wonders of unmatched beauty are neither limitless nor eternal, and deserve your respect. Excluding Yosemite Valley trails, the Whitney area has become the most popular and heavily used area in the Sierra Nevada. With this popularity comes the added responsibility of carefully protecting the alpine areas—a fragile ecology that matures slowly, one inch at a time, but that can be easily destroyed one foot (and horse hoof) at a time. We must do our part to keep this area unspoiled by following a few common-sense rules of wilderness conduct, which are outlined below. Tread lightly while exploring the backcountry and leave it as you found it.

When in the backcountry, keep in mind that the jagged crest of the Sierra Nevada serves as a natural boundary between the Sequoia and Kings Canyon National Parks on the west and the wilderness areas managed by the Forest Service on the east. These federal land managers have similar wilderness requirements but with several important differences. Since a backcountry traveler is likely to pass from one jurisdiction to another in the course of climbing Whitney, it is important to understand both sets of rules.

COMMON-SENSE RULES TO PROTECT THE FRAGILE ENVIRONMENT

- Do not cut switchbacks. They are expensive to construct and maintain; cutting them causes erosion and damage to the trail.
- Avoid creating a new campsite; use established sites, never in meadows or on vegetation. Building campsite improvements, such as rock walls, fire rings, tables, and chairs, is prohibited.
- Avoid camping under overhanging dead limbs or near leaning dead snags.
- Although many campsites are near water, select one at least 200 feet from streams and lakes. Many previously popular areas are closed to overnight camping; honor these closures.
- Visualize potential impacts when selecting a campsite and leave flowers, rocks, and other natural features undisturbed.
- There are two major causes of water contamination: soap and human/livestock waste. Soap, even biodegradable soap, should not be used in the wilderness. Clean your hands with waterless soap. Clean pots and eating utensils with boiling water. Dispose of rinse water at least 200 feet from any water source.
- The parasite *Giardia lamblia* originates from water and food contaminated by human and animal waste. Intestinal pathogens such as *Giardia lamblia* and *Escherichia coli* can live in buried waste. Use the established pit toilets where available.

Alternately, dispose of solid human waste by digging a hole six to eight inches deep and burying it. Make sure you are at least 200 feet from any water source. Pack out tampons, sanitary napkins, and used toilet paper.

- The Forest Service has established a pack-out-your-poop program for the Mount Whitney Trail and the North Fork Lone Pine Creek. It has been a huge success because of the efforts of all who have participated. When you pick up your permit for Routes 6–8, ask for this simple-to-use kit. These measures may seem extreme but are also being implemented on other high-use areas such as Mount Shasta, Mount McKinley, Mount Rainier, Mount Hood, and Grand Teton National Park.

- Backpackers are required to carry bear-resistant containers in many wilderness areas. Check with the appropriate forest service or national park ranger for information about current bear activity and requirements for bear containers. In Sequoia and Kings Canyon National Parks bear-proof food lockers have been placed at certain high-use locations. The locations of these lockers are listed at the beginning of each route description.

- Everything packed in must be packed out. When preparing for your climb, remove as much packaging material as possible. This will minimize the amount of trash you will have to pack out. Each member of your party should bring a small "garbage bag" (or stuff sack) and be responsible for carrying out his or her trash. A good wilderness citizen will also pick up additional trash found near campsites or along the trail. Wilderness travelers should leave the wilderness cleaner than when they arrived.

- Campfires have no place in the backcountry. The scarce wood supply near and above the tree line is not adequate to provide a sustainable source of wood for thousands of hikers each year. In addition, the traditional rock fire ring is an ecological hazard. Wood fires in the backcountry near and above timberline have been banned. Limit wood fires to designated areas at campgrounds. Use only dead and downed wood, and do not build a new fire ring or add rocks to an existing ring. Do not burn plastic or paper with foil; pack it out.

- Dogs, other pets, and firearms are not allowed in the national parks.

AIL TIPS FOR A SINGLE-DAY ASCENT

vo routes in this guidebook, the Mount Whitney Trail (Route 8) and the Mountaineers Route (Route 6), are appropriate for a single-day ascent. Many hikers successfully ascend the peak in one day. Conversely, large numbers attempt but fail to summit the peak because a day ascent is just too long and strenuous. Only hikers in superior physical condition should consider such a climb.

When setting out to climb Whitney in one day, it is important to get a predawn start. If you do not, your chance for success is greatly diminished and you could find yourself still on the mountain well past dark. To emphasize the importance of an early start, the following experience illustrates what occurs all too often. In 2007, our party was camped at Trail Camp in full view of the ninety-seven switchbacks leading to Trail Crest. When we went to bed at 9:00 PM, there were five hikers straggling down the trail past our camp, their headlamps on with another 6.3 miles to go to reach Whitney Portal. By chance, I took one last look up the trail toward Trail Crest and spotted three more headlamps near the top moving slowly down the trail. At 11:00 PM, I was suddenly awakened and looked out the tent. The three hikers were finally passing through Trail Camp, headed for Whitney Portal. In two hours, they had covered only 2 miles—a rate of 1 mile per hour. Who knows when they reached their car? Possibly 4:00 or 5:00 the next morning.

The following tips will increase your potential for a successful climb to the summit.

- See your doctor for a prescription of Diamox (125 mg). Take half a pill twice a day for two days before your climb and the day of the climb. If you experience mountain sickness symptoms during the ascent, take another 125 mg Diamox pill. This may help relieve your symptoms. If not, descend immediately. Refer to Chapter 3 for a more complete discussion of mountain sickness.
- If you have not been to 14,000 feet before, take a preparatory trip. Ascend to 12,000 feet and camp above 10,000 feet.
 - Camp above 8000 feet (or as high as possible) for two nights before your climb. On the day before the climb, take an easy hike.
- Wear your most comfortable trail-hiking shoes or light boots on the Whitney Trail. Wear light- to medium-weight hiking boots on the Mountaineers Route.
- Take an extra pair of socks and change socks for the descent.
- Take moleskin or medical tape and use it at the first hint of a hot spot to prevent a blister from forming.
- Get an early start; start by 4:00 AM. Many hikers take twelve to

sixteen hours to complete a round-trip. If you leave promptly by 4:00 AM, a sixteen-hour day will get you back to your car by 8:00 PM. A later start at 6:00 AM may put you back at the car at 10:00 PM!

- Take an LED headlamp with extra batteries.
- Drink plenty of fluids before and throughout the hike.
- Take two quarts of water or sport drink, and powdered sport drink mix to supplement the water.
- Take iodine tablets to purify the additional water you will drink.
- Eat small portions of food and eat often.
- Take 200–400 mg of ibuprofen with lunch and another 200–400 mg in the late afternoon when the aches and pains of the day start to accumulate.
- As the long day wears on, your legs and feet will become tired and "heavy." Stop and lie down next to a tree or large boulder. Relax, revitalize, and rejuvenate your legs and feet by elevating them for five minutes or more by propping them on a nearby rock or tree.

Two hikers approaching Fin Dome Pass and Sixty Lake Basin

The higher your legs are elevated the better. You may look peculiar with your feet pointing skyward, but this will refresh your legs and feet. Rise slowly; sudden movement could cause temporary dizziness and loss of balance.

MOONLIGHT ASCENT

A moonlight ascent is a rewarding way to trek via the Whitney Trail. Arriving on the summit to view the awakening of a new day and the magnificent golden hues of the sunrise is a gratifying experience.

Select a cloudless night with a full moon. Wait a couple hours after moonrise before heading out. This will provide a moon-illuminated trail on the eastern slopes at the start. Later on, the moonlight will touch the western slopes in time to light your crossing at Trail Crest.

Summer nights can be cold, especially if a brisk wind is blowing. Plan for freezing temperatures above 10,000 feet. The coldest time of the night is just before sunrise. If you are on schedule, you will be on or near the summit, the coldest place on the mountain, at the coldest time of the night. Take gloves, a wind parka, wind pants, and a fleece jacket with hood. Carry an LED headlamp with extra batteries. Take ample food and water and follow the applicable recommendations listed under "Trail Tips for a Single-Day Ascent."

3 BEING PREPARED

Rise early. Fix a time-table to which you must try to keep.
One seldom regrets having made an early start, but one
always regrets having set off too late; first for reasons of
safety—the adage 'it is later than you think' is very true in
the mountains—but also because of the strange beauty of the
moment: the day comes to replace the night, the peaks gradu-
ally lighten, it is the hour of mystery but also of hope. Setting
off by lantern-light, witnessing the birth of a new day as one
climbs to meet the sun, this is a wonderful experience.
—Gaston Rébuffat, *from* On Snow and Rock, 1963

IN HIS BOOK **EXTREME ALPINISM**, Mark Twight offers some insightful advice for both the casual and serious climber: On the climb, live in the present. Strip away the thoughts and trivia of everyday life. Block from your mind the normal responses developed from years of day-to-day living in a mundane world. These automatic responses may not always be appropriate in the harsh mountain environment. Maintain an intense level of awareness of the mountain and be open to all that is around you.

A critical climbing mistake made by many is to anticipate the outcome. Better not to worry whether the climbing will be easy or difficult, whether you will succeed or fail. Anticipating failure, fear, your perceived deficiencies, and imagined mountain challenges will predestine you to failure. Accept, and be prepared to react to, whatever obstacles the mountain offers. Your training, planning, preparation, and mountain awareness will allow you to react to each difficulty when it occurs.

By knowing what to expect, the dangers of mountain travel can be substantially minimized or completely avoided, and the problems successfully mastered before they become uncontrolled emergencies. Equipped with the information that follows, you will be prepared to handle any challenge the mountain throws at you, including hypothermia, mountain sickness, dehydration, snow blindness, lightning, protecting your food from bears, and much more.

MOUNTAIN MEDICINE
Hypothermia
If not adequately protected against the elements (thunderstorms, snowstorms, sleet, hail, rain, and wind), a wet and tired hiker is at risk of developing hypothermia. Hypothermia can become a serious medical

Looking across Hamilton Lake toward Kaweah Gap from the High Sierra Trail

problem, especially when one is above the tree line. If a hiker becomes wet, even a light wind can quickly strip the body of its core heat. Surprisingly, hypothermia often occurs at ambient air temperatures above freezing.

The symptoms of hypothermia are decreased mental acuity, reduced physical ability, slowness, tiredness, confusion, and, after shivering has ceased, coma and death. Hypothermia occurs when the core body temperature decreases to a level that normal muscular and cerebral functions are impaired. As the core body temperature drops, various symptoms of hypothermia appear, such as a lack of muscular coordination, weakness, a slow stumbling pace, mild confusion, and apathy. As the condition worsens, frequent stumbling and mental sluggishness with slow thought and speech intensify. Hallucinations may develop. Shivering is often uncontrollable. In the final stages, cerebral function deteriorates and death results from cessation of effective heart function.

Effective water- and wind-resistant clothing for your head, hands, body, and feet is critical. Compounding the environmental factors is moisture from perspiration. Whether your clothing gets wet from precipitation or perspiration, the result is the same: risk of hypothermia. Keep yourself and your clothing dry. Wear a synthetic wicking layer next to your skin, a layer such as pile or fleece for insulation, and a breathable waterproof layer on the exterior. Remove or add layers as conditions dictate. Keeping well nourished and hydrated is critical for maintaining normal body temperature in harsh conditions.

Do not hike alone. A hypothermic person quickly loses the ability to think rationally and may not take the necessary actions to save his or her life. A partner is invaluable in recognizing the early danger signs of hypothermia and can take the necessary critical life-saving actions.

If symptoms of hypothermia appear, seek shelter immediately to stop further heat loss. Place the victim inside a tent or hut so that he is protected from the wind, cold, and precipitation. Replace the victim's wet clothing with dry clothing and place him in a sleeping bag. Provide warm fluids. Avoid caffeinated drinks because they act as a diuretic and contribute to loss of body fluids through urination. Previously experts advised sharing body heat through body-to-body contact in a sleeping bag. However, surface rewarming (e.g., body-to-body contact, hot water bottles to the skin) suppresses shivering, which is believed to be the safest method of rewarming the body core. If the hypothermia appears to be severe, rapidly plan a rescue.

Mountain Sickness

In addition to hypothermia, mountain sickness (altitude sickness) is another concern for those ascending Whitney. Mountain sickness undoubtedly defeats more people than any other factor. Reviewing the records of those receiving permits, two out of every three falter before reaching the summit. This is a high failure rate considering that there are excellent trails to the top. So many are unsuccessful because of poor planning, inadequate conditioning, and mountain sickness. The deck is stacked against a poorly prepared hiker who drives from near sea level to South Lake at 9768 feet (Route 1), Onion Valley trailhead at 9200 feet (Routes 3 and 4), Whitney Portal at 8365 feet (Routes 6–9), or Horseshoe Meadow at 10,000 feet (Routes 10 and 11) and immediately begins to hike. Many arrive at camp the first night feeling nauseous and dizzy with a splitting headache and no energy or desire to continue.

Mountain sickness is caused by hypobaric hypoxia (reduced atmospheric pressure due to increased altitude that results in the lack of oxygen available to the body). The mechanism by which the reduced oxygen level produces the various symptoms of mountain sickness is not completely known, but the evidence suggests some alteration in the cells lining the small blood vessels that allows water to leave the blood vessels and accumulate in the tissues in an abnormal manner.

Mountain sickness is not a specific disorder but a group of widely varying symptoms caused by a rapid rise in elevation. It is a continuum of symptoms of increasing severity. What begins as a mild problem may progress into something much worse. Acute mountain sickness, generalized edema, disordered sleep, high-altitude pulmonary edema (HAPE), and high-altitude cerebral edema (HACE) represent the spectrum of altitude-related problems ranging from the less serious to the often fatal. Although individual susceptibility to mountain sickness is highly variable, hikers who have had one or more episodes, young children, and women in their premenstrual phase are at highest risk.

Acute Mountain Sickness—The symptoms of mild AMS are similar to those of a hangover or the flu: lack of energy, loss of appetite, mild headache, nausea, dizziness, shortness of breath, general feeling of lassitude, and disturbed sleep. These symptoms generally resolve over twenty-four to forty-eight hours at a given altitude and go away more quickly if one descends. Victims experiencing moderate mountain sickness involving severe headache, nausea, and vomiting must descend immediately.

On several occasions at the 12,000-foot Trail Camp, hikers in my party had all the symptoms—severe headache, dizziness, shortness of breath, extreme lethargy, puffy and swollen faces and hands, and the inability to drink or eat even small portions without vomiting. Even though it was getting dark, it was determined that they should hike down the mountain immediately (with assistance) until they showed signs of improvement. In each case, improvements were realized after dropping 1000–2000 feet.

General Edema—This is a harmless disorder occurring during the first couple of days at high altitude. Edema is an abnormal collection of fluid in the extracellular, extravascular compartment, typically in dependent parts of the extremities. Edema probably is caused by the increased permeability of small blood vessels and reduced kidney function resulting from reduced oxygen concentrations in the blood. This fluid retention can cause a noticeable weight gain of four or more pounds. The excess fluid retention can cause a swelling of the face, eyelids, ankles, feet, fingers, and hands. Urine output may be scanty despite adequate fluid intake. In the absence of AMS, edema can be treated effectively with a diuretic.

Disordered Sleep—This is as troublesome to the person experiencing the symptoms as it is to his or her tent mate. The symptoms include fitful sleep, Cheyne–Stokes respirations (periods of not breathing for up to sixty seconds followed by rapid breathing while asleep), and a sense of general tiredness the next morning. In some hikers, it is the only symptom of high altitude, and it may persist the entire time while at elevation. Presumably, the mechanism causing disordered sleep is cerebral hypoxia. Diamox/acetazolamide (125 mg) taken before going to sleep may help to reduce the symptoms.

HAPE and HACE—With high-altitude pulmonary edema, the air sacs in the lungs fill with fluid that has oozed through the walls of the pulmonary capillaries. As air sacs become filled with fluid, the oxygen transfer to the pulmonary capillaries is blocked, resulting in cyanosis (decreased oxygen saturation of hemoglobin, with a bluish cast to the lips and nail beds). Symptoms are inordinate shortness of breath and a dry, nonproductive cough or a cough producing a small amount of pink-tinged sputum (caused by blood from the lungs). Without immediate treatment, HAPE may eventually lead to severe hypoxia, coma, and death. Treatment is immediate descent.

With high-altitude cerebral edema, fluid is retained in the brain cavity, causing swelling inside the skull. It is characterized by severe headache, nausea, vomiting, mental confusion, poor judgment, ataxia (clumsy or uncoordinated gait), and eventually coma and death. Without immediate treatment, HACE may quickly lead to coma and death. Descending immediately to a lower altitude often can make a significant difference.

Both HAPE and HACE are rare in California, occurring in only about 0.5 percent and 0.1 percent, respectively, of hikers venturing above 8000 feet. But both are true emergencies necessitating immediate descent and prompt medical attention. Descent usually cures these mountain emergencies miraculously. Do not delay descent because of nightfall, inconvenience, experimenting with medications, or expectation of a rescue. In descending 1000 to 3000 feet, the victim must always be accompanied by one or more individuals and, in severe cases, carried. Even a modest descent can improve the victim's condition markedly and save his or her life.

Prevention and Recovery—There are several things you can do to help prevent or reduce the severity of the various forms of mountain sickness. Prepare for the climb by taking several acclimatization hikes to 12,000 feet. Camp two nights above 8000 feet immediately before the climb. While on the mountain, take your time by planning to spend at least two nights above 11,000 feet before going for the summit. These measures will decrease the incidence of AMS and will improve your party's chance for success as you ascend to over 14,000 feet on Whitney.

Drink plenty of water or your favorite sport drink two days before the climb and during the ascent. Research suggests that there is a direct correlation between fluid intake and susceptibility to altitude sickness. Ample fluid intake is also essential for preventing dehydration.

Take Diamox/acetazolamide (a mild diuretic that acidifies the blood) 65–125 mg twice a day for those who suffer repeatedly from unpleasant symptoms despite a slow ascent. This prescription medication can be taken a day or two before the climb and until maximum altitude is attained or for three to five days, whichever is less. Side effects include a tingling of the face and fingers and frequent urination.

The following measures may help alleviate the discomfort associated with mountain sickness and may promote recovery.

- Avoid heavy exertion but maintain light activity (such as walking) to increase circulation. The natural tendency is to lie down and rest, but this reduces circulation.
- Drink plenty of water, more than you think is necessary. A sport drink also is beneficial.
- Eat light meals, avoiding too much fat. Warm soups are excellent.
- Take an aspirin, acetaminophen, or ibuprofen for symptom relief.
- Monitor closely for HAPE or HACE. If early signs are apparent, the victim must be taken 1000 to 3000 feet lower. If an immediate improvement is not observed, remove the victim from the mountain.
- Administer Diamox/acetazolamide 125 mg twice a day.

Sunburn

Sunburn is more easily prevented than treated. Apply sunblock lotion frequently and generously during the day. Use a sunblock that provides the greatest amount of protection (SPF 40 or greater), and one that protects against both ultraviolet A and B rays. Sunblock in conjunction with a wide-brimmed hat and fabric that hangs down is effective in preventing sunburn to the face and neck. Apply aloe vera gel to sunburned and wind-chapped skin, and a moisturizer/protectant such as Blistex Daily Conditioning Treatment to face and lips to promote healing before going to bed and in the morning.

Snow Blindness

Snow blindness is a potential problem whenever large amounts of snow remain on the ground. In the simplest terms, snow blindness is sunburn

Opposite: On our way to Sixty Lakes Basin, these bighorn sheep rams allowed us to watch and photograph them.

of the epithelial layer (cornea) of the eye. To protect against the damaging effects of the ultraviolet rays, it is important to wear sunglasses when traveling on snow. Even when it is cloudy and snowing, snow blindness can occur after a few hours of unprotected exposure. Snow blindness can be extremely painful. Even the dim light of a lone candle can be infinitely unpleasant and vexatious. Treatment is an eye patch over the affected eye for twenty-four to forty-eight hours. In most cases, the eyes heal quickly with no lingering damage or side effects. When snow is not present it is also a good practice to wear sunglasses when hiking at altitude because there is significantly less atmosphere to filter the effects of ultraviolet rays.

Aches and Pains

You will experience aches, pains, and sore muscles and joints during and after your hike. Ibuprofen is the wonder drug for hikers and climbers. Taken with food once or twice during the day, this over-the-counter miracle brings welcome relief to the common ills associated with strenuous climbing and hiking. A 200- to 400-mg dose at midday acts as a powerful second wind for the tired and sore hiker. Another 200–400 mg taken before bed helps reduce stiffness and greatly improves the quality of sleep. Always take ibuprofen with food and ample amounts of water to reduce the drug's effect on your kidneys. Five to ten minutes of stretching exercises at the end of the hike as part of the cooling-down process, and then again before bedtime, is also helpful in reducing stiffness and improving sleep.

Dehydration

Losses of two to four liters of liquid per day from perspiration, breathing, and urination are common for backcountry hikers. Dehydration is further compounded by the symptoms of mountain sickness: nausea, vomiting, and a dulling of the thirst sensation that accompanies a loss of appetite. Studies suggest that dehydration contributes to depression, impaired judgment, and other psychological changes that occur at high altitudes.

Inadequate fluid replacement results in reduced circulating blood volume, the symptoms of which are decreased work capacity, feelings of exhaustion, and ultimately dizziness. Two days before your ascent, drink more water than usual—up to 1 to 2 extra quarts per day. During your excursion, drink generous amounts of water to maintain your strength and endurance and to reduce your susceptibility to mountain sickness. Supplementing the water with an electrolyte sport drink helps replace daily fluid losses. Soup with breakfast and dinner also aids with water and mineral repletion.

WATER SAFETY

Whether the water from a mountain stream, alpine lake, or snow bank is safe to drink is a major apprehension for outdoor enthusiasts. Most have heard about *Giardia lamblia* or *giardiasis* but many are largely misinformed about the organism. The Forest Service and National Park Service are also concerned about this issue and have sponsored the Sierra Nevada Wilderness Education Project to inform wilderness travelers about water purification protocols and provide critical information necessary to plan a safe and successful excursion into the wild. The link to the website is provided in Appendix 5.

There are several acceptable methods for treating water: iodine tablets or EPA-approved chlorine dioxide, filtering, and boiling. All are effective against the waterborne protozoan *Giardia lamblia* and its associated intestinal disorder, giardiasis.

Medical research has established that iodine tablets and chlorine dioxide are highly effective agents for sterilizing drinking water. They are effective against: viruses, bacteria, and *Giardia*. In extremely cold water, allow ten to thirty minutes for iodine tablets to dissolve. To speed the process, break the tablets into small pieces. If you do not like the flavor left by the iodine, use a neutralizing tablet that eliminates the offending taste or drop in a small flake of vitamin C. Vitamin C eliminates the iodine taste and provides a pleasant sweet taste to the water. A powdered sport drink will also eliminate the iodine flavor. Iodine tablets and chlorine dioxide are the least expensive way to treat drinking water, and their weight in your pack is negligible.

Filtering water is a reasonable method to purify water for *Giardia* but filters have several drawbacks: they do not remove waterborne viruses, may not be effective against bacteria depending on the pore size of the filter, are costly, heavy, bulky, and time consuming to use. Filtering alone does not ensure safe drinking water; iodine or chlorine-based purification is also needed.

Boiling water kills almost all infectious microorganisms, including *Giardia* cysts. However, it is inconvenient and time-consuming unless done in the preparation of a meal. *Giardia* cysts are highly susceptible to heat, and simply bringing water to 176 degrees Fahrenheit for two minutes or to 190 degrees Fahrenheit for a minute will kill them. At 10,000 feet, water boils at 194 degrees Fahrenheit, and at 14,000 feet at 187 degrees Fahrenheit.

There are several newer state-of-the-art devices that also purify water effectively. These have bright futures and may soon replace filters as a popular method of water purification. One device uses a combination

of salt and electricity while another uses ultraviolet rays. These devices are expensive and take up space in your pack but weigh less than bulky filters and are easier to use.

Proper personal hygiene is just as important in avoiding giardiasis and other backcountry illnesses as treating the water. Asymptomatic carriers can spread the disease without knowing it. Cooks and food handlers can easily spread giardiasis when good hygiene is not practiced. This is consistent with recent findings that a majority of giardiasis cases are caused by fecal-oral or foodborne transmission. In the backcountry, use antibacterial waterless soap after each nature call and before preparing and eating meals.

LIGHTNING

The first recorded fatality from a lightning bolt on Mount Whitney was on July 26, 1904, when a member of a scientific party was struck and killed on the summit. More recently, a climber was killed by a lightning strike as he sought shelter in the stone hut on the summit. The summit hut has since been grounded but is still considered unsafe during a lightning storm. In July 2005, lightning in the Whitney region along the John Muir Trail (JMT) killed a Boy Scout and an assistant scout leader.

Although lightning is not one of the main concerns of hikers, it has caused a number of serious (and mostly avoidable) accidents and should be a major consideration when thunderheads form. The very nature of a mountain ascent places climbers in locations that are frequent targets of lightning: high and exposed peaks and ridges.

There are three types of lightning hazard: a direct strike, ground currents, and induced currents (in the immediate vicinity of a strike). Lightning is electricity, and when 100 billion electrons strike a peak or tree, they spread instantaneously in all directions. The electrical discharge radiates outward and downward, decreasing rapidly as the distance from the strike increases.

Two factors determine the potential extent of injury from lightning: the amount of current received and the part of the body affected. The most serious threat is current running from one hand to the other, passing through the heart and lungs, or from head to foot, passing through the vital organs. This is serious even if the amount of current is small. A hiker can survive a larger amount of current if it does not pass through vital organs.

The first rule is to avoid areas that might be hit by lightning. Seek a

Opposite: Dusy Basin is filled with water courses, meadows, and lakes (Route 1).

location with nearby projections or masses that are significantly higher and closer than your head to any clouds. In a forest, the best place is among the shorter trees. Along a ridge, the best location is in the middle because the ends are more susceptible to strikes. The following are additional useful tips for hikers caught in a lightning storm:

- if a lightning storm is approaching, descend quickly to a safe location away from the summit and off exposed ridges.
- if caught in an exposed position, seek a location with nearby projections or masses that are significantly higher than your head.
- avoid moist areas, including crevices and gullies.
- sit, crouch, or stand on an insulating object such as a coiled rope, sleeping bag, or sleeping pad.
- occupy as small an area as possible. Keep your feet close together and hands off the ground.
- stay out of small depressions; choose instead a narrow, slight rise to avoid ground currents. A small detached rock on a scree slope is excellent.
- stay away from overhangs and out of small caves.
- when on a ledge, crouch at the outer edge, at least 4 feet from the rock wall.

WILDLIFE ENCOUNTERS
Bears

Adult black bears roaming the mountains of California can weigh up to 350 pounds and come in various shades of brown, black, and cinnamon. *Generally*, they are not as dangerous or aggressive as the grizzly bear, but they can inflict serious damage to parked cars (in search of stored food) and can devour a week's supply of your food in a matter of minutes.

In the Sierra Nevada near Mount Whitney, a bear's natural habitat is below 10,000 feet. These elevations support an environment that includes a wide variety of trees, brush, shrubs, grasslands, and bogs that produce berries, acorns, grubs, bugs, and insects necessary for a bear's survival. Terrain above the tree line does not support the necessary food-producing habitats, so it is normally free of bears.

Bears are an ever-present problem at certain trailhead parking lots, campgrounds, and backcountry campsites. Many have become adept at breaking into parked cars and bringing down bear bags hung from tree limbs. Bears have learned to recognize the shape of ice chests and have broken into cars for an empty ice chest. Do not leave food, toiletries, sunscreen, soap, garbage, an empty ice chest, or anything with a smell in a parked car or in your tent.

Use the bear-proof storage boxes provided at many trailheads to store food and other distinctive-smelling items. For certain backcountry destinations with a history of bear activity, the Forest Service and National Park Service require hikers to carry preapproved bear-resistant food containers. Check with these agencies to determine on which trails you are required to tote your own bear-resistant food containers. Portable bear-proof canisters are available for rent or purchase from forest service and national park visitor centers.

The National Park Service has placed bear-proof food storage boxes at many wilderness locations that are notorious for bears. Nearly forty bear-proof food storage boxes have been placed in twenty-five national park wilderness locations along Routes 1–5 and 10–15. Bear-proof box locations are described in Chapters 5 and 6 at the start of each route description.

There are no bear-proof food storage boxes on Routes 6–9 because these trails are ostensibly located in Forest Service wilderness areas. For a variety of reasons the Forest Service has not followed the lead of the National Park Service in placing bear-proof food storage boxes at overnight locations where there are high concentrations of backpackers and bears.

When wilderness bear-proof food storage boxes or portable bear-resistance food containers are not available, use the counterbalance method to hang food from a tree limb. The counterbalance method can be effective, if done correctly, but many bears have been successful at outsmarting many elaborate methods hikers have used to hang their food.

If you come upon a bear in the backcountry or catch a bear in the act of raiding your camp, make yourself look big by holding up your arms and standing on a large rock or picnic table. Yell and make noise; become annoying enough to make the bear leave. If a bear swipes your food, however, do not attempt to retrieve it.

Mountain Lions

The same advice for dealing with a bear applies in the event of a rare encounter with a mountain lion. Face the cat, make yourself look as big as you can by raising your arms, putting on a backpack, and standing on a large object, and make a lot of noise. More than likely the cat will quickly leave the area. Under no circumstance should you turn your back or run.

Other Critters

Marmots, chipmunks, mice, blue jays, ravens, and other small, mischievous critters can also feast on a backpacker's food if it is not properly protected. When hanging food to protect against marmots and chipmunks, also keep in mind blue jays and ravens. A hanging food bag may be an open invitation for our flying friends.

Certain trailhead parking areas, especially at Mineral King (Route 15), are plagued by an overabundance of marmots. Marmots have been known to damage cars by climbing into the engine compartment and eating rubber hoses and wires. If you park your car for any length of time at Mineral King, consider placing chicken wire or mesh completely around it to keep the critters out. Ask the National Park Service for information and advice about marmot damage to parked cars.

Insects

Mosquitoes, biting midges, and gnats can be a problem early in the hiking season near meadows, along creeks, or anywhere water exists. Mosquitoes are the most bothersome in June and July but by August and September the problem resolves itself. Take mosquito repellent or sunscreen with mosquito repellent.

4 WHITNEY IN WINTER

*Mountaineering is one of the finest sports imaginable but
to practise it without technique is a form of more or less
deliberate suicide. Technique encourages prudence; it also
obviates fatigue and useless or dangerous halts and, far from
excluding it, it permits meditation. It is not an end in itself
but the means of promoting safety as much in the individual
climb as on the rope.*

—*Gaston Rébuffat, from* On Snow and Rock, *1963*

DURING THE WINTER WHEN MOST outdoor enthusiasts are heading toward
the rather pedestrian ski- and snowboard-slopes of a resort, the challenges of deep snow, steep ice, and harsh weather are drawing more
climbers to Mount Whitney. Even when only a couple feet of snow
cover the ground at the trailhead, ten to fifteen feet may have accumulated high on the mountain. In these conditions, the ascent will be
challenging, but skiers, snowboarders, and snowshoers will experience
a surreal descent across the snow-covered terrain. You will be struck by

The east face of Mount Whitney and camp at Iceberg Lake in the winter

the stark beauty of the mountain covered in a deep blanket of snow as well as the prospect of nearly complete solitude not often realized during the popular summer months. Although the demands are great, the rewards of a successful winter ascent more than offset the difficulties you are likely to encounter.

For the purposes of this discussion, winter extends from November 16 through May 15. Although the Sierra Nevada is known for its long stretches of stable and sunny weather, these periods of benign weather are often followed by a series of powerful winter storms. Abrupt changes in weather can occur rapidly and can catch a climber by surprise but hopefully not ill prepared.

A winter visitor should be an experienced cross-country traveler and proficient at routefinding over rugged terrain. Competency in the use of map and compass is critical. At the higher elevations, trails will be completely buried by deep snow, so you will be forging your own route. If you are caught in a storm, your visibility could be reduced to a few feet. Without the proper skills, experience, and navigational tools, one can easily become confused and eventually lost, possibly perishing in the harsh environment.

SAFETY AND SURVIVAL

If you spend any amount of time in the mountains during the winter, you are likely to be caught in a major storm. All your planning and prudence cannot guarantee you will avoid an unanticipated storm that surprises even the weather forecasters. At the first sign of a major storm, retreat from the mountain. If this is not possible, descend to a lower elevation among the protection of trees to pitch your tent or build a snow shelter. Make sure that you are not in a run-out avalanche zone. Dig down among the trees and construct a level tent platform below the natural grade of the snow. Cut snow blocks and surround your tent with these blocks, placing them on the windward side of the tent.

Plan to stay a day or more—stay until the storm stops and the avalanche danger decreases. Remember that avalanche risk is at its greatest on steep slopes during and immediately after a storm. It is astounding how bleak and emotionally discouraging it can be in the middle of a storm and how wonderful it can become within twenty-four or forty-eight hours when the storm passes and the sun shines. Do not panic— stay put and wait out the storm.

Being caught during a violent storm in an exposed position above the tree line can be dangerous. Winds can reach eighty to one-hundred-plus miles per hour and the temperature can drop below zero Fahrenheit. I have experienced heavy snows, high winds, and temperatures dropping to minus ten degrees Fahrenheit at 12,000 feet as late as the first week in May. On numerous occasions, in March, April, and May, I have been caught in horrific storms and pinned in my tent for one to three days. We have survived with little or no damage to our shelter, but on several occasions gale-force winds have snapped tent poles, collapsed tents, and shredded a tent fly.

SNOW SHELTERS

On the first day of winter, on the summit of Lassen Peak, an igloo that Gene Leach and I constructed saved our lives and that of two climbing partners when a powerful storm, packing hurricane-force winds, swept across the summit plateau in the middle of the night. Snow is an excellent insulator and I did not know that it was storming outside until our two climbing partners sought refuge in our igloo—their tent had just been destroyed by the perilous storm. On another occasion in the Trinity Alps, an igloo again saved my life when a storm dumped eighteen inches of snow. Without the protection of the igloo, Dick Everest and I likely would have perished.

An igloo or snow cave is an excellent shelter to protect a backcountry traveler from the fiercest winds and coldest storms. The temperature outside can drop below zero but inside the temperature will hover around thirty degrees. The inside of the snow shelter will warm slightly with a candle and will jump to forty or more degrees when you are cooking a meal.

Use the following guidelines, developed by Gene Leach, to construct an igloo. You will need two energetic workers, a snow shovel, a snow saw per person, and heavy-duty rubber gloves. To keep dry during construction, put on a windbreaker or Goretex parka and pants.

- Finding the right snow texture and consistency for cutting snow blocks is critical. The best snow is usually found on a north-facing slope. Snow melted by the sun during the day and refrozen at night contains ice crystals and does not bond well or make good snow blocks.

- Stomp out the area where you plan to build the igloo. Draw a circle with the radius equal to the length of a ski pole. For more than two people, a slightly larger radius is suggested.

- Cut snow blocks two feet by one foot by one foot. Place the blocks around the circle you drew in the snow. This first row of blocks forms the base of the igloo.

- After completing the first row of snow blocks, use a snow saw to shape this row into a circular ramp. This ramp will start at snow level and finish one block high. Begin the ramp by cutting the first block flush with the surrounding snow. Proceed around the row of blocks, carving a ramp that curves gradually upward until it finishes even with the top of the final block, adjacent to the starting point.

■ Start the second row by placing the first block on the lowest point of the circular ramp; continue placing snow blocks around the circle to create the second row.

■ Beginning with the second row, use a snow saw to slope or angle the top of the blocks inward toward the center of the igloo, so that an imaginary line running parallel along the top of each block would pass through the center of the igloo.

■ For the next row of blocks and all subsequent rows, make sure the slope of the top block points to the center of the igloo.

■ When bonding a snow block to its neighbor, it may be necessary to make a small fresh cut because the ends of the blocks tend to ice up quickly, preventing a good bond from forming.

■ Each new block is supported both by the blocks beneath it and by its neighbor to one side. It is the support of the block to one side that allows you to angle each row of blocks in a little farther.

■ One member of the group should stay inside to support, trim, and fit each block while the other member cuts and carries the blocks.

■ It takes about to two hours for two workers to construct an igloo. It is tiring work for the one cutting and carrying the blocks, but it is rewarding when you come to the last few blocks that are laid nearly horizontal overhead.

■ Cut an entrance. Fill the cracks with snow. If the bonding has been good, a strong structure now exists.

■ Make a small vent in the top.

The following describes the "T" method of snow-cave construction. One energetic worker can build a snow cave but a second helper is desirable. A snow shovel, a snow saw, and heavy-duty rubber gloves are all that are needed. To keep dry, put on a windbreaker or Goretex parka and pants. Even though the process of building a snow cave takes about one and a half to two hours, the final comfort and pleasure make it worth the effort—inside is certainly warmer than the cold winter night! Select a site facing away from the sun with a slope of forty-five degrees or greater.

■ Start by cutting a rectangle, approximately six feet high by two feet wide, into the snowbank. This will be the entrance to the snow cave (this is the main stem of the "T"). The combination of cutting blocks with a lightweight snow saw and lifting the blocks of snow out with a shovel is more efficient than simply digging with a shovel.

- Dig and cut into the bank far enough so your head is now inside when you are standing up. At waist height, make the initial cuts for the left and right side bars (left and right arms of the "T"). Each side bar should be about two feet wide by two feet high by two feet deep. The initial purpose of the side bars is to initialize a platform on each side for sleeping and to open up the construction area so that excess snow dug from the cave can be removed easily. Picture a "T". The main stem is about six feet high and two feet wide. Each side bar is about two feet high (with the top of the side bar flush with the top of the main stem of the "T") and two feet long. The resulting "T" is about six feet high and six feet across the top.
- The rest of the work is time-consuming and tiring. Enlarge each sleeping platform by cutting back into the slope. To create the necessary headroom above the sleeping platforms, cut upward, enlarging the ceiling. These chunks of snow will fall onto the newly formed sleeping platform and are easily moved out of the snow cave. By this process, you will construct sleeping platforms with a domed ceiling providing ample headroom for sitting.
- When finished with the internal construction, use the saved snow blocks to seal both side bars of the "T," leaving only the vertical entrance exposed. The top portion of the entrance can also be sealed to give more protection from the elements. The resulting crawl space can be covered with a small tarp or plugged with a pack.
- Position sleeping pads and sleeping bags on the two platforms. Set up the stove, making certain there is an air vent in the ceiling. Light a candle. You are now ready to enjoy your shelter and the evening in comfort.

WHEN IS THE BEST TIME TO GO?

During December, January, and February, the days are short and the nights long and cold. The weather is unsettled and storms are frequent. New snow is being added to the snowpack with regularity. Travel over the soft, unconsolidated snow may be difficult even on backcountry skis or snowshoes.

With this in mind, March through May is the preferred time for a winter ascent of Mount Whitney. The days are longer, the nights are shorter, the avalanche risk is generally lower, and the snow is compacting, thereby improving backcountry travel. The weather during these months is more stable but be mindful that strong winter storms often pummel the high country in March, April, and early May.

An ascent of Whitney during this time is an excellent opportunity

Looking toward Mount Newcomb from Sky-Blue Lake during a winter circumnavigation of Whitney

to experience the solitude and grandeur of the peak. This is when the winter snow turns to velvetlike spring corn, providing exquisite skiing and snowboarding. With snow covering the brush, boulders, and talus, a winter mountaineer can proceed with confidence and freedom, without the geologic impediments experienced during the summer.

Another consideration is the condition of the roads that provide access to the trailheads. These roads are not plowed, so you will be able to drive only to the snow line or the first major snowbank blocking the road. An ascent in the early months of winter could require a considerable hike up the road to reach the trailhead.

Avalanche danger is an ever-present consideration and unconsolidated snow during the early winter months increases this risk. Avalanches can also occur later in the winter season within a week following a major storm or on a warm day when the snow and rocks are heated by the sun. I have triggered major avalanches on the east face of Lassen Peak and Echo Col in April and May. On another occasion, my American Eskimo dog, Prince, was swept down the east face of Red and White Mountain in April by an avalanche that was started by the warming of the rocks beneath the snow. Fortunately, he survived an 800-foot rough and tumble ride down the mountain to climb and ski with me again.

Avalanches during the winter of 2004–05 produced the first backcountry ski deaths on the eastside of the Sierra in many years. A friend of mine, an experienced backcountry skier, died in an avalanche near the Sierra Club hut on Anderson Peak (near Donner Lake) in February. Two other experienced skiers, including a guide, died in a massive avalanche near the top of Elderberry Canyon on Mount Tom that same year. On both occasions, an unusually large amount of fresh snow had accumulated on a hard icy layer of old snow. When the skiers crossed these heavily laden slopes, they triggered the disastrous slides.

To recap, the best time for a winter ascent is in the later months of the winter season when the snow has begun to firm up, it has not stormed for ten days or more, and stable weather is forecast. Depending on the amount of snow that accumulates during the winter season, there can be ample snow for skiing, snowboarding, and snowshoeing into May.

AVALANCHE AWARENESS

Everyone going into the backcountry during the winter must recognize and understand the risks. Before considering a winter expedition, learn all you can by reading and taking several avalanche courses that stress hazard evaluation and self-rescue techniques. Avalanche awareness is developed through education, observation, and winter mountain experience. Appendix 5 lists guides that provide avalanche training and Appendix 8 includes several excellent reference books on the subject.

It is critical that you recognize avalanche terrain and the associated risk factors. John Moynier, in *Avalanche Aware: Safe Travel in Avalanche Country*, states that avalanche evaluation is a function of four fundamental factors: terrain (slope angle, slope aspect); weather (current and past weather, temperature, precipitation, wind); snowpack (depth, types of layers, physical condition of the snow); and human judgment. Understanding these factors will help you make good judgments about when and where to go. These four factors are discussed below.

Terrain

When planning a trip, if at all possible choose a route that avoids avalanche terrain. Favor a route that follows a ridge or wide valley. Stay clear of likely slide paths and run-out zones. Densely timbered slopes are generally safer than open slopes. Slopes thirty to fifty degrees are the most likely to slide. Even low-angled slopes can be unsafe if threatened by steeper slopes above.

Slope aspect is an important consideration in determining avalanche hazard. Sunny slopes are more likely to slide immediately after a storm and are the quickest to stabilize. North slopes are less likely to be affected by the sun and are more likely to conceal weak layers of poorly bonded snow crystals during cold weather.

Orientation to the prevailing wind direction is also a significant factor. Windward slopes are likely to be scoured during storms. On leeward slopes, the wind often deposits thick layers of snow known as slabs. These pose the single greatest avalanche concern for backcountry travelers.

The wind can also form large and potentially dangerous cornices on ridges. These features can be unstable and may threaten more moderate slopes below. When traveling along a ridge, stay back from the edge as a snow cornice may be overhanging the lee side of the ridge. The soft area just below a cornice is often a slab, formed by the eddying effect of the wind. When a cornice collapses, it can trigger an avalanche in the unstable slab below.

Weather

Any substantial change in the weather should be noted and carefully evaluated because it could have a dramatic impact on the stability of the slope. Rain, warm winds, or a sudden increase in temperature can lead to decreased stability of the snowpack. These factors affect the relative density of surface layers and the bonding capabilities of the crystals within a given layer of the snowpack.

Most slides occur during or immediately after a storm. Snow falling at a rate of an inch an hour or twelve inches in twenty-four hours is a serious warning sign. Moderate winds can compound the danger by transporting snow from one area to another, often depositing dangerous slabs on lee slopes in a short time.

Snowpack

An important clue to snowpack stability is evidence of recent avalanches. Fresh fractures, blocks of debris, and large snowballs are other important clues that conditions are unstable. Widespread settling of the snow around tree branches or exposed cliffs should be taken as an indication of potential instability. Cracks forming in the snow or "whoomphing" sounds may indicate potentially dangerous slab conditions overlying weaker layers.

The layers of snow within the pack is another important indicator. Poor bonding between the layers is a common cause of avalanches.

Human Judgment

Experience, knowledge, and judgment become your guide when traveling in the backcountry. Gather all the information you can before you go. Check the National Weather Service website, get a local avalanche forecast, and call the Forest Service for snow conditions. Form an opinion about the snow's stability before leaving the trailhead. Be prepared to augment or even overhaul your assessment along the way. Don't be too stubborn to leave the mountain for another day, if conditions dictate.

If you must travel in a hazardous area, limit your exposure. Cross one at a time with avalanche beacons on transmit and all eyes on the person crossing. Take advantage of safer areas such as dense timber, rock outcroppings, ridges, and wide valleys. If you must ascend or descend a

Telemark skiing down a chute in the headwall on Mount Pickering

dangerous slope, stay close to the outer edge and choose a vertical line of ascent. Ascending straight up or descending down the fall line is much safer than cutting the slope with traverses. Don't assume a slope is safe just because someone else has traveled through the area.

Make sure everyone in your group carries an avalanche transceiver (beacon), shovel, and avalanche probes, and knows how to use them.

WINTER GEAR

Compared with a relatively uncomplicated climb of Whitney in the summer, a winter assault takes on the trappings of a mini-expedition. Warmer clothing and additional specialized equipment is required. This translates to a heavier backpack, slower travel, additional effort on your part, and more time spent on the mountain to reach the summit. The following discussion covers the equipment critical for a successful winter climb. A complete list of equipment is contained in Appendix 3. For additional information on equipment, route descriptions, and winter conditions on Whitney, refer to my book *50 Classic Backcountry Ski and Snowboard Summits in California: Mount Shasta to Mount Whitney*.

Skis, Snowboards, Snowshoes, and Poles

Struggling through deep unconsolidated snow while sinking to your knees with each step is a serious impediment to your success and is no fun even for the most impassioned outdoor enthusiast. Using snowshoes, backcountry skis, or a split-board snowboard can help solve this problem.

Leave your skinny, cross-country skis and leather boots at home. New technology has turned yesterday's state-of-the-art equipment into dinosaurs. The advent of plastic backcountry ski boots and shorter/wider skis is opening up entirely new and steeper terrain heretofore considered off limits for most backcountry skiers. Split-boards allow snowboarders to access the backcountry nearly as easily as telemark skiers. Skis and split-boards need to be augmented with climbing skins for uphill travel. Light, state-of-the-art snowshoes also make it possible for non-skiers/boarders to ascend over soft snow to Whitney's lofty summit. Snowshoers should also use ski poles for improved balance.

Ice Ax and Crampons

Lightweight aluminum has replaced steel to greatly reduce the weight of crampons and ice axes. Some ice axes now weigh less than a pound and a pair of crampons less than one and a half pounds. You will need both these items above 12,000 feet, where hard-packed snow and icy conditions are likely to prevail.

Internal-Frame Backpack

With snowshoes, mountaineering skis, or a snowboard, an internal-frame pack is preferable. Compared to an external-frame pack, it is less prone to shift on your back. The unexpected shifting of your backpack can cause a loss of balance at an inopportune time. When purchasing a pack, look for a seventy-liter or larger backpack weighing less than four pounds with a removable back pad. This pad can be used to augment your sleeping pad for increased comfort.

Sleeping Bag and Pad

Select a sleeping bag that is rated to zero degrees Fahrenheit. The nights are long and cold, so a warm bag is critical. A down bag with a Dryloft shell is best. The Dryloft fabric keeps the down dry from the blowing snow and spindrift that can make their way inside your tent during a storm. Without Dryloft, take a bivy sack weighing eight ounces or less to protect the bag. A synthetic-filled bag is less expensive but is heavy and bulky.

A three-quarter-length or full-length, self-inflating pad is recommended. The removable pad from your backpack can be used to augment your sleeping pad.

Soft-Shell Pants and Soft-Shell Jackets

Soft-shell clothing is made of tightly woven fabrics (polyester, Cordura, nylon, wool, microfleece, and Lycra) that are durable, warm, wind-resistant, water-resistant, and breathable. Soft-shell outer-layer garments are superior in any season but are especially valuable in the winter. In case of wet weather, the soft-shell jacket should be augmented with a watertight parka.

A soft-shell jacket with a hood is favored. The hood provides the wind protection and added warmth necessary for your head and neck on a cold winter day.

Storm-Proof Hard-Shell Parka

A watertight, storm-proof parka with a hood should be taken in case of wet weather. A lightweight parka worn over a soft-shell jacket will protect you against the most violent storm.

Hanging Stove with Two-Quart Cooking Pot

The traditional single-burner backpack stove that uses white gas or pressurized canister gas is adequate in stable weather. However, in a storm with gale-force winds, cooking with these stoves is undesirable, miserable, and nearly impossible. I have spent too many hours cooking breakfast and dinner outside my tent in blizzard conditions. But no longer do I have to suffer miserably in the elements. A hanging stove suspended from the ceiling of the tent is the answer. I now stay warm and dry in the tent in a down bag, cooking breakfast and dinner in a two-quart cooking pot on my hanging stove. An added benefit is that the stove will warm the tent to a pleasant temperature while you relax.

Shelter

A freestanding, three- or four-season tent with three or four poles is critical. The importance of a sturdy tent in the face of a snowstorm with sixty-mile-per-hour winds cannot be overstated. Your life may depend on it. Most three- and four-pole tents weight seven to nine pounds. This is too much. Look for a two-person tent that weighs four to six pounds. The challenge is to find a tent that is roomy, sturdy, lightweight, and economical. There are a few on the market but further improvements are welcome from the manufacturers.

Floorless single-pole "tents" are not serious shelters for a climb of Whitney in the winter. In stable weather they would be adequate but are unacceptable during a winter storm. They are unable to withstand a strong windstorm and would collapse from its force.

Personal Locator Beacon

This is an emergency device to be used as a last resort to signal distress to Search and Rescue. When turned on, the beacon automatically transmits your personalized, digitally coded distress signal, which uniquely identifies your beacon, your name, address, contact information, and your precise location (UTM coordinates) using GPS technology.

Avalanche Beacon

As discussed in "Avalanche Awareness" above, an avalanche transceiver is strongly recommended. Practice using the instrument before heading into the mountains.

WINTER ROUTES

The best routes for a winter ascent are those that start from Whitney Portal or Horseshoe Meadow. Routes 6–10 are the shortest and most direct. However, the roads to these trailheads are not plowed, so you will be able to drive only to the snow line. The Horseshoe Meadow Road climbs to 10,000 feet while the Whitney Portal Road attains 8365 feet. The amount of snowfall during the winter and the date of your trip will dictate how far you will have to walk along the road to reach the trailhead. For trips starting at the Whitney Portal, you may be required to hike an additional 3.6 miles to reach the trailhead.

By the end of March the snow at the lower elevations begins to melt, allowing better access. However, be aware that a major storm can strike at any time, stranding you and your vehicle. On one occasion a friend and I drove up the Horseshoe Meadow Road to the snow line, and hiked and skied to Horseshoe Meadow to climb Cirque Peak. That night it snowed eighteen inches. The next day in a blizzard we retreated to the car. Unfortunately, it was stuck in deep snow so we spent a night in the car. The following morning we skied and hiked all the way to Lone Pine. It took two 4-wheel-drive tow trucks with chains to pull the car out. Before leaving on your trip, contact the Forest Service office for a report on road conditions and check the weather report.

Below is a brief description of Routes 6–10 and what you might expect to encounter. For more details about each route, refer to the specific route descriptions in Chapter 5.

Route 6—Mountaineers Route

The Mountaineers Route and the Mount Whitney Trail (Route 8) are the most direct routes to the summit and are the logical choices for a winter ascent. The Mountaineers Route is steeper and more difficult than the Whitney Trail. The steep couloir on the Mountaineers Route can be avalanche-prone, especially the top several hundred feet. Because the couloir and north face receive little direct sunlight, the snow is slow to stabilize.

From Iceberg Lake climb the prominent Mountaineers couloir, positioned on the northeast face and right shoulder of Whitney, to a notch at 14,090 feet (visible from Iceberg Lake). At this notch, angle west descending slightly and then turn left toward the summit, climbing a gully that becomes extremely steep and icy near the top. To avoid this steep segment, traverse west across the north face to the summit ridge. Gain the ridge west of the summit. The traverse is exposed and there is a risk of avalanche on its steep slopes. Once you have attained the ridge, follow the ridge for ten minutes to the summit.

Route 7—Circumnavigation Route of Whitney

Follow Route 7 to Iceberg Lake. Continue over the Whitney-Russell Col to Arctic Lake and Guitar Lake. From Guitar Lake turn west and ascend steep slopes to Trail Crest and follow the John Muir Trail to the summit. Oftentimes, even in the middle of winter, the trail may have bare patches as fierce winds scour the mountain preventing snow from

accumulating. From the summit, return to Trail Crest and descend the Whitney Trail to complete your circumnavigation of the peak. The steep section below Trail Crest has the greatest avalanche risk.

Route 8—Mount Whitney Trail

The Whitney Trail is the easiest wintertime route. However, it is not without its difficulties and one must be cautious of the avalanche potential on the steeper terrain especially the steep slope between Trail Camp and Trail Crest. Make sure the weather has been stable for several weeks before attempting the climb to ensure avalanche risk is minimized.

Route 9—Meysan Lake Route

This is a surprisingly good route to reach Sky-Blue Lake and Mount Whitney in the winter. Ascend either the Mallory–Irvine Pass or LeConte–Mallory Pass. In some ways the climb above Meysan Lake to LeConte–Mallory Pass is made easier in the winter because the gullies are full of snow, allowing you to avoid the loose talus. This is the recommended winter option. However, the steep gullies that must be climbed to reach either pass are avalanche chutes and are potentially dangerous during and after a snowstorm.

From Sky-Blue Lake it is possible to climb Whitney in a day; however, it will be a strenuous one. Move your camp to upper Crabtree Lake to improve your chances of success.

Routes 6, 7, 9, and 10

Combining Routes 6, 7, 9, and 10 into a single trip is my favorite wintertime route around Whitney. It provides an opportunity to ascend Whitney via the Mountaineers couloir or a less difficult climb up the west slopes from Guitar Lake. Follow Route 6 to Iceberg Lake and, if you choose, ascend the Mountaineers couloir to the summit. Descend/ski/snowboard back to Iceberg Lake.

At Iceberg Lake, proceed over the Whitney–Russell Col and descend past Arctic Lake to Guitar Lake (Route 7). Here you have the option of climbing the west slopes to Trail Crest following the John Muir Trail to the summit. From Trail Crest you can pick up Route 9 and descend to upper Crabtree Lake via Discovery Pass. Better yet, you can return to Guitar Lake and follow Route 10 by traversing into Crabtree Lakes basin and ascending this beautiful valley to upper Crabtree Lake, Crabtree Pass, and down to Sky-Blue Lake. From Sky-Blue Lake follow Route 9

Opposite: A frozen Sky-Blue Lake in winter

over Mallory–Irvine Pass or LeConte–Mallory Pass to Meysan Lake and out to the Whitney Portal Campground.

This is an awesome route through spectacular terrain. Because of the remoteness of the area, only experienced winter travelers should attempt this route. Make sure the weather has been stable for a couple of weeks and that the report is for good weather for another week before heading out to enjoy the mountain.

Route 10–New Army Pass Route

Provided you can drive close to Horseshoe Meadow, this route provides a two-day approach to the base of Whitney via New Army Pass, Sky-Blue Lake, and upper Crabtree Lake. From either lake, an ascent of Whitney via Discovery Pass is possible, but it will be strenuous. A longer but less difficult route would be to descend past the various Crabtree Lakes to Crabtree Meadow and pick up the route of the JMT to the summit.

5 EASTSIDE TRAILHEADS

*For many, [mountaineering] is the fulfillment of childhood
dreams; for others, an opportunity to grow in the face of difficulty. In the mountains await adventure and mystery. . . .
The challenge of mountaineering offers you a chance to learn
about yourself outside the confines of the modern world.
[However, we must recognize that] mountaineering takes
place in an environment indifferent to human needs, and not
everyone is willing to pay the price for its rich physical and
spiritual rewards.*

— Mountaineering: The Freedom of the Hills,
7th Edition, 2003

IF YOU HAVE NOT VISITED THE EAST SIDE of the Sierra Nevada, the drive
along US 395 will be a wonderful discovery. The area is replete with natural wonders and awesome vistas. Traveling from north to south, you will
enjoy Lake Tahoe, Twin Lakes, Mono Lake, Mono Craters, Tioga Pass (the
gateway to Yosemite National Park high country), Mammoth Lakes, the
Minarets, Devils Postpile National Monument, Hot Creek, South Lake,
and Lake Sabrina. Along the drive the jagged east face escarpment of the
Sierra Nevada increases in height and grandeur, culminating atop Mount
Whitney. At Lone Pine, 60 miles south of Bishop, Whitney's spectacular
summit rises 10,000 feet above the Owens Valley.

Generally, the hiking routes originating on the east side of the Sierra
Nevada are shorter and start higher than their counterparts originating
on the west side. The eastside sits in the rain and snow shadow of the
precipitous wall formed by the high Sierra and is therefore arid. This
is in stark contrast to the west side of the range, where the terrain is
gentler, the approaches longer, and the heavily timbered mountains are
blessed with ample rain and snow each year.

The John Muir Trail (JMT) begins in Yosemite Valley and culminates
on the summit of Whitney nearly 220 trail miles south of its starting
point. The JMT traverses more than 7000 square miles of high mountain
grandeur. Both the east- and westside routes eventually join the JMT at
some point (except Route 6) before topping out on Whitney.

Various eastside routes share common trail segments. For instance,
Routes 1–5 have different starting points but join the JMT for the final
ascent. Route 1 (Bishop Pass Trail), Route 2 (Taboose Pass Trail), Route
3 (Kearsarge Pass Trail), Route 4 (University Pass Route), and Route 5

(Shepherd Pass Trail) join the JMT 73, 53, 30, 27, and 17 trail miles, respectively, north of Whitney.

Route 6 (Mountaineers Route) and Route 7 (Circumnavigation Route of Whitney) start at Whitney Portal and share a common approach for the first 4.8 miles. Route 6 ascends directly to Whitney's summit via a steep couloir above Iceberg Lake, never touching the JMT, whereas Route 7 crosses the Whitney–Russell Col, joining the JMT at Guitar Lake about 5.5 miles from the summit. Route 8 (Whitney Trail) is the main eastside trail to the summit and the most popular trail in the Sierra Nevada (excluding the trails in Yosemite Valley). It joins the JMT 2 miles from the summit. Route 9 (Meysan Lake Route) and Route 10 (New Army Pass Route) start at different trailheads but share a common cross-country route up Rock Creek, past beautiful Sky-Blue Lake and upper Crabtree Lake before reaching the JMT for the final ascent. Route 11 (Cottonwood Pass Trail) approaches from the south and joins the JMT at the Crabtree Meadow Ranger Station about 8 trail miles from the summit.

All routes can be completed by descending the Mount Whitney Trail (Route 8) for a finish at Whitney Portal. Consequently, hikers starting at trailheads other than Whitney Portal (Routes 1–5, 10, and 11) will

University Peak as seen from the Kearsarge Pass Trail (Route 3)

Kearsarge Lakes and Mount Brewer as viewed from Kearsarge Pass (Route 3)

require a shuttle (see Appendix 5). In addition, descending the Whitney Trail at the end of your adventure means you will be subject to the Trail Crest exit quota (see Chapter 2).

Road access to the eleven eastside trailheads is via five major east–west arterials from the towns of Bishop, Big Pine, Independence, and Lone Pine located along US 395. Bishop, one of the largest towns on the eastside of the Sierra Nevada, is situated 200 miles south of Reno, Nevada, and about 270 miles north of Los Angeles, California. Big Pine, Independence, and Lone Pine are 15, 45, and 60 miles south of Bishop. The following table summarizes the east–west access roads to the eleven eastside trailheads.

EASTSIDE ACCESS ROADS

Route Name	Trailhead, Elevation	Access Roads*	Nearest Town on US 395 From US 395 to Trailhead
1. Bishop Pass Trail	South Lake, 9,768 ft	South Lake Road	Bishop, 22.3 miles
2. Taboose Pass Trail	Taboose Creek, 5,480 ft	Taboose Creek Road	Big Pine/Independence, 5.7 miles
3. Kearsarge Pass Trail	Onion Valley, 9,200 ft	Onion Valley Road	Independence, 13.5 miles
4. University Pass Route	Onion Valley, 9,200 ft	Onion Valley Road	Independence, 13.5 miles
5. Shepherd Pass Trail	Symmes Creek, 6,300 ft	Onion Valley Road to Foothill Road	Independence, 9.0 miles
6. Circumnavigation Route of Whitney	Whitney Portal, 8,365 ft	Whitney Portal Road	Lone Pine, 13.0 miles
7. Mountaineers Route	Whitney Portal, 8,365 ft	Whitney Portal Road	Lone Pine, 13.0 miles
8. Mount Whitney Trail	Whitney Portal, 8,365 ft	Whitney Portal Road	Lone Pine, 13.0 miles
9. Meysan Lake Route	Lower Whitney Creek Campground, 6,880 ft	Whitney Portal Road	Lone Pine, 12.0 miles
10. New Army Pass Route	Horseshoe Meadow Road, 10,040 ft	Whitney Portal Road to Horseshoe Meadow Road	Lone Pine, 24.5 miles
11. Cottonwood Pass Trail	Horseshoe Meadow Road, 9,920 ft	Whitney Portal Road to Horseshoe Meadow Road	Lone Pine, 24.0 miles

*All access roads are paved except Foothill Road to Shepherd Pass Trail and Taboose Creek Road. Both are dirt roads passable with a sedan.

ROUTE 1: BISHOP PASS TRAIL
(CHAPTER 7: MAPS, ROUTES 1-5)

Start .... South Lake, 9768 feet
End .... Whitney Portal, 8365 feet
Rating .... Trail hiking (C-1)
Distance .... 96.4 miles
Elevation gain/loss ...... 20,911 feet/-22,314 feet
Trip duration .... 7-10 days
Maps .... Tom Harrison Maps—MonoDivide High
                                  Country, Kings Canyon High Country,
                                  Mount Whitney High Country Trail Map
Access road/town .... SR 168 and South Lake Road/Bishop
Car shuttle .... Yes

TRAIL PROFILE

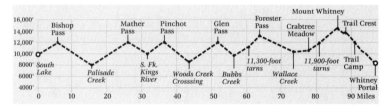

IN A NUTSHELL

Although this is a long and strenuous route covering 96 miles and 21,000 feet of elevation gain, it is a classic Sierra Nevada trek passing through some of the finest mountain scenery in America. Along this magnificent trail you will pass dozens of glistening alpine lakes, countless idyllic mountain meadows, and traverse many lofty passes with panoramic views of the pristine wilderness.

The route begins gently by passing mountain lakes and wildflower-laden meadows before ascending steeply to the Sierra Nevada Crest at Bishop Pass. On the other side of the pass, Dusy Basin, perched high above the LeConte Canyon overlooking the glacier-carved Black Divide, is a spectacular area brimming with lakes, tarns, meadows, and streams. This serene setting is one of the most picturesque in the Sierra Nevada.

Continue your descent and join the JMT in LeConte Canyon alongside the Middle Fork Kings River. Overall you will ascend six mountain passes (Bishop, Mather, Pinchot, Glen, Forester, and Trail Crest) and trek past more than twenty-six alpine lakes before reaching the summit of Whitney. Dusy Basin, Palisade Lakes, Rae Lakes, Sixty Lake Basin, Vidette Meadow to Forester Pass, Crabtree Meadow, and Guitar Lake are some of my favorite areas along the way.

A rugged cross-country variation (Variation V1.1) that traverses large talus immediately beneath the precipitous peaks of the Palisades region is included for the most experienced and athletic backpacker. For peak baggers, route descriptions for three 14,000-foot peaks (Mount Sill, Split Mountain, and Mount Muir) have been included. To augment your rest days, enjoyable side trips to Bench Lake, Center Basin, and Sixty Lake Basin are described.

To complete the 96-mile adventure following the suggested nine-day hiking itinerary, you would need to average about 11 miles and 2300 feet of elevation gain each day. Consider adding a rest day or two along the way to recuperate and relax. The extra day(s) would allow you to explore a specific area by taking a side trip without the burden of carrying your backpack.

HOW TO GET THERE

From US 395 in the town of Bishop, turn west onto SR 168 (to South Lake/ Lake Sabrina). Follow this paved road for 15 miles and turn left for South Lake. Continue 7 more miles to South Lake and the Bishop Pass trailhead. Overnight parking is available at the trailhead. However, if the lot is full, you will have to park along the road near Parchers Rainbow Village, about 1.2 miles away.

TRAILHEAD FACILITIES

A boat ramp, toilets, and drinking water are available at the trailhead. Parchers Rainbow Village, with basic meals, hot showers, and a pack station, is located about 1.2 miles north of the trailhead. Bishop Creek Lodge and Creekside RV Park are about 5 miles north of the trailhead. There are numerous Forest Service campgrounds along the paved road between Bishop and South Lake.

BEAR-PROOF WILDERNESS FOOD STORAGE BOX LOCATIONS

- Woods Creek crossing at JMT: Two boxes are on the south side of the footbridge.
- Arrowhead Lake: One box is on the east shore next to the trail.
- Lower Rae Lake: One box is on the east shore, west of the trail.
- Middle Rae Lake: Two boxes are about 200 yards on the west side of the JMT about 0.2 mile south of the ranger station. Look for the sign pointing the way.
- Vidette Meadow: Two boxes are in lower Vidette Meadow about 0.1 mile and 0.2 mile east of the Bubbs Creek Trail/JMT junction

on the downhill side of the JMT. A third box is in upper Vidette Meadow about 1.0 mile southeast of the Bubbs Creek Trail/JMT junction above a series of switchbacks around 9800 feet.

- Center Basin Trail: One box is below the JMT approximately 150 yards south of the unmarked Center Basin trail junction (0.25 mile north of the Center Basin Creek crossing).
- Tyndall Creek Crossing: One box is west of the JMT, about 350 feet north of the creek.
- Tyndall Creek Frog Ponds: One box is about 0.5 mile south of Tyndall Creek crossing on the east side of the trail.
- Wallace Creek Crossing: One box is west of the trail about 100 feet south of the creek crossing.
- Crabtree Meadow: One box is southeast of the creek and about 0.1 mile south of the Crabtree Patrol Cabin near the creek crossing.

TRAIL PROFILE TABLE

Milepost	Distance (miles)	Cumulative (miles)	Elevation (feet)	Gain/Loss (feet)
Day 1				
South Lake	0.0	0.0	9,768	0/0
Bishop Pass	6.0	6.0	11,960	2,192/0
Lower Dusy Basin	3.0	9.0	10,700	0/-1,260
Day 2				
LeConte Canyon R.S.	3.6	12.6	8,720	0/-1,980
Palisade Creek	3.3	15.9	8,040	0/-680
Palisade Lakes	6.2	22.1	10,613	2,573/0
Day 3				
Mather Pass	4.0	26.1	12,100	1,487/0
S.F. Kings River	5.5	31.6	10,020	0/-2,080
Pinchot Pass	4.6	36.2	12,130	2,110/0
Day 4				
Woods Creek Crossing	7.1	43.3	8,520	0/-3610
Middle Rae Lake	5.7	49.0	10,500	1,980/0
Day 5				
Glen Pass	2.6	51.6	11,978	1478/0
Bubbs Creek	4.5	56.1	9,600	0/-2,378
11,300-foot tarns	4.4	60.5	11,300	1,700/0

continued on next page

Milepost	Distance (miles)	Cumulative (miles)	Elevation (feet)	Gain/Loss (feet)
Day 6				
Forester Pass	3.0	63.5	13,180	1,880/0
Shepherd Pass Trail	5.0	68.5	10,880	0/-2,300
Wallace Creek	4.7	73.2	10,400	680/-1,160
Day 7				
Crabtree Meadow	4.2	77.4	10,640	680/-440
11,900-foot tarns	3.0	80.4	11,900	1,380/-120
Day 8—Summit Day				
Mount Whitney Trail	3.0	83.4	13,480	1,580/0
Whitney Summit	2.0	85.4	14,491	1,011/0
Trail Camp	4.7	90.1	12,040	180/-2,631
Day 9				
Whitney Portal	6.3	96.4	8,365	0/-3,675
Totals	**96.4**	**96.4**	—	**20,911/-22,314**

ROUTE DESCRIPTION

Day 1—South Lake to lower Dusy Basin, 9.0 miles, 2192/-1260 feet

The trek begins alongside the shore of South Lake. Numerous peaks surround the lake, providing inspiring views as you hike along the trail. Colorful wildflowers line the trail in the summer and the aspen trees turn various shades of brilliant red/yellow/gold in the fall.

Hike past the junction to Treasure Lakes and continue to Long Lake. Long Lake is a popular destination for day hikers and anglers. This elongated lake points the way to Bishop Pass. Mount Agassiz and the Inconsolable Range on the left and the precipitous rock face of Mount Goode on the right define the pass.

Spearhead Lake and Saddlerock Lake, the latter dotted with many rock islands, are quickly reached. The north and east faces of Mount Goode dominate the view. Pass the spur trail to Bishop Lake at 4.5 miles. The trail now begins its steep climb to Bishop Pass by ascending a series of rocky switchbacks as it snakes its way up the nose of a rocky cliff. Not much grows in this harsh environment except mountain heather and a few whitebark pine. Hike across the rock-strewn saddle, noting the lack of vegetation except for tiny low-growing alpine plants, flowers, and an occasional conifer. The trail enters Kings Canyon National Park at the pass.

From this high point overlooking Columbine Peak, Giraud Peak, and LeConte Canyon, the trail drops 3200 feet in 6.6 miles to the Middle Fork Kings River. Begin your descent to Dusy Basin, a gem replete with tarns, lakes, meadows, and streams. Those wishing to take Varia-

Alpine streams, tarns, meadows, wildflowers, and wildlife abound in Dusy Basin.

tion V1.1 to Palisade Basin and Mount Sill (Peak Scramble PS1.1) leave the trail near the upper end of Dusy Basin. Otherwise, continue the descent through Dusy Basin. There are good areas to camp from 11,300 feet down to 10,700 feet. Aim to camp in lower Dusy Basin about 3 miles below Bishop Pass.

Day 2—Lower Dusy Basin to Palisade Lakes, 13.1 miles, 2573/-2660 feet

At the lower end of Dusy Basin, the large natural bench forming the basin gives way to a steep-walled canyon. At this point the trail descends steeply, via a series of switchbacks, into the LeConte Canyon. You will cross a bridge immediately below a beautiful waterfall near 10,240 feet. As you look out over the canyon you will see the rugged granite walls of Langille Peak, Mount McDuffie, and The Citadel. Look directly below and you will see a path of destruction caused by a major avalanche that demolished thousands of trees. This avalanche appears to have started above the waterfall, wiping out everything in its path for several miles.

One summer afternoon our party was caught in a thunderstorm around the 9600-foot level. We sought shelter in a grove of trees for an hour to keep dry. While we watched the storm in the canyon far below, a large tree was struck by lightning and was immediately vaporized. A large smoke and vapor cloud hung over the spot and slowly drifted up and out of the canyon—an amazing sight and experience. Not long after, the canyon was filled with smoke from the fire that had been started. This was the same day that a Boy Scout and assistant scout leader were struck by lightning and killed farther south on the JMT in the Whitney region.

Continue your descent to the JMT. The LeConte Canyon Ranger Station is near this trail junction along the Middle Fork Kings River. Turn left (south) and begin your hike through the canyon. The trail gradually descends along the river for 3.3 miles to Palisade Creek. Here the canyon is more than 4000 feet deep. At Palisade Creek the trail makes a sharp turn to the left (east) and begins a gradual ascent alongside this beautiful stream. You will pass many meadows, including aptly named Deer Meadow, where there are many excellent camping opportunities. You can expect to see numerous deer along this stretch of trail. On a climb of Devils Crag, I saw a dozen mule deer bucks—some of the largest I have ever seen—in the Rambaud Creek drainage.

One-half mile past Deer Meadow and Glacier Creek, the trail steepens as it ascends 1400 feet to Palisade Lakes. Look for a camp near one of the two lakes or continue a short distance beyond and camp on a bench overlooking the lakes.

Day 3—Palisade Lakes to Pinchot Pass, 14.1 miles, 3597/-2080 feet

The Palisade Lakes are nestled in a beautiful cirque at the head of Palisade Creek, surrounded by granite walls on three sides. The rugged escarpment of the Palisades crest towers 3500 feet to the east. Slightly lower but nearly as impressive, glaciated peaks rise from the canyon to the west while Mather Pass blocks passage southward. It is believed that a sheepherder and his burro successfully navigated this difficult crossing in 1897. In 1921 the pass was named after Stephen Mather, the first director of the National Park Service.

Follow the JMT along the northeast shore of the two Palisade Lakes. The stream flowing into the upper lake at its midpoint drains a beautiful basin below The Thumb and Mount Bolton Brown. At the upper end of the second lake begin the 1500-foot ascent to Mather Pass. Over the last mile the trail steepens to reach the apex of the pass via a series of switchbacks.

The views improve as you climb. Look back on the Palisades group and view portions of the route you just completed with a new respect and perspective. Survey the terrain's ruggedness and marvel that you were able to navigate through it.

From the pass, the trail drops swiftly through switchbacks to the

Upper Basin, where the trail begins to level out at the 11,600-foot level. At the 11,598-foot lake, a short distance east of the trail and directly below Split Mountain (Peak Scramble PS1.2), there are excellent campsites. You will also find numerous places to camp as you continue down the trail to the South Fork Kings River crossing.

The trail continues its descent alongside numerous small rivulets that begin in the basin below Mather Pass. These seemingly inconsequential runnels are not particularly noteworthy until you realize they are the headwaters of the mighty South Fork Kings River. As you descend the trail and hop from rock to rock to cross this evolving river, keep in mind that the water at your feet will soon be flowing through one of the deepest canyons in North America. The South Fork Kings River flows through a wild and scenic canyon more than 8000 feet deep. A portion of this canyon can be viewed on the drive to Roads End and the trailhead for Routes 12 and 13.

The walking is pleasant over tundra-like terrain with flourishing wildflowers scattered throughout the many meadows and grassy benches. The scenery is superb and the hiking relaxing, with excellent views of Vennacher Needle and Mount Ruskin on your right, and Split Mountain and Cardinal Mountain on your left.

At 10,020 feet the trail crosses the South Fork Kings River and begins its 2100-foot ascent to Pinchot Pass. In high water, this crossing can be a challenge. You may have to walk upstream or downstream to find a log or suitable place to cross. After about 700 feet of climbing, the trail passes the Taboose Trail junction (Route 2) and the trail to Bench Lake (Side Trip ST1.1). Continue past these junctions and ascend through meadows and past several small lakes to Lake Marjorie (11,132 feet). At the lake, Pinchot Pass comes into view. Mount Wynne to the east and Crater Mountain to the west frame the red- and black-rocked pass. As you ascend past Lake Marjorie and the tarns immediately above the lake, shift gears for the climb to Pinchot Pass. As you approach the pass, the trail makes a series of climbing switchbacks alongside a small stream flowing from a tarn perched northeast of the pass near the 12,000-foot level. Where the path crosses this small stream, it is a short climb to the pass. At Pinchot Pass you will be presented with magnificent views of where you just came from and where you are now headed.

There are numerous places to camp from Bench Lake to the pass. It is a 1.5-mile hike to Bench Lake and campsites with spectacular views of Arrow Peak. There are also good camping opportunities at the lower and upper end of Lake Marjorie and at the lower end of the two tarns above Lake Marjorie. The lower end of the tarn immediately above Lake

Marjorie looks particularly inviting with its view northward to Mount Ruskin and Mather Pass. The small tarn northeast of the pass at 11,920 feet is a secluded spot to camp out of view of the trail. Leave the trail where the path crosses the stream (at 11,840 + feet) and follow it for 0.25 mile to the tarn.

Day 4—Pinchot Pass to middle Rae Lake, 12.8 miles, 1980/-3610 feet

After the initial descent of the steep and rocky south slope of Pinchot Pass, the track passes through a manicured parklike setting with small streams, lush meadows, tarns, wildflowers, deer, coyotes, rabbits, chipmunks, marmots, and hawks. From the summit of Mount Perkins I counted more than fifteen small lakes and tarns between Pinchot Pass and Twin Lakes. As you look down into this basin you may be able to see the route of the old trail that passed directly through the meadows and alongside many of these small lakes. Because of damage to the meadows, the path was relocated to pass above them.

As you near Twin Lakes you will begin to see the shark-finned shape of Mount Clarence King. At the time Bolton Brown made the first ascent of the peak in August 1898, it was considered the most difficult rock-climbing feat in North America. The summit is Class 5.4.

From the meadow and shore of a small lake (10,880 feet) west of the trail, there are excellent views of Mount Clarence King. While I was camping here to photograph this majestic peak, several small deer and a buck walked into my photo at sunrise, a duck swam across the tarn, and an owl flew overhead while I cooked dinner.

It is a short distance to Twin Lakes where you will find excellent fishing and many good campsites. Reach the Sawmill Pass Trail junction at 3.7 miles. Sawmill Pass Trail provides east–west access to the JMT, but it is a brutal 7000-foot climb from the desert floor trailhead to Sawmill Pass.

Hike along the JMT for another 3.4 miles to Woods Creek crossing (with bridge). The Woods Creek Trail (Route 12, Variation V12.1), coming from Roads End in Kings Canyon, joins the JMT here. This is a favorite camping spot for JMT trekkers.

At the trail junction, make a sharp turn to the left (southeast) and cross Woods Creek. Begin the gradual ascent to Rae Lakes. You will be hiking through a beautiful valley sandwiched between the towering summits of the Sierra Nevada Crest (Mount Baxter, Diamond Peak, Black Mountain, Dragon Peak) to the east and the rugged pinnacles of the King Spur (Mount Clarence King, Mount Cotter, Mount Gardiner) to the west.

The Baxter Pass Trail is another long and difficult trail that provides access to the JMT. From its trailhead in Owens Valley, it is a 6000-foot climb

Baxter Pass. This trail joins the JMT at Dollar Lake. Consider camping at Dollar Lake, Arrowhead Lake, lower Rae Lake, or middle Rae Lake. Each lake has a bear-proof food storage box.

Rae Lakes are set in a stunningly beautiful canyon surrounded by towering peaks. Mount Rixford and Dragon Peak are striped with veins of multi-colored black, brown, yellow, and gray rocks, making the area uniquely picturesque. The lakes, meadows, surrounding peaks, and rock formations add to the splendor. Early morning light on Rae Lakes and the textured rock cliffs of Painted Lady provide unique color for exceptional photographs. Because of the area's special beauty this is an ideal area for a rest day or a side trip to Sixty Lake Basin (Side Trip ST1.2).

Early-day mountaineer Norman Clyde, for whom many natural features in the Sierra Nevada have been named, and who made more first ascents of Sierra Nevada peaks than anyone then or now, was so impressed with the grandeur of this area that he described it as follows: "Rae Lake possesses one of the most wildly picturesque settings of any in the Sierra."

Day 5—Rae Lakes to 11,300-foot tarns, 11.5 miles, 3178/-2378 feet

Hike around the shore of middle Rae Lake and follow the trail along the narrow spit of land separating upper from middle Rae Lakes. Cross the stream that flows between the lakes.

Pass the Sixty Lake Basin trail junction (Side Trip ST1.2) and ascend a series of switchbacks to Glen Pass, a climb of 1440 feet. The views of Rae Lakes, Sixty Lake Basin, Mount Clarence King, and Mount Cotter are stunning. At Glen Pass you will enjoy unbelievable views of the unique Sierra Nevada topography, which was formed millions of years ago by huge granite blocks being thrust upward thousands of feet and tilted on edge, and then carved by thousands of years of glacial action. There is no better example of this than looking southeast from the pass toward Kearsarge Pinnacles, Kearsarge Lakes, and University Peak. The views are most dramatic in the early morning light when the long shadows accentuate the unique terrain.

On the descent from Glen Pass to Vidette Meadow, the trail passes through rugged terrain, past several tarns at 11,500 feet and 11,300 feet, the Kearsarge Pass Trail, Charlotte Lake Trail, and the trail to Bullfrog Lake and Kearsarge Lakes (Route 3). Beyond these trail junctions, the JMT drops steeply to Vidette Meadow and Bubbs Creek. As you descend into the deep canyon you will enjoy many fine vistas. In the distance, the glacier-covered slopes of Mount Brewer rise prominently above the surrounding summits. On July 2, 1864, it was on these slopes that William

Brewer and his Geologic Field Survey party first sighted Mount Whitney and identified it as the highest peak in the Sierra Nevada.

The closer views of East Vidette, Deerhorn Mountain, the Kings–Kern Divide, and Bubbs Creek canyon are inspiring. East Vidette is not the highest peak in the area but is one of the most striking with its classic lines thrusting skyward. Examine the steep-walled Bubbs Creek canyon sandwiched between the East Spur and the Sierra Nevada Crest. The JMT follows this beautiful valley before ascending to Forester Pass.

At Bubbs Creek the JMT turns left (east) and soon reaches Vidette Meadow. Route 12 (Bubbs Creek Trail), coming from the west in Kings Canyon, joins the JMT here. In Vidette Meadow there are several bear-proof food storage boxes, and rightfully so, as this beautiful meadow is notorious for brazen bears that will help themselves to your unprotected food.

The hike up the north side of the Kings–Kern Divide to Forester Pass is a rewarding ascent. From Vidette Meadow the trail climbs gradually beneath a forest of lodgepole pine and past lush meadows, colorful wildflowers, and cascading streams. The towering summits of University Peak, East Vidette, Mount Stanford, Junction Peak, and Basin Peak rise precipitously above the canyon floor.

Upper Rae Lake and Painted Lady as viewed from the trail to Sixty Lake Basin

Between Vidette Meadow and the Center Basin trail junction there is evidence of several massive avalanches that have wreaked havoc across the landscape. Hundreds of large trees have been uprooted or snapped like toothpicks. Their dead carcasses are spread across the mountainside as lasting evidence of the power of an out-of-control avalanche. These avalanches originated high on the canyon walls before plunging down the steep granite cliffs to Bubbs Creek. The avalanches were so powerful that they did not stop at the bottom of the canyon but continued across Bubbs Creek and up the opposite side of the canyon, spreading their destruction across the trail.

Pass the unmarked trail to Center Basin and Golden Bear Lake (Side Trip ST1.3). This is also where Route 4 from Onion Valley via University Pass joins the JMT. The trail junction is at 10,500 feet about 150 yards north of a bear box that is located below the trail. The trail junction is also about 0.25 mile north of the Center Basin stream crossing. There are many camping opportunities between Vidette Meadow and Center Basin Trail.

The JMT continues to gradually ascend the canyon for another 1.75 miles to a large bench area between 11,200 and 11,300 feet containing several tarns and a beautiful alpine meadow. This is an ideal place to camp before the steep climb to Forester Pass. Just before reaching the alpine meadow, you will see several campsites hacked out of the hillside on the right side of the trail. Continue past these sites and follow the trail as it turns left and comes alongside a fork of Bubbs Creek. There are numerous camping opportunities in this alpine meadow area with majestic views of the canyon below and the rugged summits above. The largest tarn is located just above 11,200 feet on the left side of the trail but is not visible until you pass it.

Day 6—11,300-foot tarns to Wallace Creek, 12.7 miles, 2560/-3460 feet

Above the tarns, the trail steepens as it ascends to Forester Pass. Forester Pass is the highest pass on the JMT as it crests the Kings–Kern Divide at 13,120 feet. Here the trail passes from Kings Canyon National Park to Sequoia National Park. Stop and look back to soak in the views and examine the terrain that you have just traversed. Look south to what lies ahead. The terrain opens up and you should be able to see all the way to Crabtree Meadow, about 10 miles away.

The south side of Forester Pass is steep, with the trail winding its way through steep granite cliffs. The trail quickly descends more than 600 feet but eases off as it passes a tarn at 12,500 feet and two large unnamed lakes near 12,200 feet. Reach the Shepherd Pass Trail (Route 5) in another 4 miles.

If you plan to climb Mount Tyndall, hike up the Shepherd Pass Trail (Peak Scramble PS5.1). This lovely 3-mile hike passes through meadows and along streams over gradual terrain.

The JMT continues past the Tyndall Creek tarns, Tawny Point, and crosses the Bighorn Plateau before dropping down to Wright Creek and Wallace Creek. This section of the trail includes some short climbs and descents over gentle terrain. From Bighorn Plateau there are rewarding views of the Kern Canyon, the Great Western Divide, and the Kaweah Peaks.

Day 7—Wallace Creek to 11,900-foot tarns, 7.2 miles, 2060/-560 feet

From Wallace Creek, the trail climbs about 500 feet in the first mile and then drops gradually to Sandy Meadow. The trail again climbs gradually to a trail junction 3.3 miles from Wallace Creek. At this point, the Pacific Crest Trail continues south, and the JMT turns east (left) toward Whitney. Turn left and hike 0.9 mile to Crabtree Meadow and the ranger station.

Crabtree Meadow is a large alpine meadow stretching 1.5 miles along Whitney Creek. You are likely to see mule deer grazing in the lush meadows. Crabtree Meadow is positioned beneath the towering walls of Mounts Hitchcock and Young and is an excellent place to camp. From the meadow, the trail begins its long and steady ascent, nearly 4000 feet over 8.5 miles, of the western slope of Mount Whitney.

Hike along Whitney Creek, gradually gaining elevation to Timberline Lake. Due to overuse, the lake is closed to camping. Sighting across this beautiful lake, your view will be of the Arctic Lake recess and the sheer southwest face of Mount Russell. From Timberline Lake, sandwiched between granite cliffs and timber, the trail gains 500 feet to Guitar Lake. Continue past Guitar Lake for about 0.3 mile and camp near a tarn at the 11,600-foot level or continue to the 11,900-foot level, where there are several excellent campsites near several more tarns. Although there are good campsites at Guitar Lake, it is beneficial to camp as high as possible, as your next-day ascent of Whitney will be long and arduous.

Day 8—11,900-foot tarns to Whitney summit to Trail Camp, 9.7 miles, 2771/-2631 feet

From the tarns, the JMT climbs steadily up the steep west slopes of Whitney for 3.0 miles. The switchbacks seem to go on forever but they finally end at the Whitney Trail junction near Trail Crest. The views of

Hitchcock Lakes, Guitar Lake, and the mountain panorama improve as you gain elevation. The trail is impressive as it climbs through talus, large rock faces, and impressive granite towers. This trail segment and the ninety-seven switchbacks on the other side (east side) of the mountain between Trail Camp and Trail Crest are engineering marvels and tributes to the workers who built them (see photo on page 141).

There are only 2 more miles to the summit and a little more than 1000 feet of elevation gain. The most difficult hiking is over as the JMT gradually reaches the highest point in the Lower 48. Stash your pack and head for the summit. If you are not suffering from the altitude, the climb will be enjoyable as the trail snakes its way through impressive rock towers and past "windows" in the Sierra Nevada crest that provide breathtaking views of Trail Camp, the Mount Whitney Trail, and the Owens Valley, far below. On the other hand, this may be the most strenuous portion of the trip because the altitude may have depleted your energy, strength, and desire to continue.

As you make your way to the summit, the trail passes within a couple hundred feet of Mount Muir, providing an excellent opportunity to bag another 14,000-foot peak (Peak Scramble PS1.3).

Ascend the last switchbacks of the JMT and arrive at the stone hut on the summit. Congratulations, you are standing on the highest point in the land—at 14,491 feet you are nearly three miles above sea level. On the summit you will be greeted with impressive views of Mount Langley and Mount Muir to the south; the Kaweah Peaks and Sawtooth Peak to the west; Mount Russell, Tulainyo Lake (to the right of Mount Russell), the highest large alpine lake in the Sierra Nevada, Mount Williamson, Milestone Mountain, Table Mountain, and Thunder Mountain to the north; and Trail Camp, Mount Whitney Trail switchbacks, Consultation Lake, and Owens Valley to the east. If the weather is pleasant, spend some time on top and take in the scenery. This is a significant accomplishment you will long remember. Whip out your cell phone and call home.

Return to your pack and hike out the Whitney Trail (Route 8). When exiting the trail, your wilderness permit will be subject to the exit quota requirement of Trail Crest (refer to Chapter 2). At Trail Crest (the boundary of Sequoia National Park), the Whitney Trail begins its steep descent of ninety-seven switchbacks down and around precipitous cliffs, over glaciated granite slabs, and past talus blocks to Trail Camp at 12,000 feet. If you are not too tired, continue past Trail Camp for 2 more miles and stop at Outpost Camp or continue to Lone Pine Lake for a swim. Both areas are less crowded than Trail Camp.

Day 9—Trail Camp to Whitney Portal, 6.3 miles, 0/-3675 feet

It is practically all downhill from here back to civilization. Refer to Route 8 for a complete description of the trail.

VARIATIONS, SIDE TRIPS, PEAK SCRAMBLES

Variation V1.1 (Palisade Basin), 7.9 miles cross-country with two passes (C-2) and one pass (C-2+)

This is a strenuous cross-country route that stays high above the LeConte Canyon. It crosses Thunderbolt Pass (12,400 feet), Potluck Pass (12,120 feet), and Cirque Pass (12,000 feet) before joining the JMT at Palisade Lakes. This alternate route cuts off 8.2 miles and about 1000 feet of climbing, but because it is over difficult terrain it is not a time-saving detour. However, the solitude and exceptional scenery are primary attractions for choosing this route.

Descend the south side of Bishop Pass and leave the trail at 11,400 feet near the upper end of Dusy Basin. Head east toward the 11,393-foot lake. Hike along the left shore of the lake and follow the lake's inlet stream to Thunderbolt Pass. The hiking is primarily over mixed terrain of small meadows and benches, granite slabs, and talus. The way becomes more difficult with car-sized boulders as you approach Thunderbolt Pass (Class 2).

Thunderbolt Pass is located 0.4 mile west-southwest of Thunderbolt Peak at the toe of the steep granite wall guarding access to the 14,000-foot summits high above. From the top of the pass, descend the southeast side by following ledges that angle to the right (south) down to a small tarn at 12,000 feet. This is a lovely place to camp and can be used as a base camp to climb Thunderbolt, North Palisade, and Mount Sill.

From the tarn, traverse beneath North Palisade, staying near the 12,000-foot level. The terrain is wild and the talus blocks impressively large, but reasonable progress can be made through the Palisade Basin to Potluck Pass.

From Potluck Pass, traverse northeast, scrambling along ledges to reach the basin immediately above the 11,676-foot lake. Reach easier terrain at the 11,900-foot level and hike down to the 11,676-foot lake.

The 11,676-foot lake is a lovely place to stop and camp. This unique setting offers solitude, beauty, and spectacular scenery. I have vivid memories of camping at the lake while circumnavigating the Palisades on mountaineering skis one blizzard-filled week. On that eventful trip we camped at the exposed outlet of the lake because it was the only place we could find a small trickle of running water. After we had climbed and skied from near the summit of Mount Sill, a powerful winter storm rapidly moved in and engulfed the Sierra Nevada. The storm pinned our party for three nights and two days while a blizzard battered our tent. We left the perilous confines of the tent only when nature beckoned and to repair the wind-damaged tent poles.

Presumably during the summer this lake would be safe and inviting, making it a beautiful base camp for a scramble to the summit of Mount Sill (Peak Scramble PS1.1).

From the outlet of the 11,676-foot lake, head southeast, angling left across ledges to Cirque Pass. The pass is located about 0.9 miles southwest of Palisade Crest. It is not as obvious as one would expect, but it is the notch northeast of the 12,220-foot peak. At the pass, you will have a prominent view of North Palisade and the steep wall and cliffs below this highly coveted peak.

On the southeast side of Cirque Pass (Class 2+), descend a gully and follow granite slabs to a tarn at 11,360 feet. Upon reaching a 300-foot cliff, scramble down its western edge following a series of ledges that zigzag down the far-right side. Angle toward the lower end of the lower Palisade Lake and join the JMT below the lake. The difficulties of climbing down from Cirque Pass can be avoided by taking an alternate route over Chimney Pass, which is directly above Cirque Pass.

Side Trip ST1.1 (Bench Lake)

Near the Taboose Trail and JMT junction, turn southwest onto the trail heading to Bench Lake. It is an easy 1.5-mile hike to this lovely lake, which is a favorite of anglers. Bench Lake, with its beautiful views of Arrow Peak, rests on a natural shelf perched high above the South Fork Kings River canyon. A sunrise view across the lake to Arrow Peak is exhilarating. I have fond memories of skiing across a frozen Bench Lake in the winter on my way to climb and ski from the summit of Arrow Peak.

Side Trip ST1.2 (Sixty Lake Basin)

Sixty Lake Basin is one of my favorite places in the Sierra Nevada. During the summer of 2005, our party was fortunate to photograph ten bighorn sheep near Fin Dome Pass on our way into the basin to climb Mount Gardner and Clarence King. We watched these rams for thirty minutes while they played and butted heads. Each head strike was surprisingly powerful and the crack of the horns astoundingly loud. Another memorable experience in this isolated basin took place during the winter of 2004–05, when I ascended and then skied down the east ridge of Mount Cotter.

Between middle and upper Rae Lakes, head northwest on the trail

A beautiful tarn and Mount Cotter in Sixty Lake Basin

to the basin. The trail ascends Fin Dome Pass, a climb of about 500 feet. From this 12,000-foot pass the trail makes a gentle descent into the basin. There are many good campsites at the lakes near where the trail makes a sharp right turn to the north (2.5 miles). Beyond this point the trail is difficult to follow, but it tracks alongside the stream flowing from the upper lakes in the basin for another 1.5 miles. For the more adventurous, near the end of the trail head southwest and then west up a side stream to two spectacular tarns (near 11,600 feet) immediately below the precipitous east face of Mount Clarence King.

Side Trip ST1.3 (Center Basin)

This is the original route of the JMT. In 1915 the trail through Center Basin, over Junction Pass (northeast of Junction Peak), and over Shepherd Pass was opened. In 1931 the JMT was rerouted over Forester Pass (west of Junction Peak) thereby bypassing Junction Pass and Shepherd Pass. This is a beautiful basin of lakes, tarns, and meadows popular with ambitious hikers and anglers. The jagged ridges linking University Peak, Mount Bradley, Mount Keith, Junction Peak, and Center Peak form this isolated basin. An unmarked trail leaves the JMT about 2.5 miles southeast of Vidette Meadow near 10,500 feet. The trail gains 700 feet over 2 miles before reaching the outlet of Golden Bear Lake. The unmaintained trail continues for another mile but slowly disappears into the tundra-like landscape.

Peak Scramble PS1.1 (Mount Sill, 14,153 feet)

From the 11,676-foot lake, about 2 miles south of Mount Sill, ascend the valley hiking north. The valley narrows and steepens and turns to the northwest near 12,600 feet. Near 13,000 feet gain the upper glacier cirque and ascend to the toe of the glacier. Skirt the right side of the glacier and turn north-northeast and ascend steeply to the summit. The upper portion of the mountain contains large talus blocks (Class 2 +).

Peak Scramble PS1.2 (Split Mountain, 14,058 feet)

On the south side of Mather Pass, leave the trail near 11,600 feet and hike eastward toward the 11,598-foot lake. Continue hiking east and gain the gentle saddle between Mount Prater and Split Mountain. At the saddle, head south scrambling over Class 2 terrain to the summit of this 14,000 footer. The ambitious can also climb Prater from the saddle.

Peak Scramble PS1.3 (Mount Muir, 14,012 feet)

From the junction of the JMT and the Mount Whitney Trail, head north along the JMT toward Whitney. Ascend two switchbacks and proceed to a large rock cairn marking the cutoff to Mount Muir. The summit is visible from the trail. Climb a shallow gully of loose scree and head toward the notch in the ridge to the right of the main summit. From this notch, angle left and climb a small chimney. Traverse left across a sloping ledge. Climb a crack to your right, gaining the small summit block. There is room for only three or four carefully placed climbers on the top at any one time. The top 50 feet of climbing is easy Class 3. From the summit there are impressive views of the east face of Mount Muir, the ninety-seven switchbacks in the Whitney Trail, Trail Camp, Consultation Lake, Arc Pass, Whitney Portal, and the Owens Valley, far below.

ROUTE 2: TABOOSE PASS TRAIL

(CHAPTER 7: MAPS, ROUTES 1-5)

Start...............................Taboose Creek, 5480 feet
End...............................Whitney Portal, 8365 feet
Rating...........................Trail hiking (C-1)
Distance.......................75.4 miles
Elevation gain/loss......20,279/-17,394 feet
Trip duration...............5-8 days
Maps............................Tom Harrison Maps—Kings Canyon High
Country, Mount Whitney High Country
Trail Map
Access road/town........Taboose Creek Road/Big Pine
Car shuttle...................Yes

TRAIL PROFILE

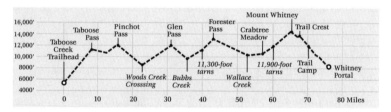

IN A NUTSHELL

The Taboose Pass Trail begins among the high desert sagebrush scrub and chaparral at the relatively low elevation of 5480 feet. You will ascend 6000 feet over 8 miles while passing through several climatic life zones before reaching Taboose Pass at 11,360 feet. The upper portions of the path traverse endless fields of talus and are exceptionally rocky. Midweight hiking boots will protect the soles of your feet and may help prevent you from accidentally turning an ankle on the rough cobblestones. Once over the pass the route becomes easier and descends gently to the JMT, where it turns south and follows Route 1 to Whitney.

This route is 21 miles shorter than Route 1. It includes a visit to beautiful Rae Lakes; however, you will miss some of the highlights of the longer Route 1, such as Dusy Basin, LeConte Canyon, and Palisade Lakes.

By averaging 9.5 miles a day, you can complete Route 2 in eight days. This is a realistic and manageable itinerary. Following a more challenging schedule, a strong hiker averaging 14–15 miles a day can complete the trip in five or six days.

HOW TO GET THERE

On US 395, about halfway between Big Pine and Independence, turn west onto Taboose Creek Road. Proceed past the Taboose Creek Campground. The pavement ends in 1.2 miles. Bear right at each of the two Ys (1.6 and 1.7 miles, respectively, from US 395). Pass through a barbed-wire gate and leave it as you found it, open or closed. At a third Y the left fork is signed for Goodale Creek. Take the right fork and continue about 2 miles to the end of the road. The road is rough in places but is passable by car.

TRAILHEAD FACILITIES

There are no facilities at the trailhead.

BEAR-PROOF WILDERNESS FOOD STORAGE BOX LOCATIONS

- Woods Creek crossing at JMT: Two boxes are on the south side of the footbridge.
- Arrowhead Lake: One box is on the east shore next to the trail.
- Lower Rae Lake: One box is on the east shore, west of the trail.
- Middle Rae Lake: Two boxes are located about 200 yards on the west side of the JMT about 0.2 mile south of the ranger station. Look for the sign pointing the way.
- Vidette Meadow: Two boxes are in lower Vidette Meadow about 0.1 mile and 0.2 mile east of the Bubbs Creek Trail/JMT junction on the downhill side of the JMT. A third box is positioned in upper Vidette Meadow about 1 mile southeast of the Bubbs Creek Trail/JMT junction above a series of switchbacks around 9800 feet.
- Center Basin Trail: One box is below the JMT approximately 150 yards south of the unmarked Center Basin trail junction (0.25 mile north of the Center Basin Creek crossing).
- Tyndall Creek Crossing: One box is west of the JMT, about 350 feet north of the creek.
- Tyndall Creek Frog Ponds: One box is about 0.5 mile south of Tyndall Creek Crossing on the east side of the trail.
- Wallace Creek Crossing: One box is west of the trail about 100 feet south of the creek crossing.
- Crabtree Meadow: One box is southeast of the creek and about 0.1 mile south of the Crabtree Patrol Cabin near the creek crossing.

TRAIL PROFILE TABLE

Milepost	Distance (miles)	Cumulative (miles)	Elevation (feet)	Gain/Loss (feet)
Day 1				
Taboose Creek TH	0.0	0.0	5,480	0/0
Taboose Pass	8.0	8.0	11,360	6,120/-240
Day 2				
JMT	3.6	11.6	10,760	240/-840
Pinchot Pass	3.6	15.2	12,130	1,370/0
Day 3				
Woods Creek Crossing	7.1	22.3	8,520	0/-3,610
Middle Rae Lake	5.7	28.0	10,500	1,980/0
Day 4				
Glen Pass	2.6	30.6	11,978	1,478/0
Bubbs Creek	4.5	35.1	9,600	0/-2,378
11,300-foot tarns	4.4	39.5	11,300	1,700/0
Day 5				
Forester Pass	3.0	42.5	13,180	1,880/0
Shepherd Pass Trail	5.0	47.5	10,880	0/-2,300
Wallace Creek	4.7	52.2	10,400	680/-1,160
Day 6				
Crabtree Meadow	4.2	56.4	10,640	680/-440
11,900-foot tarns	3.0	59.4	11,900	1,380/-120
Day 7—Summit Day				
Mount Whitney Trail	3.0	62.4	13,480	1,580/0
Whitney Summit	2.0	64.4	14,491	1,011/0
Trail Camp	4.7	69.1	12,040	180/-2,631
Day 8				
Whitney Portal	6.3	75.4	8,365	0/-3,675
Totals	**75.4**	**75.4**	**—**	**20,279/-17,394**

ROUTE DESCRIPTION

Day 1—Taboose Creek Trailhead to Taboose Pass,
8.0 miles, 5880/-0 feet

The trail begins in the high desert, which is in full bloom in early season. The red, blue, yellow, and lavender colors of thistle and cactus are striking. The low-elevation start among the chaparral and sagebrush scrub is discouraging, but the trail will slowly transport you to cooler temperatures. An early morning start will help you avoid the low-elevation afternoon heat.

The trail ascends an alluvial fan of decomposed granite sand following along the right (north) side of Taboose Creek for about 3.5 miles. At 8400 feet the trail crosses Taboose Creek and climbs steeply to 9100 feet, where the path crosses back to the other side of the stream. These crossings may be tricky in early season when stream flows are high from snowmelt. There are two small tent platforms at the upper stream crossing.

The nature of the terrain changes markedly after the first, and then again after the second, stream crossing as the canyon narrows and becomes more rugged. The sandy track turns into a rough and rocky one as it crosses endless fields of talus that are rough on the feet and ankles.

Above the second crossing, the creek flows over a cliff and through a slot forming an impressive ribbon waterfall. Above the waterfall, near 9600 feet, is a natural bench with a group of stately lodgepole pine. Several tent platforms have been hacked out of the cement-like hillside. Near 10,400 feet the stream flows over a nearly flat rock "meadow." Across the stream in a grouping of trees are two tent platforms.

Continue the relentless climb across talus fields to 11,200 feet. Here you think you are near the pass, but the trail continues for another 0.5 mile, snaking its way around and over glaciated granite outcroppings and past several tarns to finally reach the pass. There are camping opportunities near the upper tarn on the east side of the pass or continue down the west side on gentle terrain to camp.

Day 2—Taboose Pass to Pinchot Pass, 7.2 miles, 1370/-600 feet

Today is a relative easy day compared with the arduous climb of Day 1. From Taboose Pass descend through gentle terrain and meadows. Deer often graze in these meadows. You will have grand views of Kings Canyon National Park, Arrow Peak, and Mount Ruskin. In about 1.2 miles the path reaches a nearly level meadow area with small rivulets of running water. At a 90-degree angle to your left and about 100 yards across the meadow is a large squarish boulder. At this point the trail forks. Take the left fork. If you miss this junction you will end up hiking several extra miles and climbing an additional 800 feet to get back on route. Follow the trail to the left and cross the meadow and stream flowing from near the pass. Follow this trail to the JMT and turn south toward Pinchot Pass. In 0.1 mile you will come to the junction to Bench Lake (ST1.1).

Continue hiking toward Lake Marjorie. Camp at this lake or at the tarns closer to Pinchot Pass (refer to Route 1, Day 3). If you feel strong, ascend Pinchot Pass and hike down to Twin Lakes, which are an additional 2.7 miles beyond the pass. Rugged peaks surround the lakes, and beautiful

Mount Clarence King and an unnamed tarn along the John Muir Trail above Twin Lakes

meadows and stands of evergreen trees make this an ideal place to stop for the night.

Day 3—Pinchot Pass to middle Rae Lake, 12.8 miles, 1980/-3610 feet

Refer to Route 1, Day 4, for a description of this trail segment. See ST1.2 for an enjoyable side trip to Sixty Lake Basin.

Day 4—Rae Lakes to 11,300-foot tarns, 11.5 miles, 3178/-2378 feet

Refer to Route 1, Day 5, for a description of this trail segment. Refer to ST1.3 for a side trip to Center Basin and Golden Bear Lake.

Day 5—11,300-foot tarns to Wallace Creek, 12.7 miles, 2560/-3460 feet

Refer to Route 1, Day 6, for a description of this trail segment. Refer to Peak Scramble PS5.1 for the route description to climb Mount Tyndall.

Day 6—Wallace Creek to 11,900-foot tarns, 7.2 miles, 2060/-560 feet

Refer to Route 1, Day 7, for a description of this trail segment.

Day 7–11,900-foot tarns to Trail Camp, 9.7 miles, 2771/-2631 feet
Refer to Route 1, Day 8, for a description of this trail segment. If you plan to climb Mount Muir, refer to Peak Scramble PS1.3.

Day 8–Trail Camp to Whitney Portal, 6.3 miles, 0/-3675 feet
Refer to Route 8 for a description of the Mount Whitney Trail.

ROUTE 3: KEARSARGE PASS TRAIL
(CHAPTER 7: MAPS, ROUTES 1-5)

Start..............................Onion Valley, 9200 feet
End................................Whitney Portal, 8365 feet
Rating...........................Trail hiking (C-1)
Distance.......................50.6 miles
Elevation gain/loss......11,651/-12,486 feet
Trip duration...............4–7 days
Maps.............................Tom Harrison Maps—Kings Canyon High Country, Mount Whitney High Country Trail Map
Access road/town........Onion Valley Road/Independence
Car shuttle...................Yes

TRAIL PROFILE

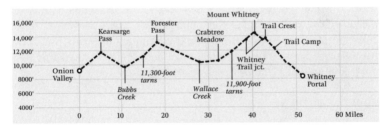

IN A NUTSHELL
Once an Indian trading route, Kearsarge Pass Trail now provides access via a high-elevation trailhead to beautiful Kearsarge Lakes basin, the spectacular backcountry of the John Muir Wilderness, and Kings Canyon National Park. From the 9200-foot trailhead at Onion Valley, the trail ascends nearly 2600 feet to Kearsarge Pass and then quickly descends 2200 feet past Kearsarge Lakes and Bullfrog Lake to Vidette Meadow along Bubbs Creek. This route joins Routes 1 and 2

near Bullfrog Lake and follows the JMT the rest of the way to Mount Whitney.

From Vidette Meadow, the route ascends the beautiful glaciated valley of Bubbs Creek, gaining 3500 feet to Forester Pass, the highest passage on the JMT. Here the trail crosses the rugged Kings–Kern Divide, traversing from Kings Canyon National Park into Sequoia National Park. The trail then drops 2100 feet to Tyndall Creek, Wallace Creek, and Crabtree Meadow. From this large alpine meadow at the foot of Mounts Hitchock, Young, and Whitney, the JMT starts its long ascent of the west slope of Whitney, passing Timberline Lake and Guitar Lake. From the lake shaped like a guitar, the trail climbs nearly 3000 feet over 5.5 miles on its way to the apex of California.

Because the Onion Valley trailhead provides a high-elevation starting point, it is popular with backpackers and anglers. Wilderness permit quotas fill quickly each year. To secure your preferred date, make reservations early.

Route 3 is 46 miles and 25 miles shorter than Routes 1 and 2, respectively, and can be completed in six days by averaging 9 miles per day, a realistic itinerary that is manageable for most. Following a more challenging schedule, a strong hiker averaging 14–15 miles a day can complete the trip in four days.

The shortest trans-Sierra hike from road end to road end is Onion Valley trailhead to Roads End in Kings Canyon National Park. This hike starts at Onion Valley, ascends Kearsarge Pass, descends to Vidette Meadow, and descends via the Bubbs Creek Trail, passing through Junction Meadow (Bubbs Creek), and continuing to Roads End. This trans-Sierra classic traverses portions of both Route 3 (Kearsarge Pass Trail) and Route 12 (Bubbs Creek Trail).

HOW TO GET THERE

From the small community of Independence on US 395 (45 miles south of Bishop), turn west on Market Street (Onion Valley Road) and drive 13.5 miles to the end of the road at Onion Valley. The paved road usually is open from May to November.

TRAILHEAD FACILITIES

Potable water is available at the trailhead. A twenty-nine-unit campground is located nearby. Metal bear-proof food lockers are provided at the campsites. The campground usually is open May through September. The fifty-two-unit Lower and Upper Grays Meadow Campground is located 6 miles west of Independence on the Onion Valley Road.

BEAR-PROOF WILDERNESS FOOD STORAGE BOX LOCATIONS

- Kearsarge Lakes: One box is on the Kearsarge Lakes lateral trail at the south end of the upper lake, a second box is on the north shore of the largest lake, and a third box is on the north shore of the lowest small lake.
- Vidette Meadow: Two boxes are in lower Vidette Meadow about 0.1 mile and 0.2 mile east of the Bubbs Creek Trail/JMT junction on the downhill side of the JMT. A third box is in upper Vidette Meadow about 1 mile southeast of the Bubbs Creek Trail/JMT junction above a series of switchbacks around 9800 feet.
- Center Basin Trail: One box is below the JMT approximately 150 yards south of the unmarked Center Basin trail junction (0.25 mile north of the Center Basin Creek crossing).
- Tyndall Creek Crossing: One box is west of the JMT, about 350 feet north of the creek.
- Tyndall Creek Frog Ponds: One box is about 0.5 mile south of Tyndall Creek crossing on the east side of the trail.
- Wallace Creek Crossing: One box is west of the trail about 100 feet south of the creek crossing.
- Crabtree Meadow: One box is southeast of the creek and about 0.1 mile south of the Crabtree Patrol Cabin near the creek crossing.

TRAIL PROFILE TABLE

Milepost	Distance (miles)	Cumulative (miles)	Elevation (feet)	Gain/Loss (feet)
Day 1				
Onion Valley	0.0	0.0	9,200	0/0
Kearsarge Pass	5.0	5.0	11,760	2,560/0
Kearsarge Lakes	1.4	6.4	10,896	0/-864
Day 2				
Bubbs Creek	3.9	10.3	9,600	0/-1,296
11,300-foot tarns	4.4	14.7	11,300	1,700/0
Day 3				
Forester Pass	3.0	17.7	13,180	1,880/0
Shepherd Pass Trail	5.0	22.7	10,880	0/-2,200
Wallace Creek	4.7	27.4	10,400	680/-1,160

continued on next page

Milepost	Distance (miles)	Cumulative (miles)	Elevation (feet)	Gain/Loss (feet)
Day 4				
Crabtree Meadow	4.2	31.6	10,640	680/-440
11,900-foot tarns	3.0	34.6	11,900	1,380/-120
Day 5—Summit Day				
Mount Whitney Trail	3.0	37.6	13,480	1,580/0
Whitney Summit	2.0	39.6	14,491	1,011/0
Trail Camp	4.7	44.3	12,040	180/-2,631
Day 6				
Whitney Portal	6.3	50.6	8,365	0/-3,675
Totals	**50.6**	**50.6**	**—**	**11,651/-12,486**

ROUTE DESCRIPTION

Day 1—Onion Valley to Kearsarge Lakes, 6.4 miles, 2560/-864 feet

The trail gains elevation steadily (2560 feet over 5 miles) as it climbs from Onion Valley to Kearsarge Pass. The trail begins by ascending a series of switchbacks passing Little Pothole Lake, Gilbert Lake, and Flower Lake. In the first couple of miles, deer often are seen early in the morning or near dusk.

Bears also roam the area. One night while sleeping under the stars at Gilbert Lake, I was awakened with a start at 1:00 AM by a bear sniffing my empty pack and sleeping bag. I let out a frantic shout that undoubtedly could be heard for miles. The bear turned and ran—surely, he was as startled as I. Needless to say, even though our food was properly stashed in bear canisters or hanging twenty-five feet up in a tree, I did not sleep much the remainder of the night.

The trail ascends high above Heart Lake by way of more switchbacks, providing great views of this aptly named lake. Farther along a large glacial moraine acts as a natural dam holding back the waters of Big Pothole Lake. The path passes Big Pothole Lake, making its final climb to Kearsarge Pass. On the ascent to Kearsarge Pass you are rewarded with an impressive view of University Peak (13,632 feet).

At Kearsarge Pass the trail crosses from the John Muir Wilderness to Kings Canyon National Park. There are great views into the national park, including Kearsarge Pinnacles, Kearsarge Lakes, Bullfrog Lake, Mount Brewer, and North Guard.

From the pass descend several switchbacks before reaching the trail junction to Kearsarge Lakes and Bullfrog Lake. Take the left fork, continuing the descent to Kearsarge Lakes. Several bear-proof food lockers are located at the lakes.

Bullfrog Lake on the west side of Kearsarge Pass and Mount Brewer

Bullfrog Lake is closed to camping so stop at Kearsarge Lakes or continue down to Vidette Meadow.

Day 2—Kearsarge Lakes to 11,300-foot tarns, 8.3 miles, 1700/-1296 feet

From Kearsarge Lakes, hike 2.4 miles over gentle terrain past Bullfrog Lake. At the junction with the JMT, turn left (south). The trail drops steeply over the next 1.5 miles to Bubbs Creek and Vidette Meadow, offering many fine vistas along the way. At Bubbs Creek, Route 12 (Bubbs Creek Trail) joins the JMT from Roads End.

Continue following the JMT southward for the next 4.4 miles, ascending through the Bubbs Creek canyon to the 11,300-foot tarns below Forester Pass. For details of the route and information about camping opportunities from Vidette Meadow to the tarns and a side trip into Center Basin (ST1.3), refer to Day 5 of Route 1.

Day 3—11,300-foot tarns to Wallace Creek, 12.7 miles, 2560/-3460 feet

Refer to Route 1, Day 6, for a description of this trail segment. To climb Mount Tyndall, refer to Peak Scramble PS5.1.

Day 4—Wallace Creek to 11,900-foot tarns, 7.2 miles, 2060/-560 feet

Refer to Route 1, Day 7, for a description of this trail segment.

Day 5—11,900-foot tarns to Trail Camp, 9.7 miles, 2771/-2631 feet

Refer to Route 1, Day 8. If you plan a climb of Mount Muir, refer to Peak Scramble PS1.3.

Day 6—Trail Camp to Whitney Portal, 6.3 miles, 0/-3675 feet

Refer to Route 8 for a complete description of the Whitney Trail.

ROUTE 4: UNIVERSITY PASS ROUTE
(CHAPTER 7: MAPS, ROUTES 1–5)

Start.............................Onion Valley, 9200 feet
End...............................Whitney Portal, 8365 feet
Rating..........................39.4 miles trail hiking (C-1) and 3.6 miles x-c with one pass (C-2)
Distance........................43 miles
Elevation gain/loss......11,631/-12,466 feet
Trip duration...............4–6 days
Maps.............................Tom Harrison Maps—Kings Canyon High Country and Mount Whitney High Country
Access road/town........Onion Valley Road/Independence
Car shuttle...................Yes

TRAIL PROFILE

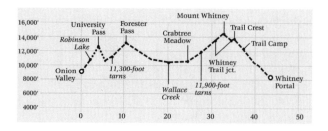

IN A NUTSHELL

As in Route 3, this excursion starts at Onion Valley but bypasses Kearsarge Pass and the deep recess of Vidette Meadow. Instead, Route 4 follows the unmaintained trail to Robinson Lake, and then ascends cross-country to University Pass (12,640 feet). From University Pass it descends through a steep gully and over loose scree to Center Basin and the JMT.

This route is 7.6 miles shorter than the Kearsarge Pass Trail but contains rugged cross-country travel. Only experienced and strong cross-country hikers should attempt this route. Others will find the Kearsarge Pass Trail the better choice.

The cross-country route above Robinson Lake (class 2) is over large talus boulders and scree. It is relatively short, 3.6 miles, but rugged, steep, and strenuous. Take an ice ax for the scramble up University Pass. There is usually snow in the couloir through August.

HOW TO GET THERE

From the town of Independence on US 395 (45 miles south of Bishop), turn west on Market Street (Onion Valley Road) and drive 13.5 miles to Onion Valley, located at the end of the road. The paved road usually is open from May to November.

TRAILHEAD FACILITIES

Potable water is available at Onion Valley. The twenty-nine-unit Onion Valley Campground is located near the trailhead. Metal bear-proof food lockers are located at the campsites. The campground is usually open May through September. The fifty-two-unit Lower and Upper Grays Meadow Campground is located 6 miles west of Independence on Onion Valley Road and usually is open March through October.

BEAR-PROOF WILDERNESS FOOD STORAGE BOX LOCATIONS

- Center Basin Trail: One box is below the JMT approximately 150 yards south of the unmarked Center Basin trail junction (0.25 mile north of the Center Basin Creek crossing).
- Tyndall Creek Crossing: One box is west of the JMT about 350 feet north of the creek.
- Tyndall Creek Frog Ponds: One box is about 0.5 mile south of Tyndall Creek crossing on the east side of the trail.
- Wallace Creek Crossing: One box is west of the JMT about 100 feet south of the creek crossing.
- Crabtree Meadow: One box is southeast of the creek and about 0.1 mile south of the Crabtree Patrol Cabin near the creek crossing.

TRAIL PROFILE TABLE

Milepost	Distance (miles)	Cumulative (miles)	Elevation (feet)	Gain/Loss (feet)
Day 1				
Onion Valley	0.0	0.0	9,200	0/0
Robinson Lake	2.0	2.0	10,500	1,300/0
University Pass	1.8 x-c	3.8	12,640	2,140/0
JMT	1.8 x-c	5.6	10,500	0/-2,140
11,300-foot tarns	1.5	7.1	11,300	800/0
Day 2				
Forester Pass	3.0	10.1	13,180	1,880/0
Shepherd Pass Trail	5.0	15.1	10,880	0/-2,300
Wallace Creek	4.7	19.8	10,400	680/-1,160
Day 3				
Crabtree Meadow	4.2	24.0	10,640	680/-440
11,900-foot tarns	3.0	27.0	11,900	1,380/-120
Day 4—Summit Day				
Mount Whitney Trail	3.0	30.0	13,480	1,580/0
Whitney Summit	2.0	32.0	14,491	1,011/0
Trail Camp	4.7	36.7	12,040	180/-2,631
Day 5				
Whitney Portal	6.3	43.0	8,365	0/-3,675
Totals	**43.0**	**43.0**	**—**	**11,631/-12,466**

ROUTE DESCRIPTION

Day 1—Onion Valley to 11,300-foot tarns, 7.1 miles, 4240/-2140 feet
The Robinson Lake Trail has not been maintained for many years, and there is some brush, but it is passable. The trail begins at the eastern end of the Onion Valley Campground next to campsite 8. The trail immediately crosses the creek flowing from Robinson Lake and ascends wooded slopes to a large hanging valley. This short, steep trail passes through large stands of virgin timber and groves of aspen. Deer are common in the area and may be seen early in the morning. As you ascend, you will see evidence of powerful avalanches that, over the years, have swept down the steep slopes of Independence Peak, uprooting hundreds of trees.

The trail ends at Robinson Lake, signaling the start of the rugged cross-country route from Robinson Lake over University Pass to Center Basin. Hike around the right side of Robinson Lake, passing beneath a large stand of mature foxtail pine. Ascend steeply alongside the stream flowing into Robinson Lake climbing over talus and granite cliffs.

From above Robinson Lake, University Pass is on the left.

Near 11,400 feet, hike alongside the creek and ascend into a hidden glacial cirque at the base of University Peak. Large talus boulders make the travel tedious. Two prominent passes become visible. University Pass is the lowest point (and first gap) northwest (right) of the 13,362-foot peak. The second pass, farther to the right of the peak, is not as steep and is easier to climb. Both passes lead to Center Basin. Depending on the amount of snowfall the previous winter, snow may remain in these two gullies into August. Take an ice ax and possibly crampons.

At University Pass, the route enters Sequoia National Park. Descend the west side of the pass via a steep chute filled with loose scree and rock. Exercise caution in the gully. From the second pass, descend gradually, angling to your left. Hike over decomposed granite sand and rock. Soon you will come to the top of a large, open gully. Descend steeply down scree, sand, and loose rocks to the northernmost tarn in Center Basin at 11,120 feet. At the base of either chute head south to the Center Basin trail. There are excellent opportunities to camp near Golden Bear

Lake or the various tarns in Center Basin (see Side Trip ST1.3 for more information about Center Basin).

Follow the Center Basin Trail west to the JMT. At the junction with the JMT, turn south (left) and begin the magnificent climb up this beautiful canyon to the tarns and alpine meadow located on a large bench between 11,200 and 11,300 feet. The trail ascends gradually with spectacular views of the meadows along Bubbs Creek and the towering peaks overhead. There are places to camp at the junction of the JMT/Center Basin Trail, but more picturesque options await at the 11,300-foot tarns. For more details, refer to Route 1, Day 5.

Day 2—11,300-foot tarns to Wallace Creek, 12.7 miles, 2560/-3460 feet

Refer to Route 1, Day 6, for a description of this trail segment. If you plan to climb Mount Tyndall, refer to Peak Scramble PS5.1 for the route description.

Day 3—Wallace Creek to 11,900-foot tarns, 7.2 miles, 2060/-560 feet

Refer to Route 1, Day 7, for a description of this trail segment.

Day 4—11,900-foot tarns to Trail Camp, 9.7 miles, 2771/-2631 feet

Refer to Route 1, Day 8, for a description of this trail segment. If you plan to climb Mount Muir, refer to Peak Scramble PS1.3.

Day 5—Trail Camp to Whitney Portal, 6.3 miles, 0/-3675 feet

Refer to Route 8 for a description of the Whitney Trail.

ROUTE 5: SHEPHERD PASS TRAIL

(CHAPTER 7: MAPS, ROUTES 1-5)

Start..............................Symmes Creek, 6240 feet
End...............................Whitney Portal, 8365 feet
Rating..........................Trail hiking (C-1)
Distance.......................41.8 miles
Elevation gain/loss......11,711/-9646 feet
Trip duration...............4–6 days
Maps............................Tom Harrison Maps—Mount Whitney High Country
Access road/town........Onion Valley Road and Foothill Road/Independence
Car shuttle..................Yes

TRAIL PROFILE

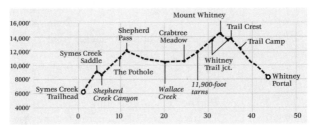

IN A NUTSHELL

The Shepherd Pass Trail is long, arduous, and discouraging. The trail gains more than 6000 feet before reaching Shepherd Pass after 9.7 difficult miles. The trail begins at Symmes Creek and follows the creek for a mile, crossing the stream four times before ascending steeply to the saddle dividing Symmes Creek and Shepherd Creek. At the Symmes–Shepherd saddle (located several miles east of the Sierra Nevada crest), the trail drops 500 feet to Shepherd Creek, losing precious elevation you fought to climb only a short time before. From this new low point, the trail gains 3300 feet in 5.5 miles to Shepherd Pass. From the pass, it is an easy and enjoyable 4.2-mile hike through meadows alongside Tyndall Creek to the JMT.

This route affords an excellent opportunity to climb Mount Tyndall (14,018 feet). Refer to Peak Scramble PS5.1. It is also easier to obtain a wilderness permit for Shepherd Pass Trail especially if you are departing during midweek.

HOW TO GET THERE

From the town of Independence (45 miles south of Bishop) on US 395, turn west on Market Street (Onion Valley Road). Drive 4.3 miles to Foothill Road and turn left (south). Follow this dirt road for 1.3 miles and turn right at a fork in the road. Proceed 1.6 miles to a horse corral. Continue past the corral for 0.4 mile to the next fork. Turn right (west) and drive 0.5 mile to the next fork and turn right again. In 0.9 mile you will arrive at the end of the road and the trailhead for the Shepherd Pass Trail. The dirt road to the trailhead is passable in a sedan.

TRAILHEAD FACILITIES

There are no trailhead facilities.

BEAR-PROOF WILDERNESS FOOD STORAGE BOX LOCATIONS

- Tyndall Creek Crossing: One box is west of the JMT about 350 feet north of the creek.
- Tyndall Creek Frog Ponds: One box is about 0.5 mile south of Tyndall Creek crossing on the east side of the trail.
- Wallace Creek Crossing: One box is west of the trail about 100 feet south of the creek crossing.
- Crabtree Meadow: One box is southeast of the creek and about 0.1 mile south of the Crabtree Patrol Cabin near the creek crossing.

TRAIL PROFILE TABLE

Milepost	Distance (miles)	Cumulative (miles)	Elevation (feet)	Gain/Loss (feet)
Day 1				
Symmes Creek TH	0.0	0.0	6,300	0/0
Symmes Creek Saddle	3.0	3.0	9,200	2,900/0
Shepherd Creek Cny	1.2	4.2	8,700	0/-500
The Pothole	3.5	7.7	10,840	2,140/0
Day 2				
Shepherd Pass	2.0	9.7	12,000	1,160/0
JMT	4.2	13.9	10,880	0/-1,120
Wallace Creek	4.7	18.6	10,400	680/-1,160
Day 3				
Crabtree Meadow	4.2	22.8	10,640	680/-440
11,900-foot tarns	3.0	25.8	11,900	1,380/-120
Day 4—Summit Day				
Mount Whitney Trail	3.0	28.8	13,480	1,580/0
Whitney Summit	2.0	30.8	14,491	1,011/0
Trail Camp	4.7	35.5	12,040	180/-2,631
Day 5				
Whitney Portal	6.3	41.8	8,365	0/-3,675
Totals	**41.8**	**41.8**	—	**11,711/-9646**

ROUTE DESCRIPTION

Day 1—Symmes Creek to The Pothole, 7.7 miles, 5040/-500 feet

There are two starting points for the Shepherd Pass trail: one for hikers and one for stock. The one for stock starts near a corral at the 5700-foot level and adds 1.3 miles to the approach. The hiker's trail begins farther up the road at 6300 feet.

The trail traverses some wild country. In the first mile (from the hiker's trailhead) the trail and Symmes Creek pass through an impressive narrows just wide enough for the trail and the little creek. In this narrow canyon with cliffs towering overhead, the trail follows Symmes Creek, crossing it four times before starting a 2-mile climb via numerous switchbacks to a saddle in the ridge dividing Symmes Creek and Shepherd Creek. The trail is steep but not unpleasant because it is on the north (cool) side of the ridge and is shaded by large evergreen trees. Once you leave Symmes Creek there is no water for about 4 miles so make sure your water bottles are full.

At the crest of the ridge (9200 feet) the trail levels off. From this point, the trail traverses 0.25 mile to a broad sandy saddle where the trail moves to the hot southerly exposure. Here the virgin forest coverage gives way to mountain mahogany and chaparral. Little shade from the hot summer sun can be found. In another 0.25 mile the trail passes through a distinctive notch where it begins a rapid descent to Shepherd Creek, dropping nearly 500 feet.

From this new low point (8700 feet), the trail begins a 1700-foot climb to Anvil Camp. Near Anvil Camp the trail crosses Shepherd Creek for the first time. In a mile the trail crosses the creek again near The Pothole. Campsites are available at Anvil Camp and The Pothole, but if you can, continue to the large lake at 12,000 feet, immediately southwest of Shepherd Pass.

Day 2—The Pothole to Wallace Creek, 10.9 miles, 1840/-2280 feet

From The Pothole, the trail ascends through moraines, talus, boulder fields, and snowfields (in June and July) to Shepherd Pass and Sequoia National Park. East of the crest the trail enters the Bighorn Sheep Zoological Area. Please respect the area closures.

After Shepherd Pass, it is an easy and enjoyable walk over gentle terrain alongside Tyndall Creek to the JMT. Meadows, creeks, flowers, and beautiful vistas highlight this segment. The trail drops only 1000 feet in

Mount Tyndall from near Shepherd Pass (Photo by Sierra Richins)

4.2 miles. If you plan on climbing Mount Tyndall, leave the trail about 0.5 mile southwest of Shepherd Pass (PS5.1).

At the junction with the JMT, turn left (south) onto the JMT and follow it as it goes past Tyndall Creek tarns, Tawny Point, and crosses the Bighorn Plateau before dropping down to Wright Creek and Wallace Creek.

Day 3—Wallace Creek to 11,900-foot tarns, 7.2 miles, 2060/-560 feet
Refer to Route 1, Day 7, for a description of this trail segment.

Day 4—11,900-foot tarns to Trail Camp, 9.7 miles, 2771/-2631 feet
Refer to Route 1, Day 8, for a description of this trail segment. If you plan to climb Mount Muir, refer to Peak Scramble PS1.3.

Day 5—Trail Camp to Whitney Portal, 6.3 miles, 0/-3675 feet
Refer to Route 8 for a description of the Mount Whitney Trail.

VARIATIONS, SIDE TRIPS, PEAK SCRAMBLES
Peak Scramble PS5.1 (Mount Tyndall, 14,019 feet)
From Shepherd Pass continue southwest down the trail for about 0.5 mile and angle southeast toward the toe of the northwest ridge. This is the obvious ridge to the right of the north face. Ascend the broad northwest slope (to the right of the ridge) to the summit ridge and follow it to the summit scrambling over large granite blocks. Stay on the crest of the summit ridge or drop down slightly onto the southwest slopes. There are a couple of short sections along the summit ridge where there is some exposure (Class 2 scrambling).

For those climbing the peak from Routes 1–4 and 12, from the JMT ascend the gentle Shepherd Pass Trail for about 3 miles and angle east to the base of the northwest slope before beginning the obvious climb.

ROUTE 6: MOUNTAINEERS ROUTE
(CHAPTER 7: MAPS, ROUTES 6–9)
Start..............................Whitney Portal, 8365 feet
End..............................Whitney Portal, 8365 feet
Rating..........................1.6 miles trail hiking (C-1) and 10.8 miles x-c
                                    (C-2/3)
Distance........................12.4 miles
Elevation gain/loss......6126/-6126 feet
Trip duration...............1–3 days

Maps..............................Tom Harrison Maps—Mount Whitney High
Country or Mount Whitney Zone
Access road/town........Whitney Portal Road/Lone Pine
Car shuttle ....No

TRAIL PROFILE

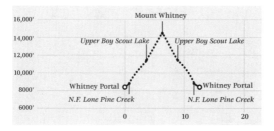

IN A NUTSHELL

The Mountaineers Route ascends the distinctive couloir on the northeast face and right shoulder of Mount Whitney. It can be readily seen from US 395, the town of Lone Pine, and the Whitney Portal Road. In the winter and spring it is a challenging snow couloir for backcountry skiers and snowboarders. In the summer and fall it is a favorite rock scramble used by many climbers. This route is also becoming more popular as a winter and early season climb. Mountain guides are also taking clients to the summit via this route.

In the autumn of 1873, John Muir made the fifth ascent of Mount Whitney and the first ascent of what is today known as the Mountaineers Route. On foot, without a sleeping bag and modern equipment, Muir completed the round-trip from Independence (not Lone Pine) to the summit and back in just four days. Two years later he made another first ascent, that of Whitney's north face via the Whitney–Russell Col. After completing these climbs, he wrote:

"For climbers there is a canyon which comes down from the north shoulder of the Whitney peak. Well-seasoned limbs will enjoy the climb of 9000 feet required for this direct route, but soft, succulent people should go the mule way." (In the 1800s the standard route up Whitney was from the west, i.e., the mule way.)

The Mountaineers Route provides the most direct access to the lofty summit. Rated Class 2 + /3, this and the east ridge climb of Mount Russell (Peak Scramble PS6.1) are the most difficult routes included in this guide. Only hearty hikers with routefinding experience using a map and

compass should attempt this challenging cross-country trek.

The Mountaineers Route follows an unmaintained climbers trail that is not always obvious. In the route description below, 1927 UTM grid coordinates have been provided at key points along the way. Refer to Chapter 1 "How To Use This Guidebook" and the glossary (Appendix 7) for a brief explanation of UTM grid coordinates.

The Mountaineers Route above Iceberg Lake will contain snow or ice in early season and possibly later, so take an ice ax and crampons. Check with the Forest Service for snow and ice conditions on this part of the mountain. Because of the popularity of the route and the risk of rock fall, also consider wearing a helmet.

The climb can be completed in a single day but it also is a wonderful two- or three-day trip with the opportunity for a summit bid of Mount Russell.

This route also provides an excellent opportunity to complete a traverse of Whitney's summit. Ascend the Mountaineers Route and descend the Mount Whitney Trail (Route 8). (A wilderness permit is required to descend the Whitney Trail; refer to "Trail Crest Exit Quota" in Chapter 2.) A traverse is best completed on a single-day climb so that you do not have to carry a backpack with your gear over the summit.

The popularity of the North Fork Lone Pine Creek and the confined area has prompted the Forest Service to establish a pack-out-your-poop program. It has been extremely successful because of the efforts of all those that have participated. Ask for a kit when you pick up your permit for Routes 6, 7, and 8.

Due to the limited number of permits issued for the North Fork Lone Pine Creek and the growing popularity, make your permit reservation well in advance of your departure date.

HOW TO GET THERE

From the traffic light in Lone Pine on US 395, turn west and proceed 13 miles to the end of the Whitney Portal Road. The paved road is usually open from May to early November. In the winter the last 3.6 miles of the road may be blocked to vehicle traffic at the 6500-foot level due to snow, ice, boulders, and slides.

TRAILHEAD FACILITIES

The Whitney Portal Store supplies basic meals, souvenirs, maps, bear-proof canisters, and showers. There is a picnic area with barbecue grills,

Opposite: As viewed from Iceberg Lake, the Mountaineers Route ascends the couloir on the right.

tables, and a fishing pond near the store. There are bear-proof food storage boxes near the trailhead and parking lots. One mile to the east is a forty-four–unit campground with piped water and vault toilets.

BEAR-PROOF WILDERNESS FOOD STORAGE BOX LOCATIONS
There are no bear-proof food storage boxes on this route, except near the trailhead.

TRAIL PROFILE TABLE

Milepost	Distance (miles)	Cumulative (miles)	Elevation (feet)	Gain/Loss (feet)
Day 1				
Whitney Portal	0.0	0.0	8,365	0/0
N.F. Lone Pine Creek	0.8	0.8	8,730	365/0
Upper Boy Scout Lake	2.8 x-c	3.6	11,300	2,570/0
Day 2—Summit Day				
Whitney Summit	2.6 x-c	6.2	14,491	3,191/0
Upper Boy Scout Lake	2.6 x-c	8.8	11,300	0/-3,191
Day 3				
Whitney Portal	3.6 x-c	12.4	8,365	0/-2,935
Totals	**12.4**	**12.4**	**—**	**6,126/-6,126**

ROUTE DESCRIPTION
Day 1–Whitney Portal to Upper Boy Scout Lake, 3.6 miles, 2935/0 feet
The trail starts east of the Whitney Portal Store near several large Forest Service signs. The first 0.8 mile follows the Mount Whitney Trail and gently gains elevation. The trail begins by heading northeast, away from Mount Whitney, but soon switchbacks toward the west and the crest of the Sierra Nevada. After about 0.5 mile, the trail crosses Carillon Creek. Continue up the trail to the next stream, the North Fork Lone Pine Creek.

Leave the Whitney Trail (UTM 388674mE and 4049567mN) before crossing the North Fork Lone Pine Creek. Follow an unmaintained climbers trail that ascends this steep and rugged canyon. Although the use trail (climbers trail) can be readily followed in most places, it often disappears into thick brush or rocky talus slopes. Pay close attention to the route so you do not get caught in an endless tangle of water birch. I have observed many hikers who failed to make a critical turn and ended up fighting through the nearly impenetrable brush.

From the Whitney Trail, follow the climbers trail as it ascends the north side of the North Fork Lone Pine Creek. After about 0.3 mile, cross the creek to its south side at 9115 feet (UTM 388336 and 4049525) and continue through brush and talus. The climbers trail climbs steeply up and away from the stream, ascending to the base of the large cliffs and granite slabs perched above the canyon floor on the left. As you hike along the toe of these cliffs you will see a Matterhorn-shaped rock in the streambed mostly hidden by willows and water birch. Traverse into the creek bottom and cross the stream at 9560 feet (UTM 388023 and 4049422) below this distinctive rock. This second crossing is about 0.3 mile above the first crossing.

Here the stream is divided into three rivulets. The last one flows over a large boulder forming a mini ten-foot waterfall. Cross all three rivulets to reach the base of the granite wall on the north side (right) and then ascend along the toe of the wall. Ascend past the large Matterhorn-shaped rock working your way up between the granite cliff on your right and the willows and water birch on your left. Continue about 60 feet above the pointed granite boulder to a break in the cliff at 9655 feet (UTM 387986 and 4049452).

Leave the streambed and climb the wide crack to a large tree on a granite ledge. Traverse east across the rock ledges (known as the Ebersbacher Ledges), on the north side of the creek. Continue traversing east until it is possible to climb up to the next level of ledges, turning back upstream heading west. The top of the ledges is at 9700 feet (UTM 388073 and 4049523). Ascend as high as possible and hike along the base of this upper granite wall. Continue along the toe of the cliff until you reach Lower Boy Scout Lake (10,345 feet). Cross the stream at the lake's outlet (UTM 387432 and 4049348). There are spots to camp beneath a stand of foxtail pine on the south side of the lake.

The segment from Lower Boy Scout Lake to Upper Boy Scout Lake is steep but not as steep as the section you just climbed. It passes over talus, large boulders, an occasional brush field, and up-sloping granite slabs. From the southwest end of Lower Boy Scout Lake there are several use trails that cross the talus. Follow the lower trail that stays just above the stream and willows. As you climb, locate a gigantic boulder and two smaller ones in the middle of a talus field. The route ascends directly below these three monster-sized rocks. From this point, climb over large boulders and through willows to the stream and ascend smooth granite slabs situated between the brush and the creek. Ascend several hundred feet on these granite slabs and then cross to the north side of the main creek. Follow the route to Upper Boy Scout Lake, avoiding the willows and brush along the way.

Upper Boy Scout Lake (UTM 386273 and 4049010) is an excellent place to camp and provides a prime opportunity to climb Mount Russell (Peak Scramble PS6.1). Camp at the lower end of the lake on either side of the outlet stream.

Day 2—Upper Boy Scout Lake to Whitney summit and return, 5.2 miles, 3191/-3191 feet

From the lower end of Upper Boy Scout Lake, hike south skirting below a rock buttress before turning west. As you gain elevation, the views of the great east face of Whitney and the four needles to the south of Whitney come into view. The route to Iceberg Lake passes below the magnificent near-vertical east face of Aiguille Extra, Third Needle, Crooks Peak (previously, Day Needle), Keeler Needle, and Whitney.

Continue hiking in a westerly direction. Near 12,000 feet climb steeply up a glacial moraine of boulders and sand for about 60 feet. From the top of the moraine there is an upper route and a lower route. The preferred route is the lower use trail that drops down slightly and meets the creek near 12,000 feet. There are good campsites here but water may not be available in the fall. Follow the drainage past a waterfall and a wall of weeping water (on your right) until you reach the last water seeping from the cliff. At this point there is a break in the cliff. Ascend loose scree on the left side of this last water. As the slope narrows into a slot with running water, traverse left on a ledge climbing out of the wet gully. Follow the use trail through cliffs to the lower end of Iceberg Lake at 12,640 feet (UTM 385142 and 4048917).

Located at the base of Whitney's sheer east face, Iceberg Lake is an impressive place to camp, relax, explore, and take photographs. From Iceberg Lake, technical rock climbers ascend various Class 5 routes on the east face of Whitney. You may be able to see some roped climbers high on the rock or others scrambling up the Mountaineers Route.

On a recent climb of Whitney, we watched a group of five climbers from New Hampshire attempt the East Face (a roped climb). When they were part way up, a thunderstorm hit the mountain (and the climbers) with rain, sleet, and hail. They halted and waited for the storm to subside. We watched them from the comfort of our tents at Iceberg Lake as they huddled on the rock face for hours, trying to stay dry. It was not until 7:00 PM that evening that they were able to start their retreat. As day turned to night, they switched on their headlamps and inched their way down the rock. They did not make it back to their Iceberg Lake base camp and tent until 1:00 AM, tired and wet, but happy to be off the vertical rock and on level ground.

A climber at the top of the Mountaineers Route near the summit ridge

From Iceberg Lake, the Mountaineers Route is the obvious large gully ascending the right shoulder of the east face of Whitney. In early season it is filled with snow and crampons and an ice ax will be needed. Later in the season the snow may melt out but check with the Forest Service for conditions. Much of the snow and loose scree can be avoided by climbing a narrow slot located about 100 yards to the left (south) of the base of the main gully (see photo on page 128). This slot has excellent handholds and merges into the main couloir about halfway up.

Scramble to the top of the couloir that ends in a notch near 14,090 feet (UTM 384326 and 4048805). Views of the east ridge and east face of Mount Russell are spectacular. From the notch, descend slightly and then turn left up the first gully. This gully is distinctive because of its water-stained brown rock. Start up on either the left or right side of the gully. If you start on the right, climb about 20 feet and then cross to the left. Climb along the left side of the gully gaining approximately 80 feet. On a natural bench covered with scree, carefully cross the gully to the right side. Ascend the rib that divides the first gully from the second gully and follow it to the summit ridge (UTM 384329 and 4048710). The route tops out north of the rock hut built by the Smithsonian Institution in 1909. Stroll to the summit (UTM 384490 and 4048710).

You have just completed one of the classic climbs in the Sierra Nevada, pioneered by John Muir more than 130 years ago. Relax and enjoy your wonderful accomplishment. And take care on the descent.

Day 3—Upper Boy Scout Lake to Whitney Portal, 3.6 miles, 0/-2935 feet

Follow your route down to Lower Boy Scout Lake and down the North Fork Lone Pine Creek to the Whitney trail and out to your starting point at Whitney Portal.

VARIATIONS, SIDE TRIPS, PEAK SCRAMBLES
Peak Scramble PS6.1 (Mount Russell, 14,088 feet)

Mount Russell is one of the finest peaks in California and a favorite of mine. There are no easy routes on its high and precipitous summit; consequently it was one of the last 14,000-foot peaks in California to be climbed. As a comparison, Mount Whitney was first climbed in 1873 but Mount Russell, Whitney's next door neighbor, was not climbed until 1926.

To ascend the mountain, leave the lower end of Upper Boy Scout Lake and head northeast for about 0.2 mile. There are numerous use trails across the loose decomposed granite scree slope. Ascend the uppermost use trail that passes through a break in the cliff band. After crossing the obvious rock band, turn northwest up broad slopes of loose scree to the Russell–Carillon Pass at 13,300 feet.

From the pass, the exposed east ridge is challenging and looks as if a rope would be required for safe climbing. However, once you begin, the route is not as difficult as it appears. The climbing is Class 2 + or easy Class 3. There are many excellent footholds and handholds along the climb. My daughter, Sierra, at age twelve completed the scramble with some minor assistance, but we did not use a rope. The route passes over the east summit. Continue climbing along the ridge until you reach the main west summit. The route lies either on the right (north side) of the east ridge or directly on top. The ridge is about 0.7 mile long and takes about 1 to 1.5 hours each way.

ROUTE 7: CIRCUMNAVIGATION ROUTE OF MOUNT WHITNEY

(CHAPTER 7: MAPS, ROUTES 6–9)

Start...............................Whitney Portal, 8365 feet

End................................Whitney Portal, 8365 feet

Rating ....17.2 miles trail hiking (C-1) and 7.4 miles x-c with one pass (C-2)

Distance........................24.6 miles

Elevation gain/loss......7866/-7866 feet

Trip duration ....3–5 days

Maps.............................Tom Harrison Maps—Mount Whitney High Country or Mount Whitney Zone

Access road/town........Whitney Portal Road/Lone Pine

Car shuttle ....No

TRAIL PROFILE

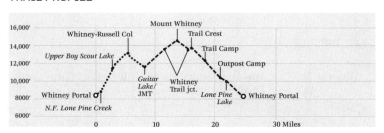

IN A NUTSHELL

The Circumnavigation Route of Whitney is one of the finest hikes featured in this guidebook and is one of my favorites. This exceptional route ascends the North Fork Lone Pine Creek, traverses beneath the spectacular east face of Whitney, crosses the Whitney–Russell Col, and passes through the seldom-visited Arctic Lake recess. This classic circuit joins the JMT near Guitar Lake and then ascends 3000 feet to Whitney's summit.

The route includes 7.4 miles of rugged cross-country travel over trailless terrain. The hiking is strenuous and should be undertaken only by experienced cross-country hikers with routefinding experience. The route also provides an excellent opportunity to climb Mount Russell

(Peak Scramble PS6.1) and to attempt the Mountaineers Route up Whitney (Route 6).

Due to the popularity of the North Fork Lone Pine Creek and the limited number of wilderness permits issued, make your reservations early.

HOW TO GET THERE

From the signal light in the town of Lone Pine on US 395 drive 13 miles west to the end of the Whitney Portal Road. The paved road is usually open from May to early November. In the winter, the last 3.6 miles of the road may be blocked to vehicle traffic at the 6500-foot level due to snow, ice, boulders, and slides.

TRAILHEAD FACILITIES

Souvenirs, maps, bear-proof canisters, and basic meals can be purchased at the Whitney Portal Store. There is a picnic area with barbecue grills, tables, and a fishing pond near the store. There are bear-proof food storage boxes near the trailhead and parking lots. One mile to the east is a forty-four-unit campground with piped water and vault toilets.

BEAR-PROOF WILDERNESS FOOD STORAGE BOX LOCATIONS

There are no bear-proof food storage boxes on this route, except at the trailhead.

TRAIL PROFILE TABLE

Milepost	Distance (miles)	Cumulative (miles)	Elevation (feet)	Gain/Loss (feet)
Day 1				
Whitney Portal	0.0	0.0	8,365	0/0
N.F. Lone Pine Creek	0.8	0.8	8,730	365/0
Upper Boy Scout Lake	2.8 x-c	3.6	11,300	2,570/0
Day 2				
Whitney–Russell Col	1.8 x-c	5.4	13,060	1,760/0
Guitar Lake	2.8 x-c	8.2	11,500	0/-1,560
Day 3				
Mount Whitney Trail	3.4	11.6	13,480	1,980/0
Whitney Summit	2.0	13.6	14,491	1,011/0
Trail Camp	4.7	18.3	12,040	180/-2,631

continued on next page

Milepost	Distance (miles)	Cumulative (miles)	Elevation (feet)	Gain/Loss (feet)
Day 4				
Whitney Portal	6.3	24.6	8,365	0/-3,675
Totals	**24.6**	**24.6**	—	**7,866/-7,866**

ROUTE DESCRIPTION

Day 1—Whitney Portal to Upper Boy Scout Lake, 3.6 miles, 2935/0 feet

Refer to Route 6, Day 1, for a description of this trail segment. Camp at Upper Boy Scout Lake or ascend another 1300 feet to Iceberg Lake. A camp at Upper Boy Scout Lake places you in excellent position to climb Mount Russell's east ridge (Peak Scramble PS6.1).

Day 2—Upper Boy Scout Lake to Guitar Lake, 4.6 miles, 1760/-1560 feet

Refer to Route 6, Day 2, for a description of the route from Upper Boy Scout Lake to Iceberg Lake.

The route from Iceberg Lake over the Whitney–Russell Col and down the valley to Arctic Lake is surprisingly gentle considering that it is sandwiched between the rugged north face of Whitney and the sheer Fishhook Arête of Mount Russell. Although the terrain you will be traversing is not particularly steep, you will have to navigate across talus that can be tedious.

Beyond Iceberg Lake the faint use trail continues to the Whitney–Russell Col but becomes more difficult to follow and completely disappears in places. Skirt the southwest shore (left side) of the lake and ascend to the notch in the ridge above the lake. At the col, you pass from the John Muir Wilderness into the Sequoia National Park.

From the col, descend across talus, scree, and granite slabs to three tarns and follow the creek to Arctic Lake. This seldom-visited valley is peaceful and relaxing. Standing below Mount Russell's Fishhook Arête and looking up at the north face of Whitney, you will be awestruck by the sheer size of these mountains and, in comparison, how small and inconsequential we humans are.

The creek flowing from Arctic Lake continues its gentle descent to Guitar Lake. There are several places to camp along this stream. A camp here will give you good views of Guitar Lake and will keep you from the crowds on the JMT. Or you could hike down to the JMT and select a campsite near Guitar Lake. Thirdly, you could hike past Guitar Lake and camp near a tarn at the 11,600-foot level or continue a bit farther to the 11,900-foot level, where there are excellent campsites near a tarn. Your next-day ascent will be long and arduous, so it is beneficial to camp as high as possible.

Day 3—Guitar Lake to Whitney summit to Trail Camp, 10.1 miles, 3171/-2631 feet

From Guitar Lake, the JMT rises steadily for 3.4 miles and nearly 2000 feet up the steep west slopes of Whitney. The views of Hitchcock Lakes, Guitar Lake, and the mountain panorama improve as you gain elevation. The trail is impressive as it climbs past large rock cliffs and striking granite towers. This segment of trail and the ninety-seven switchbacks below Trail Crest on the Whitney Trail are engineering marvels and tributes to the workers who built them.

The switchbacks seem to go on forever but they finally end at the Whitney Trail junction near Trail Crest. There are only 2.0 miles to the summit and a little more than 1000 feet of elevation gain remaining. You

Looking down the arctic recess at Arctic Lake from the summit of Mount Russell

have completed the most difficult hiking as the trail gradually ascends to the highest point in the forty-eight contiguous United States. Stash your pack and head for the summit. If you are not suffering from the altitude the climb will be enjoyable as the trail snakes through impressive rock towers and past windows in the Sierra Nevada crest that provide breath-taking views of Trail Camp, the Whitney Trail, and the Owens Valley far below. On the other hand, this may be the most strenuous portion of the trip because the altitude may have sucked the energy, strength, and desire from your body.

The trail along the west side of the crest provides an excellent opportunity to climb Mount Muir. It is a short 200-foot scramble to the top (Peak Scramble PS1.3).

Ascend the last switchbacks in the JMT and arrive at the stone hut on the summit. Congratulations, you are standing on the highest point in the Lower 48—and at 14,491 feet you are nearly three miles above sea level. On the summit of Whitney you will be greeted with impressive views of Mount Langley and Mount Muir to the south; the Kaweah Peaks and Saw-tooth Peak to the west; Mount Russell, Tulainyo Lake (the highest large alpine lake in the Sierra Nevada to the right of Mount Russell), Mount Williamson, Milestone Mountain, Table Mountain, and Thunder Mountain to the north; and Trail Camp, Mount Whitney Trail switchbacks, Consultation Lake, and Owens Valley to the east. If the weather is pleasant, spend some time on top; take in the scenery. This is an accomplishment you will long remember.

Return to your pack and hike out the Mount Whitney Trail (Route 8). At Trail Crest the Whitney Trail begins its steep descent over precipitous cliffs, glaciated granite slabs, and talus to Trail Camp. If you are not too tired, continue past Trail Camp for 2 more miles and stop at Outpost Camp or continue to Lone Pine Lake. These spots are less crowded but not as picturesque.

Day 4—Trail Camp to Whitney Portal, 6.3 miles, 0/-3675 feet

It is practically all downhill from here. To complete the circumnavigation of Whitney and return to civilization, hike down the Whitney Trail to Whitney Portal and the start of the trip. Refer to Route 8 for a description of the Mount Whitney Trail.

VARIATIONS, SIDE TRIPS, PEAK SCRAMBLES

Three climbs can be undertaken while circumnavigating Whitney: the east ridge of Mount Russell (Peak Scramble PS6.1), the Mountaineers Route on Whitney (Route 6), and Mount Muir (Peak Scramble PS1.3).

MOUNT WHITNEY TRAIL
(MAPS, ROUTES 6-9)

....	Whitney Portal, 8365 feet
...nd	Whitney Portal, 8365 feet
Rating	Trail hiking (C-1)
Distance	22 miles
Elevation gain/loss	6486/-6486 feet
Trip duration	1–3 days
Maps	Tom Harrison Maps—Mount Whitney High Country or Mount Whitney Zone
Access road/town	Whitney Portal Road/Lone Pine
Car shuttle	No

TRAIL PROFILE

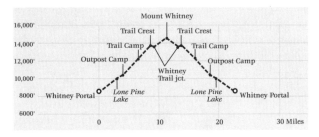

IN A NUTSHELL

Just about any highly motivated hiker in excellent physical condition can complete the climb of Mount Whitney via this footpath. A single-day climb (22-mile round-trip) is popular but may be out of the question for many. However, if you spread the climb out over two or three days it becomes more manageable.

More than 150 hikers, with high aspirations, set out from Whitney Portal for the summit each day. Because of the popularity of the Mount Whitney Trail, wilderness permits are issued through a lottery in February each year (see Chapter 2 for details). Outside Yosemite Valley, this may be the most heavily used summit trail in California. An outing via this trail should be viewed as a social event, not necessarily a wilderness experience.

Based on records kept by the Sequoia National Park and the Inyo National Forest, only about one-third of those attempting the peak reach the summit. Altitude sickness, caused by the rapid rise in elevation, is a major contributor to this low success rate. Driving from near sea level to more than 8000 feet at Whitney Portal and then ascending to 12,000 or

From the east, the Mount Whitney Trail (Route 8) ascends from Whitney Portal to Whitney's lofty summit. From the west, the John Muir Trail climbs to the summit via Guitar Lake and many switchbacks. The two trails join and become one near Trail Crest on the west side of the divide.
1. Whitney Portal; 2. Lone Pine Lake; 3. Outpost Camp; 4. Trail Camp; 5. Trail Crest; 6. Mount Whitney summit. (Photo courtesy of USDA, Inyo National Forest staff)

14,000 feet in a day may trigger mountain sickness for many hikers. This problem may be overcome by spending two nights at the Whitney Portal Campground (8000 feet) or Horseshoe Campground (9920 feet) and then camping one night at Outpost Camp (10,360 feet) or Trail Camp (12,040) before summiting. By ascending slowly, your body is more likely to adjust to the lack of oxygen at the higher elevations. Chapter 3 contains a detailed discussion of mountain sickness and preventative measures.

Even in June and July there is likely to be snow on the steep slopes between Trail Camp and Trail Crest and an ice ax, and possibly crampons, may be necessary. Contact the Forest Service for up-to-date trail conditions.

The following description provides a three-day itinerary. If you plan to complete the ascent in a single day, start by 4:00 AM. Because each hiker's pace and endurance differ from another's, it is difficult to predict how long it will take you to complete the climb. However, it is not unusual for a single-day trip to the summit and back to take twelve to sixteen hours. Refer to Chapter 2 and "Trail Tips for a Single-Day Ascent."

Since the 1960s the Forest Service maintained a solar toilet at Outpost Camp and another at Trail Camp. These convenient toilets have been removed and hikers/backpackers are now required to use pack-out-your-poop kits. These kits are supplied when you pick up your wilderness permit.

HOW TO GET THERE

From the signal light in Lone Pine on US 395, turn west and drive 13 miles to the end of the Whitney Portal Road. The paved road is usually open from May to early November. In the winter the last 3.6 miles of the road may be closed due to snow and ice.

TRAILHEAD FACILITIES

The Whitney Portal Store sells basic meals, souvenirs, maps, and bear-proof canisters. There is a picnic area with barbecue grills, tables, and a fishing pond near the store. One mile to the east is a forty-four-unit campground with piped water and vault toilets.

BEAR-PROOF WILDERNESS FOOD STORAGE BOX LOCATIONS

There are no bear-proof food storage boxes on this route, except right near the trailhead.

TRAIL PROFILE TABLE

Milepost	Distance (miles)	Cumulative (miles)	Elevation (feet)	Gain/Loss (feet)
Day 1				
Whitney Portal	0.0	0.0	8,365	0/0
Outpost Camp	3.8	3.8	10,360	1,995/0
Trail Camp	2.5	6.3	12,040	1,680/0
Day 2				
Trail Crest	2.2	8.5	13,660	1,620/0
JMT	0.5	9.0	13,480	0/-180
Whitney Summit	2.0	11.0	14,491	1,011/0
Trail Camp	4.7	15.7	12,040	180/-2,631
Day 3				
Whitney Portal	6.3	22.0	8,365	0/-3,675
Totals	**22.0**	**22.0**	—	**6,486 / -6,486**

ROUTE DESCRIPTION
Day 1—Whitney Portal to Trail Camp, 6.3 miles, 3675/0 feet

The Mount Whitney Trail starts east of the Whitney Portal Store near several large Forest Service display signs. The trail begins by heading northeast, away from the mountain, but soon switchbacks toward the west and the crest of the Sierra Nevada. After about 0.5 mile, the trail crosses Carillon Creek. At 0.8 mile the trail crosses the North Fork of Lone Pine Creek and enters the John Muir Wilderness.

The trail then begins a series of switchbacks through a brushy area of chinquapin oak, mountain mahogany, and chaparral. To the left is Lone Pine Creek cascading down a series of cataracts as it flows from Lone Pine Lake. After several switchbacks and about 2 miles of steady climbing, the trail levels off slightly. Just before reaching the trail junction to Lone Pine Lake (at 2.8 miles), the trail crosses a small stream. From this junction it is a short walk to beautiful Lone Pine Lake, perched on a glacial bench overlooking Whitney Portal and Owens Valley.

A forest consisting of foxtail pine, limber pine, Jeffrey pine, and lodgepole pine supplants the brush of the lower trail segment. Over the next mile the path gradually gains 400 feet in elevation. As you near Bighorn Park, a meadow overgrown with willows, the trail descends slightly and skirts the meadow. Cross a small stream several times and then cross Lone Pine Creek below a scenic waterfall cascading over a granite cliff. Outpost Camp (at 3.8 miles) is situated at the far end of the Bighorn Park.

Outpost Camp (10,360 feet) and Trail Camp (12,040 feet) are the two primary areas to camp along the trail. If altitude sickness is a concern, camp at Outpost Camp before moving up the mountain.

Over the next 2.5 miles the trail climbs steeply, gaining 1700 feet to Trail Camp. The scenery and vistas improve as you gain elevation. As you leave Outpost Camp, the sheer granite face of Thor Peak dominates the view. Mirror Lake lies in a lovely glacial cirque at the base of Thor Peak, 0.5 mile beyond Outpost Camp. Mirror Lake (at 4.3 miles) makes a beautiful rest stop but is closed to camping. At one time this was a popular spot to camp but it was overused, causing serious damage to the fragile lake and meadow environment.

Above Mirror Lake, the footpath ascends several switchbacks before leveling off for a short distance to cross polished granite slabs near the tree line. Here there are exceptional views of Mirror Lake, Wotans Throne, Thor Peak, and Mount Irvine. From Mirror Lake, climb 800 feet over 1 mile to the small but picturesque Trailside Meadow (at 5.3 miles) situated at 11,400 feet. No camping is permitted but it makes for a nice place to take a breather and enjoy the colorful wildflowers and lush meadow.

Ascending the Mount Whitney Trail below Lone Pine Lake

From Trailside Meadow it is another mile and a 600-foot climb to Trail Camp (at 6.3 miles). As you ascend, the scenic vistas become more expansive with views of Consultation Lake, Arc Pass, Mount McAdie, and the great east face escarpment of Mount Muir and the Sierra Nevada.

Trail Camp or near Consultation Lake are logical locations for a base camp but too many people in a confined area have adversely affected the fragile environment. Because of the concentration of campers at Trail Camp, a word of caution is warranted. When you fill your water bottles do not seek water from the nearby lake. Boiling, filtering, or treating this water with purification tablets may provide adequate safeguards but higher quality water is nearby. Walk to the upper end of the lake and hike up the inlet stream a short distance to fill your water bottles from the stream flowing into the lake. This is a better source of water.

Paradoxically, Trail Camp is the last reliable place to get water. Make sure your water bottles are full for the hike to the summit.

Day 2—Trail Camp to Whitney summit to Trail Camp, 9.4 miles, 2811/-2811 feet

Trail Camp is located above Consultation Lake and at the base of the great east face of the Sierra Nevada. The 14,000-foot Mount Muir is due west and clearly visible from the camp. Mount Whitney is to the north just out of view. From Trail Camp, the trail ascends ninety-six, ninety-seven, or ninety-eight (depending on the count) switchbacks up a granite buttress to Trail Crest. Some years ago the trail continued farther to the west before ascending the steep slope to the crest. After World War II, the trail was relocated to its current position so that it would be clear of snow for a longer period each summer and fall. The trail is not particularly steep but is unrelenting in its climb to the crest, gaining 1620 feet in 2.2 miles.

Enter Sequoia National Park at the crest. Here you are greeted with awesome views of Sequoia National Park to the west and north. The park stretches as far as the eye can see and beyond. Immediately below are the beautiful Hitchcock Lakes and Guitar Lake. Beyond these lakes are the Great Western Divide and the Kaweah Peaks.

The trail drops slightly from 13,660 to 13,480 feet to meet the JMT. The JMT, originating in Yosemite Valley about 220-trail miles to the north, passes Crabtree Meadow and Guitar Lake as it ascends the west slope of Whitney on its way to the summit.

There are only 2 miles to the summit and a little more than 1000 feet of elevation gain. The most difficult hiking is over as the JMT gradually reaches its apex. If you are not suffering from the altitude, the next 2 miles will be extremely rewarding as the trail snakes through impressive rock towers and past windows in the Sierra Nevada crest that provide breathtaking views of Trail Camp, the Whitney Trail, and the Owens Valley far below. On the other hand, this may be the most strenuous portion of the trip because the altitude may have sucked the strength, energy, and desire from your body.

The path along the west side of the crest passes within a couple hundred feet of Mount Muir providing an excellent opportunity to climb another 14,000-foot peak (Peak Scramble PS1.3).

Congratulations, you have made it to the highest point in the land. Sign

The spectacular John Muir Trail snakes around rock towers and over granite cliffs within 2 miles of the summit.

the summit register and take pictures of your historic moment. From the summit you will be greeted with impressive views of Mount Langley and Mount Muir to the south; the Kaweah Peaks and Sawtooth Peak to the west; Mount Russell, Tulainyo Lake (to the right of Mount Russell), the highest large alpine lake in the Sierra Nevada, Mount Williamson, Milestone Mountain, Table Mountain, Thunder Mountain, and Mount Brewer to the north; and Trail Camp, Mount Whitney Trail switchbacks, Consultation Lake, Arc Pass, and Owens Valley to the east. If the weather is pleasant, spend some time on top; take in the scenery and savor your accomplishment. Call home with your cell phone and celebrate.

Day 3—Trail Camp to Whitney Portal, 6.3 miles, 0/-3675 feet

Retrace your steps and hike out to Whitney Portal. It is practically all downhill. Celebrate your successful ascent.

ROUTE 9: MEYSAN LAKE ROUTE
(CHAPTER 7: MAPS, ROUTES 6-9)

Start .... Lower Whitney Portal Campground, 7880 feet
End .... Whitney Portal Campground, 7880 feet
Rating .... 14.2 miles trail hiking (C-1),14.6 miles x-c
with six passes (C-2/2 +)
Distance .... 28.8 miles
Elevation gain/loss ...... 11,961/-11,961 feet
Trip duration .... 4-6 days
Maps .... Tom Harrison Maps—Mount Whitney High
Country or Mount Whitney Zone
Access road/town .... Whitney Portal Road/Lone Pine
Car shuttle .... No

TRAIL PROFILE

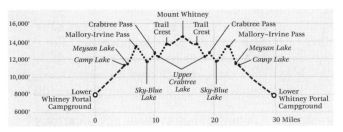

IN A NUTSHELL

This difficult trek, along with Routes 4, 6, 7, and 10, is the most strenuous in this guidebook. Only well-conditioned hikers with routefinding experience over rugged trail-less terrain should attempt this route.

After the first edition of this guidebook was published, I received feedback from several readers saying that the Meysan Lake Route was too difficult and should not be included. However, this is such a wonderful and unique route I did not want to drop it. Instead, I have included this warning and have modified the route substantially to avoid two of the sections that were the most troublesome. The steep climb over unstable scree and talus from Meysan Lake to the LeConte–Mallory Pass has been replaced with a climb over the Mallory–Irvine Pass. And the long tedious climb from upper Crabtree Lake to Discovery Pass over decomposed granite sand has been modified significantly. If you prefer to avoid this difficult ascent altogether, I have included a description of a major detour around Discovery Pass. This variation descends the spectacular Crabtree Lakes basin and joins the JMT near Crabtree Meadow (Route 10, Day 3).

With these modifications the route is less difficult than before, but it is still rugged and strenuous and should not be attempted by inexperienced cross-country travelers.

A wilderness permit should be more readily available because the hike begins and finishes at the Meysan Lake trailhead, thereby avoiding the popular Whitney Trail.

HOW TO GET THERE

From the signal light on US 395 in Lone Pine turn west onto the Whitney Portal Road and drive 12 miles to the lower end of the Whitney Portal Campground, located about 1 mile east of the end of the road. Park on the left side of the road in a designated area. The paved road usually is open from May to early November. In winter, the last 2.6 miles of the road may be blocked by snow.

TRAILHEAD FACILITIES

A forty-four-unit campground (Whitney Portal Campground) with piped water and vault toilets is located at the trailhead. One mile to the west, near the start of the Mount Whitney Trail, the Whitney Portal Store sells basic meals, souvenirs, maps, and bear-proof canisters. There is a picnic area with barbecue grills and tables, and a fishing pond near the store.

BEAR-PROOF WILDERNESS FOOD STORAGE BOX LOCATIONS

There are no bear boxes on this route.

TRAIL PROFILE TABLE

Milepost	Distance (miles)	Cumulative (miles)	Elevation (feet)	Gain/Loss (feet)
Day 1				
Whitney Portal CG	0.0	0.0	7,880	0/0
Camp Lake	5.0	5.0	11,280	3,400/0
Meysan Lake	0.6 x-c	5.6	11,500	220/0
Day 2				
Mallory–Irvine Pass	1.2 x-c	6.8	13,520	2,020/0
Sky-Blue Lake	1.8 x-c	8.6	11,545	0/-1,975
Crabtree Pass	1.2 x-c	9.8	12,560	1,015/0
Upper Crabtree Lake	0.7 x-c	10.5	12,120	0/-440

continued on next page

Milepost	Distance (miles)	Cumulative (miles)	Elevation (feet)	Gain/Loss (feet)
Day 3				
Discovery Pass	1.2 x-c	11.7	13,600	1,480/0
Trail Crest	0.2 x-c	11.9	13,660	80/-140
JMT	0.5	12.4	13,480	0/-180
Whitney Summit	2.0	14.4	14,491	1,011/0
Trail Crest	2.5	16.9	13,660	180/-1,011
Upper Crabtree Lake	1.4 x-c	18.3	12,120	140/-1,560
Day 4				
Crabtree Pass	0.7 x-c	19.0	12,560	440/0
Sky-Blue Lake	1.2 x-c	20.2	11,545	0/-1,015
Mallory–Irvine Pass	1.8 x-c	22.0	13,520	1,975/0
Meysan Lake	1.2 x-c	23.2	11,500	0/-2,020
Day 5				
Camp Lake	0.6 x-c	23.8	11,280	0/-220
Whitney Portal CG	5.0	28.8	7,880	0/-3,400
Totals	**28.8**	**28.8**	**—**	**11,961/-11,961**

ROUTE DESCRIPTION

Day 1—Whitney Portal Campground to Meysan Lake,
5.6 miles, 3620/0 feet

Park along the Whitney Portal Road, at the Meysan Lake Trail sign located near the lower end of the Whitney Portal Campground. Start by walking through the campground, following signs that direct you along a combination of roads and trails, and then past lovely summer cabins perched on the steep mountainside overlooking Owens Valley.

The elevation gain along the trail is continuous and the switchbacks are unrelenting as the trail ascends the rugged Meysan Creek canyon. The canyon is steep and its walls rise precipitously for thousands of feet. On your left, the northwest face of Lone Pine Peak towers overhead. On your right, the trail skirts below sheer granite walls that define the canyon.

After about 4 miles of strenuous hiking you will reach Grass Lake. The small lake is not readily visible from the trail, but you can follow a short spur trail to its shore. From this junction, follow the main trail as it turns right and climbs above Grass Lake on its way to Camp Lake. Camp Lake is a beautiful tarn located near a small meadow.

Continue on to Meysan Lake by skirting the right shore of Camp Lake and following the creek flowing from Meysan Lake. This is the route of an old trail to Meysan Lake. An ancient sign and sections of the long-forgotten trail are sometimes visible above Camp Lake.

Meysan Lake is a beautiful and rugged place to stop and camp for the first night. This will provide your party with a fresh start the following morning for the tedious and sometimes discouraging climb of the loose scree above the lake. The crux of the trip is this 2000-foot ascent above Meysan Lake to the high plateau and the Mallory–Irvine Pass.

Day 2—Meysan Lake to upper Crabtree Lake, 4.9 miles, 3035/-2415 feet

Four dominant peaks ring the Meysan Lake basin: Irvine, Mallory, LeConte, and Lone Pine. On the right, the vertical granite face of Mount Irvine rises from the lake. In the center, the large glacial basin is split by the rugged east ridge of Mount Mallory. To the left of this ridge are four distinctive couloirs. To the right of this ridge, but not readily visible from the lower end of Meysan Lake, is a narrow and steep gully that provides access to the upper bowl and easier terrain on Mount Irvine.

Skirt around the left (east) shore of Meysan Lake. At the south end of the lake a steep gully immediately to the right (north) of the prominent east ridge of Mount Mallory comes into view. Ascend this steep gully. A large basin ringed by the rugged ridge connecting Mount Mallory and Mount Irvine will gradually come into view. Head for the obvious low point in the ridge that is about halfway between Mallory and Irvine. It is Class 2 scrambling to the pass.

At the pass you will be looking down the northwest side to Consultation Lake and Trail Camp on the Mount Whitney Trail. Do not descend but rather scramble left (south-southwest) around sharp pinnacles and across ledges (Class 2) to less rugged terrain. Descend toward Arc Pass, staying on the south side of the ridge. Descend to the valley south of Arc Pass and turn south. Follow the valley to an unnamed lake due south of Arc Pass and then continue down to Sky-Blue Lake.

You are approaching one of the most beautiful areas of the Sierra Nevada: Rock Creek and Sky-Blue Lake. The sheer rock walls above Sky-Blue Lake are particularly inspiring at sunrise when early morning light casts a golden glow on the towering cliffs. If time allows, camp at Sky-Blue Lake to enjoy this lovely spot, saving Crabtree Pass and upper Crabtree Lake for the next day.

Not only is Sky-Blue Lake a major attraction in the area but so is near-by Iridescent Lake nestled in the Miter Basin. The scenery is superb and the fishing enticing. Not many anglers visit these waters, but I have seen trout up to eighteen inches long cruising near the shore of Iridescent Lake. The upper Rock Creek area near Solider Lake, Iridescent Lake,

The prominent east ridge of Mount Mallory, with the route to the Mallory–Irvine Col to its right and the way to Mallory–LeConte Pass to its left

Sky-Blue Lake, and Crabtree Pass are bighorn sheep habitat, and I have spotted several groups of sheep in the area.

Your next major goal is Crabtree Pass. This pass is framed by Mount McAdie and Mount Newcomb. Although not clearly visible from the lake, the pass is directly below Mount McAdie. From the upper end of Sky-Blue Lake, ascend alongside the lake's inlet stream heading generally northwest and then angling west, passing through a patchwork of beautiful miniature meadows and past several petite ponds. At a glacial moraine and two potholes at 11,920 feet, the stream turns right (north). Follow the streambed over large boulders and talus to a tarn at 12,000 feet. At the upper end of this tarn and meadow, hike northeast up gradual terrain to the outlet of the large unnamed lake at 12,129 feet. From the outlet you can look directly down on Sky-Blue Lake and up to Crabtree Pass.

Proceed around the right side of the lake to a small tarn at 12,320 feet immediately below Crabtree Pass and continue to the pass. You will see occasional rock carins marking the way and evidence of a climbers trail in many spots.

The enjoyable hike to the pass is over difficult terrain requiring a good deal of rock-scrambling skill with a pack. Lush meadows, colorful wildflowers, cascading streams, and alpine lakes provide a welcome break in the glaciated granite slabs and steep cliffs that form the rugged terrain in upper Rock Creek.

From Crabtree Pass, you can see Discovery Pinnacle high above and upper Crabtree Lake a good distance below. To descend from the pass, angle to your right (north), losing elevation gradually as you scramble over ledges and downsloping granite slabs. Follow a series of ramps working your way down and across to a large boulder field. As you approach the talus, the granite slabs you are hiking across have been undercut by a glacier, thereby forming a small cliff. If you come to an impasse and cannot find a way down to the talus, climb up until the ledges merge easily with the boulder field.

Descend on large boulders and talus to upper Crabtree Lake and walk around the right (north) side of the lake on a use trail to the outlet. There are several good campsites near the lake's outlet stream. From here, the route heads up the steep decomposed granite sand slopes to Discovery Pass. To avoid this arduous climb, descend over gentle terrain past Crabtree Lakes and join the JMT at Crabtree Meadow. This pleasant and scenic option is described in Route 10, Day 3.

Day 3—Upper Crabtree Lake to Whitney summit to upper Crabtree Lake, 7.8 miles, 2891/-2891 feet

A short distance north of the lake's outlet there is a natural ramp of decomposed granite sand and granite slabs. This ramp is clearly visible from Crabtree Pass and as you make your way around the north side of the lake. Ascend this ramp to 12,300 feet, turn sharply to your right (north-northwest) and scramble up tedious scree and decomposed granite sand to the horseshoe-shaped ridge above upper Hitchcock Lake. Ascending the loose, decomposed granite sand is tiring as you step forward and then slip back in the soft sand. It is particularly laborious with a full pack. Kick steps in the soft scree just as you would ascending a steep snow slope.

Reach the ridge at 13,120 feet and turn right. Follow the ridge toward Discovery Pinnacle. Pass the pinnacle on its right shoulder.

Traverse beneath Discovery Pinnacle, on the Mount Whitney Trail side, and regain the ridge. Hike along the ridge for a short distance before dropping down to the Whitney Trail directly below, being careful not to dislodge loose rocks onto the trail. Hike up the Whitney Trail to Trail Crest and drop down to the junction with the JMT.

There are only 2 more miles to the top. Refer to Route 8, Day 2, for a description of this trail segment.

Congratulations, you have reached the highest point in the contiguous United States. Rest and absorb the magnificent scenery, then retrace your route back to camp at upper Crabtree Lake. If you plan to descend via the Mount Whitney Trail (Route 8) hike down the trail to Trail Camp and continue to Whitney Portal.

Day 4—Upper Crabtree Lake to Meysan Lake,
4.9 miles, 2415/-3035 feet

Retrace your footsteps back to Meysan Lake via Crabtree Pass, Sky-Blue Lake, Mallory–Irvine Pass, and Meysan Lake. There is one area worth describing in detail for your return trip. From Sky-Blue Lake ascend the valley toward Arc Pass. Before reaching Arc Pass turn right (east) and climb the ridge/steep slopes to the Mallory–Irvine ridge. Because the Mallory–Irvine Pass is located immediately north of where you will gain the Mallory–Irvine ridge, the pass is not obvious when you begin your ascent. Near the crest of the ridge, scramble through pinnacles traversing left into the Mallory–Irvine Pass.

Day 5—Meysan Lake to Whitney Portal Campground,
5.6 miles, 0/-3620 feet

Follow the trail out to the campground.

VARIATIONS, SIDE TRIPS, PEAK SCRAMBLES
Variation V9.1 (LeConte–Mallory Pass), 13.6 miles cross-country
travel with six passes (C-2/2+)

Four major peaks surround the Meysan Lake basin. On the right, the vertical granite face of Mount Irvine rises from the shore of Meysan Lake. In the center the large glacial basin is split by the rugged east ridge of Mount Mallory. To the left of this ridge are four distinctive couloirs. To reach the Mallory–LeConte Pass ascend either of the two couloirs closest to the east ridge of Mallory when they contain snow, which is usually into July. A snow route is the best way to avoid the loose scree that is so tedious to climb. Crampons and ice ax will be needed.

If you did not bring an ice ax and crampons or the snow has melted, begin by climbing the third gully (counting from the east ridge of Mallory). Where the couloir steepens and downsloping slabs are encountered, traverse right along ledges to the rib dividing the third couloir from the second couloir. Follow this rib to the plateau.

The footing along the rib is loose but generally better than that found in the gullies. This 1-mile section is the crux of the route and is strenuous. Once the Mallory–LeConte plateau is attained, the correct pass is the low point on the far right near the base of Mount Mallory. From the pass descend toward the unnamed lake due south of Arc Pass and then on to Sky-Blue Lake.

There is no particular advantage to this route over the featured Route 9 unless you are able to ascend the gullies when they are filled with snow. Without snow, ascend over the Mallory–Irvine Pass.

ROUTE 10: NEW ARMY PASS ROUTE
(CHAPTER 7: MAPS, ROUTES 10-11)

Start.............................Horseshoe Meadow, 10,040 feet
End............................Whitney Portal, 8365 feet
Rating........................29.4 miles trail hiking (C-1) and 7.5 miles x-c
with one pass (C-2)
Distance......................36.9 miles
Elevation gain/loss......9051/-10,726 feet
Trip duration...............4–7 days
Maps...........................Tom Harrison Maps—Mount Whitney High
Country or Mount Whitney Zone
Access road/town........Whitney Portal Road to Horseshoe Meadow
Road/Lone Pine
Car shuttle..................Yes

TRAIL PROFILE

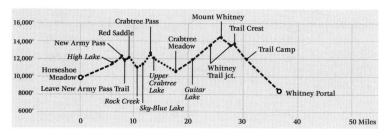

IN A NUTSHELL

Named for the cottonwood trees that were located at the original trailhead in the Owens Valley, the Cottonwood Lakes–New Army Pass Trail provides access to the southern portion of the John Muir Wilderness, Sequoia National Park, and Mount Whitney. Cottonwood Lakes are a favorite with anglers and home to the golden trout, California's state fish.

This excellent route skirts the Cottonwood Lakes basin, ascends New Army Pass, journeys through the impressive Rock Creek drainage, passes by the beautiful Sky-Blue Lake, and crosses Crabtree Pass. It descends past Crabtree Lakes on its way to Crabtree Meadow, then climbs to Guitar Lake, Trail Crest, and finally the summit of Whitney. The route also provides an excellent opportunity to climb Mount Langley, another 14,000-footer. Mount Langley was first climbed in 1871 by Clarence King, who mistakenly thought he was making the first ascent of Whitney.

Following Route 10 to Mount Whitney and returning to Horseshoe

Meadow via Route 11 is one of my favorite circuits in the region. The beauty, spectacular scenery, and variety of topography make this an outstanding adventure. Along the way you may see golden trout swimming in Cottonwood Lakes; 18-inch-long trout in Iridescent Lake and Sky-Blue Lake; bighorn sheep in the upper Rock Creek environs (upper Soldier Lake, Iridescent Lake, and Crabtree Pass); and mule deer in the Crabtree Meadow and in the lush grasslands along lower Rock Creek. Combining Routes 10 and 11 would total about 57 miles, but the 31 return miles would be along well-maintained trails and no cross-country travel would be required.

This route includes 7.5 miles of cross-country travel over rugged trailless terrain. Only hikers with routefinding experience using a map and compass should attempt this route. If you do not plan to climb Mount Langley, an alternative route would be to stay on the New Army Pass Trail to Lower Soldier Lake (Variation V10.1a).

The drive and rapid rise to 10,000 feet can cause a hiker to become lethargic with mountain sickness the first day. Spending one or two nights at the Horseshoe Meadow campground is helpful in adjusting to the altitude.

HOW TO GET THERE

From the traffic light on US 395 in Lone Pine, turn west and drive 3.5 miles up the Whitney Portal Road. Turn south (left) onto Horseshoe Meadow Road and continue 20.5 miles to Horseshoe Meadow. Just before the end of the road, turn right and proceed 0.3 mile to the Cottonwood Lakes and New Army Pass trailhead (not to be confused with the Cottonwood Pass trailhead and Route 11). The paved road usually is open from May to late October.

TRAILHEAD FACILITIES

There are twelve walk-in campground sites, toilets, and piped water near the trailhead.

BEAR-PROOF WILDERNESS FOOD STORAGE BOX LOCATIONS

- Crabtree Meadow: One box is about 0.1 mile south of the Crabtree Ranger Station southeast of the creek crossing.

Variation V10.1

- Lower Soldier Lake: A long, narrow meadow is located south of the lake along the lake's outlet stream. One box is on the east side of this meadow about 600 feet south of the lake.

- Rock Creek Lake: One box is alongside lower Rock Creek Trail at the lower end of Rock Creek Lake. The lake is about 1 mile southwest of lower Soldier Lake.

TRAIL PROFILE TABLE

Milepost	Distance (miles)	Cumulative (miles)	Elevation (feet)	Gain/Loss (feet)
Day 1				
Horseshoe Meadow	0.0	0.0	10,040	0/0
High Lake	6.0	6.0	11,500	1,700/-240
Day 2				
New Army Pass	1.6	7.6	12,320	820/0
Leave New Army Pass Trail	0.6 x-c	8.2	11,840	0/-480
Red Saddle	0.8 x-c	9.0	12,240	400/0
Rock Creek	1.6 x-c	10.6	11,120	180/-1,300
Sky-Blue Lake	1.2 x-c	11.8	11,545	425/0
Day 3				
Crabtree Pass	1.2 x-c	13.0	12,560	1,015/0
Upper Crabtree Lake	0.7 x-c	13.7	12,120	0/-440
Crabtree Meadow and JMT	4.2 x-c	17.9	10,640	480/-1,960
Guitar Lake	2.6	20.5	11,500	860/0
Day 4				
Mount Whitney Trail	3.4	23.9	13,480	1,980/0
Whitney Summit	2.0	25.9	14,491	1,011/0
Trail Camp	4.7	30.6	12,040	180/-2,631
Day 5				
Whitney Portal	6.3	36.9	8365	0/-3,675
Total	**36.9**	**36.9**	—	**9,051/-10,726**

ROUTE DESCRIPTION
Day 1—Horseshoe Meadow to High Lake, 6 miles, 1700/-240 feet
Because of the lack of camping spots with fresh water above High Lake, Day 1 is relatively short and stops for the night at Long Lake or High Lake. The shorter day should also assist in your acclimatization process. Day 2 is also short, but the hiking is over trail-less terrain and camping at Sky-Blue Lake should not be bypassed.

At the start, the trail gradually loses elevation, crosses South Fork Creek, and then ascends alongside Cottonwood Creek past Golden

Trout Camp. Beyond this camp, the trail gradually turns west and begins a moderate climb to Cottonwood Lakes basin. You will encounter several trail junctions along the way. Always take the trail heading to New Army Pass. The trail passes Cottonwood Lakes 1 and 2 before reaching Long Lake and High Lake. These two lakes are situated at the foot of the south ridge of Mount Langley and directly below New Army Pass. There is an impressive granite wall/rock face rising to the north of High Lake. Camp at Long Lake or continue a short distance to High Lake. You will encounter far fewer campers at High Lake and it is a beautiful spot to camp.

Day 2—High Lake to Sky-Blue Lake, 5.8 miles, 1825/-1780

At High Lake the trail begins a steady climb to New Army Pass. The footpath makes several long sweeps across the steep face before reaching the pass. As you near the pass, unique beehivelike rock formations come into view. The trail snakes through these unusual rock structures to reveal marvelous views of Mount Langley and Mount Whitney, and sites west across the great Central Valley to the Coast Range.

Hike down the northwest side of New Army Pass over gentle terrain. Follow the trail for ten to fifteen minutes until you are about even with Army Pass. Leave the trail and hike cross-country over decomposed granite sand and granite slabs to Army Pass and the old unmaintained

High Lake, below New Army Pass, is an excellent place to camp.

Army Pass Trail. Near the pass another unmaintained, but distinctive, trail climbs gradually in a north-northwest direction. Pick up this trail and follow it over easy terrain to a large natural beehivelike rock structure/cliff. It is as if this area was under a great sea millions of years ago. Continue on the trail as it traverses sandy slopes to an obvious red saddle near 12,320+ feet. If you plan to climb Mount Langley, leave your backpack at the red saddle and scramble up loose sand to the summit (see PS10.1).

Cross the red saddle and follow the trail as it descends steeply and switchbacks its way to a large meadow just above upper Solider Lake. In this meadow our party spotted a large group of female and immature bighorn sheep.

Walk around the right side of the meadow and enter an area of mature foxtail pine. Do not drop down to upper Soldier Lake but maintain your elevation near 11,360 feet to avoid some steep cliffs. Traverse in a westerly direction, aiming for an unseen notch and a narrow tarn (11,280 feet) located between, and north of, the two Solider Lakes. Traverse into the notch and drop down to the picturesque tarn nestled among the cliffs and perched on a bench high above Rock Creek. From this tarn, traverse into Rock Creek basin, hiking north. Rock Creek and its surroundings are magnificent as the creek snakes its way between Mount Langley, Mount LeConte, and Mount McAdie to the east and the impressive wall formed by the summits of Joe Devel, Pickering, and Newcomb to the west.

Follow Rock Creek and various use trails over gentle terrain past the outlet stream flowing from Iridescent Lake to Sky-Blue Lake. Below Sky-Blue Lake is a rock cliff that acts as a natural dam, holding the lake waters in place. The best way to ascend this obstacle is to follow the stream to the base of the cliff and climb along the toe of the cliff on the west (left) side of the outlet stream. In a short distance turn sharply right and follow granite ledges to the lake's outlet. Cross the stream and walk around the right side of Sky-Blue Lake.

There are excellent campsites at one of the loveliest spots in the Sierra Nevada. Help keep it this way by choosing your campsite carefully. Do not camp in the small meadows scattered around the lake; instead, pitch your tent on mineral soil. There are good areas near the outlet on the left (west) side of the lake and by two small ponds on the right (east) side of the lake.

Day 3—Sky-Blue Lake to Guitar Lake, 8.7 miles, 2355/-2400 feet

Although this is not a long day based on the number of miles from Sky-Blue Lake to Guitar Lake, it will be a difficult and challenging one due to the rugged cross-country travel involved. That being said, you may consider taking two days rather than one to complete this segment of the hike. If you do, there are excellent places to camp at the tarn above middle Crabtree Lake (a favorite spot of mine) or at Crabtree Meadow.

From Sky-Blue Lake, size up the route to Crabtree Pass, your next major goal. The pass is framed by the steep granite slopes of Mount McAdie and Mount Newcomb. Although not clearly visible from the lake, the pass is directly below Mount McAdie. It is an enjoyable hike to the pass, but it is over difficult terrain requiring a considerable amount of scrambling. Meadows, lakes, tarns, wildflowers, and cascading streams provide a welcome break in the glaciated granite slabs and steep cliffs that form the rugged terrain of upper Rock Creek.

From Sky-Blue Lake's outlet, walk around the right (east and north) side and ascend alongside the lake's inlet stream, heading generally northwest and then angling west through beautiful meadows and past several small ponds. At a large glacial moraine and two potholes at 11,920 feet, the stream turns right (north). Follow the streambed over large boulders and talus to a tarn at 12,000 feet. At the upper end of this tarn and meadow, hike northeast up gradual terrain to the outlet of the large unnamed lake at 12,129 feet. From the outlet you can look down on Sky-Blue Lake and up to Crabtree Pass.

Proceed around the right side of the lake to a small tarn at 12,320 feet, situated directly below Crabtree Pass, and continue to the pass. You will see an occasional rock carin marking the way and evidence of a climbers trail in many spots.

From Crabtree Pass you can see Discovery Pinnacle high above and upper Crabtree Lake a good distance below. To descend from the pass, angle to your right (north), losing elevation gradually as you scramble over ledges and downsloping granite slabs. Follow a series of ramps working your way down and across to a large talus field. As you approach the boulders, the granite slabs you are hiking across have been undercut by a glacier, thereby forming a small cliff. If you come to an impasse and cannot find a way down, climb up until the ledges merge easily with the talus field.

Descend on large boulders to upper Crabtree Lake and walk around the right (north) side of the lake on a use trail to the outlet. There are several good campsites near the lake's outlet stream.

The route now turns west down Crabtree Creek. (For a direct ascent of Whitney via the steep sandy slopes leading to Discovery Pass, refer to the description for Route 9, Day 3.) Follow the stream flowing from upper Crabtree Lake and descend this magnificent valley passing the lakes on the right (north) side. The sheer walls of Mount Newcomb and

Mount Chamberlin rise steeply overhead. A use trail in the valley becomes more pronounced as you descend.

For about 0.5 mile above middle Crabtree Lake (11,312 feet) there is one continuous granite slab along the stream that makes the walking easy. When you reach the tarn above middle Crabtree Lake, stay high and do not drop down to the lake. From the tarn, traverse to your right, gaining elevation slightly to avoid a large cliff. Once past the cliff, drop down to the use trail along the edge of the lake.

Continue to follow the stream to lower Crabtree Lake. Just above the lake you will pass through a meadow and come to a forest of ancient foxtail pine occupying the north slopes above lower Crabtree Lake. The use trail that has been spotty is now pronounced and it is easy to follow all the way to Crabtree Meadow and the JMT.

I skied up this valley on a circumnavigation of Whitney one winter and this valley and Sky-Blue Lake, along with the entire route, were stunning. I was the only one in the area and the feeling of solitude beneath these great granite walls was overwhelming. Snow and ice covered the lakes and much of the surrounding landscape, but the vertical walls were too steep to hold snow.

Follow the JMT east-northeast past Timberline Lake to Guitar Lake and select a campsite, or continue a short distance to the tarns at the 11,600-foot level or the 11,900-foot level. If your day is not too tiring, continue to the tarns. This higher camp will help reduce your next day's long and arduous ascent of Whitney.

Day 4—Guitar Lake to Whitney summit to Trail Camp, 10.1 miles, 3171/-2631 feet
Refer to Route 7, Day 3, for a description of this trail segment.

Day 5—Trail Camp to Whitney Portal, 6.3 miles, 0/-3675 feet
Refer to Route 8 for a description of the Mount Whitney Trail.

VARIATIONS, SIDE TRIPS, PEAK SCRAMBLES
Variation V10.1a (Lower Soldier Lake), 5.7 miles cross-country travel with one pass (C-2)
This variation eliminates the climb of Mount Langley and the cross-country travel to Soldier Lakes. From New Army Pass follow the trail down the northwest side as it drops steeply to the Siberian Pass Trail. Turn right (north) on the Siberian Pass Trail and travel toward Rock Creek and lower Soldier Lake. In 0.7 mile, pass a long narrow meadow located south of the lake along the lake's outlet stream. Continue past

the meadow and cross the stream flowing from lower Soldier Lake. Turn right and hike around the left (west) side of the lake. Up ahead you will see a distinctive notch in the granite cliffs in which the lake's inlet stream flows. Hike to the upper end of the lake and ascend the lake's inlet stream passing through this gap. Follow the stream to a small but beautiful tarn (11,280 feet) at the western base of The Major General. Rejoin Route 10 at the tarn and traverse into the Rock Creek basin. Follow use trails alongside Rock Creek to Sky-Blue Lake. Overall, this will add 1.5 miles but reduce the amount of elevation gain by 600 feet.

Variation V10.1b

An alternative to the gap/tarn route above lower Soldier Lake is to hike down the main trail below lower Soldier Lake to lower Rock Creek Lake. About 200 yards before the trail crosses Rock Creek and at the upper end of the meadow above Rock Creek Lake, turn right onto an unsigned use trail. Follow this trail up Rock Creek to Sky-Blue Lake.

Peak Scramble PS10.1 (Mount Langley, 14,027)

To climb Langley, drop your pack at the red sandy saddle (see Day 2 above) and climb decomposed granite slopes to the summit (Class 2). Numerous use trails cross the south slopes of the mountain. The most difficult part of the climb is the frustration of stepping up and then sliding back in the loose sand. The climbing is not technically difficult, but you may feel the altitude as you ascend the peak's upper slopes. From the summit you will have wonderful views of Cirque Peak and Mount Olancha to the south, and of course Mount Muir and Mount Whitney to the north, along with hundreds of other peaks in all directions.

ROUTE 11: COTTONWOOD PASS TRAIL
(CHAPTER 7: MAPS, ROUTES 10–11)

Start	Horseshoe Meadow, 9920 feet
End	Whitney Portal, 8365 feet
Rating	Trail hiking (C-1)
Distance	42.4 miles
Elevation gain/loss	8323/-9878 feet
Trip duration	5–7 days
Maps	Tom Harrison Maps—Mount Whitney High Country
Access road/town	Whitney Portal Road to Horseshoe Meadow Road/Lone Pine
Car shuttle	Yes

TRAIL PROFILE

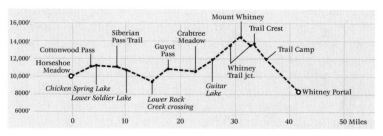

IN A NUTSHELL

This popular trail is perhaps the easiest of the routes not originating at Whitney Portal. The route (along with the New Army Pass trailhead) starts at nearly 10,000 feet, the highest starting point of any of the trips in this guidebook, and gains about 8200 feet over 31.4 miles to reach the summit of Whitney.

This footpath is a good choice for an early season ascent. Because of its southerly exposure and sun-drenched terrain, it is the earliest of the trails to open in the spring. It becomes nearly free of snow by mid-June, so it is a good trail to take in June or July.

The route begins by ascending Cottonwood Pass (a gradual climb of 1200 feet) where it picks up the Pacific Crest Trail (PCT) traversing the southwest slopes of Cirque Peak to Siberian Pass Trail. The route then turns north to lower Soldier Lake and then west descending alongside Rock Creek before starting a 1370-foot climb to Guyot Pass. From the pass the trail advances past Crabtree Meadow and the Crabtree Meadow Ranger Station, where it joins the JMT to the summit.

This route passes through magnificent stands of ancient foxtail pine near Chicken Spring Lake and many vibrant meadows along the way to Crabtree Meadow and Guitar Lake. Wildflowers are plentiful in the luxuriant meadows. The grasslands along Rock Creek and Whitney Creek, and in Crabtree Meadow seem to be favorites for herds of mule deer.

The first two days are relatively easy. This should help you acclimatize to the high elevation. Overall, I have selected a fairly leisurely itinerary (an average of 7 miles per day) so that you can include a side trip from lower Soldier Lake to Sky-Blue Lake. If you forego Sky-Blue Lake, the route could be completed in five days instead of six. Refer to Variation V10.1 for a description of the hike to Sky-Blue Lake, one of the highlights of this route.

HOW TO GET THERE

From the signal light on US 395 in Lone Pine, turn west and drive 3.5 miles up the Whitney Portal Road. Turn south onto Horseshoe Meadow Road and continue 20.5 miles to Horseshoe Meadow and the Cottonwood Pass trailhead (not to be confused with the Cottonwood Lakes and New Army Pass trailhead, Route 10, a short distance away). The paved road usually is open from May to late October.

TRAILHEAD FACILITIES

There are twelve walk-in campground sites, toilets, and piped water near the trailhead.

BEAR-PROOF WILDERNESS FOOD STORAGE BOX LOCATIONS

- Lower Soldier Lake: A long narrow meadow is situated south of the lake along the lake's outlet stream. One box is on the east side of this meadow about 600 feet south of the lake.
- Rock Creek Lake: One box is alongside lower Rock Creek Trail at the lower end of Rock Creek Lake. The lake is about 1 mile southwest of lower Soldier Lake.
- Lower Rock Creek Crossing: One box is about 5 feet southwest of the trail on the south side of the crossing.
- Lower Crabtree Meadow: A box is about 75 yards south of the Whitney Creek crossing on the west side of the PCT.
- Crabtree Meadow: One box is about 0.1 mile south of the Crabtree Patrol Cabin southeast of the creek crossing.

TRAIL PROFILE TABLE

Milepost	Distance (miles)	Cumulative (miles)	Elevation (feet)	Gain/Loss (feet)
Day 1				
Horseshoe Meadow	0.0	0.0	9,920	0/0
Cottonwood Pass	3.8	3.8	11,120	1,200/0
Chicken Spring Lake	0.7	4.5	11,242	122/0
Day 2				
Siberian Pass Trail	4.0	8.5	11,040	640/-842
Lower Soldier Lake	2.0	10.5	10,760	160/-440

continued on next page

Milepost	Distance (miles)	Cumulative (miles)	Elevation (feet)	Gain/Loss (feet)
Day 3				
Lower Rock Creek crossing	4.8	15.3	9,520	160/-1,400
Day 4				
Guyot Pass	2.8	18.1	10,890	1,370/0
Crabtree Meadow R.S. and JMT	5.3	23.4	10,640	640/-890
11,900-foot tarns	3.0	26.4	11,900	1,260/0
Day 5				
Mount Whitney Trail	3.0	29.4	13,480	1,580/0
Whitney Summit	2.0	31.4	14,491	1,011/0
Trail Camp	4.7	36.1	12,040	180/2,631
Day 6				
Whitney Portal	6.3	42.4	8,365	0/-3,675
Total	**42.4**	**42.4**	—	**8,323/-9,878**

ROUTE DESCRIPTION

Day 1—Horseshoe Meadow to Chicken Spring Lake, 4.5 miles, 1322/0 feet

For the first 2 miles the Cottonwood Pass Trail skirts Horseshoe Meadow, gaining only 200 feet in the process. At the upper end of the meadow, the trail begins its upward climb to Cottonwood Pass, gaining 1000 feet in less than 2 miles. The trail passes through some beautiful high Sierra Nevada meadow terrain with widely spaced lodgepole, limber, and foxtail pine.

At the four-way trail junction just beyond Cottonwood Pass, turn right onto the PCT toward Rock Creek. Chicken Spring Lake and its outlet creek are reached in a short distance. Ascend the outlet stream to the right side of the lake where there are numerous excellent spots to camp. Ancient foxtail pines with their distinctive red bark and thick trunks and limbs are plentiful in the cirque around the lake. These beautiful trees have withstood the test of time and the harsh environment over the centuries—heat, cold, blizzards, snow, ice, and windstorms. Some are tall and stately. Others are gnarled and deformed. Many of these giants are 2000 to 3000 years old and some of the dead trees on the ground are up to 5000 years old. Foxtail pine are a relative of the bristlecone pine, the oldest living thing on earth. The opportunities to photograph these remarkable trees abound and I have enjoyed countless hours at the lake taking pictures of them. Between Cottonwood Pass and lower Soldier Lake there is an abundance of these magnificent trees.

Many ancient foxtail pines occupy the cirque surrounding Chicken Spring Lake.

Day 2—Chicken Spring Lake to lower Soldier Lake, 6.0 miles, 800/-1282 feet

From Chicken Spring Lake there is an initial climb of 300 feet after which the path gently traverses in a northwest direction along the southwest slopes of Cirque Peak. The PCT is relatively flat with several ups and downs that slow your progress before reaching Sequoia National Park and the Siberian Pass Trail.

At the Siberian Pass Trail junction turn right (north) toward lower Soldier Lake. In about a mile, cross a stream and then the junction with the New Army Pass Trail. Arrive at a long, narrow meadow located south of lower Soldier Lake along the lake's outlet stream. Follow the use trail that skirts this meadow on the right. A bear-proof food box is located on the east side of this meadow about 600 feet south of the lake. Plan to camp in the general vicinity of the bear box.

Day 3—Lower Soldier Lake to Lower Rock Creek Crossing,
4.8 miles, 160/-1400 feet

This is a leisurely day that allows time for a side trip to beautiful Sky-Blue Lake or Iridescent Lake. These lakes are the true gems of the Sierra and a visit to their azure waters will be a trip highlight. Refer to Side Trip ST11.1 for a description of a day hike from lower Soldier Lake to Sky-Blue Lake.

Leave lower Soldier Lake and descend alongside Rock Creek. You will pass through numerous alpine meadows and oftentimes see mule deer browsing in these lush grasslands. Wildflowers are also abundant in June and July. Take your time and enjoy the scenery. There are good campsites and a bear box on the south side of the Rock Creek just before the creek crossing.

Because the next day will be strenuous, it may be beneficial to continue beyond Lower Rock Creek Crossing. If you choose to continue on, ford Rock Creek and begin the steady climb toward Guyot Pass. There is not much water along this trail segment, but you will find water at Guyot Creek, about 1.5 miles up the trail near 10,320 feet. There are good campsites among the widely spaced foxtail pine near this creek.

Day 4—Lower Rock Creek Crossing to 11,900-foot tarns,
11.1 miles, 3270/-890 feet

Cross Rock Creek and begin the ascent to Guyot Pass, a climb of 1370 feet over 2.8 miles. The hike out of the Rock Creek canyon is steep for the first 600 feet. After this initial climb, the rate of ascent slackens. Near the 10,320-foot level, the trail crosses Guyot Creek. Continue the ascent to Guyot Pass. At the pass, one can climb the ridge, over easy terrain, to the summit of Mount Guyot with its 360-degree views of the Sierra Nevada and Mount Whitney.

From Guyot Pass, the PCT skirts Guyot Flat and gradually descends to lower Crabtree Meadow. About 0.5 miles before Whitney Creek, as you round a bend in the trail at the top of a slight rise, Mount Whitney comes briefly into view for the first time. Descend to Crabtree Meadow and ford Whitney Creek. This is the perfect spot to stop and wash off the dust in the cooling stream.

At the trail junction in Crabtree Meadow, take the right fork heading to the Crabtree Meadow Ranger Station. It is about 1.3 miles. Before reaching the ranger station, turn left and cross Whitney Creek. Join the JMT and turn right toward Timberline and Guitar lakes. From this trail junction it is about 1 mile to Timberline Lake. The area around Timberline Lake is closed to camping. From the lake, the JMT climbs another 500 feet to

Guitar Lake. Camp at Guitar Lake or, if you are not too tired, continue to the tarns at 11,600 feet or at 11,900 feet. A higher camp will shorten your next day's long and arduous ascent of Whitney.

Day 5—11,900-foot tarns to Whitney summit to Trail Camp, 9.7 miles, 2771/-2631 feet

From the tarns, the JMT climbs steadily for 3.0 miles and 1580 feet up the steep west slopes of Whitney. The switchbacks seem endless but they finally end at the junction with the Whitney Trail. The views of Hitchcock Lakes, Guitar Lake, and the mountain panorama improve as you gain elevation. The trail itself is impressive as it climbs past imposing granite towers. This segment of trail and the ninety-seven switchbacks on the Whitney Trail on the other side of the crest are engineering marvels and tributes to the workers who built them.

There are only 2 more miles to the summit and a little more than 1000 feet of climbing. The most difficult work is over as the trail gradually reaches the highest point in the Lower 48. Stash your pack and head for the summit. If you are not suffering from the altitude, the next 2 miles will be enjoyable as the trail snakes through impressive rock towers and past windows in the Sierra Nevada crest that provide breathtaking views of Trail Camp, the Whitney Trail, and the Owens Valley far below. On the other hand, this may be the most strenuous portion of the trip because the altitude may have depleted your strength, energy, and desire to continue.

The trail along the west side of the crest provides an excellent opportunity to scramble up Mount Muir (PS1.3) positioned a couple hundred feet above the trail.

From the summit of Whitney you will be greeted with gratifying views of Mount Langley and Mount Muir to the south; the Kaweah Peaks and Sawtooth Peak to the west; Mount Russell, Tulainyo Lake (to the right of Russell and the highest large alpine lake in the Sierra Nevada), Mount Williamson, Milestone Mountain, Table Mountain, and Thunder Mountain to the north; and Trail Camp, Mount Whitney Trail switchbacks, Consultation Lake, and Owens Valley to the east. If the weather is pleasant, spend some time on top; take in the scenery and savor your accomplishment.

After an hour on the summit it is time to consider the hike out. Return to your pack and hike down to Trail Camp.

Day 6—Trail Camp to Whitney Portal, 6.3 miles, 0/-3675 feet

Hike out to the Whitney Portal. It is all downhill from here. See Route 8 for a description of the Mount Whitney Trail.

VARIATIONS, SIDE TRIPS, PEAK SCRAMBLES

Variation V11.1 (return to Horseshoe Meadow)

Instead of carrying your fully loaded pack to Trail Crest, leave it at your high camp (the 11,900-foot tarns, Guitar Lake, or Crabtree Meadow) and ascend Whitney's west slopes with a light daypack. After climbing Whitney, return to your high camp instead of descending via the Mount Whitney Trail. Retrieve your gear and over the next couple of days retrace your steps back to your starting point in Horseshoe Meadow. The advantage to this variation is that you can secure a wilderness permit more easily because a Whitney Trail exit permit (see Chapter 2) is not required. For this round-trip, plan on six to eight days and 62.8 miles.

Side Trip ST11.1 (Sky-Blue Lake)

Hike to the upper end of lower Soldier Lake and ascend the lake's inlet stream. Angle left through a distinctive gap in the granite. Follow the stream through this gap to the beautiful tarn (11,280 feet) located 0.5 mile northeast of lower Soldier Lake. Traverse into the Rock Creek basin and follow use trails alongside Rock Creek to Sky-Blue Lake. For more details see Route 10, Day 2.

6 WESTSIDE TRAILHEADS

*Walk away quietly in any direction and taste the freedom
of the mountaineer. Camp out among the grasses and
gentians of glacial meadows, in craggy garden nooks full of
nature's darlings. Climb the mountains and get their good
tidings, Nature's peace will flow into you as sunshine flows
into trees. The winds will blow their own freshness into you
and the storms their energy, while cares will drop off like
autumn leaves. As age comes on, one source of enjoyment
after another is closed, but nature's sources never fail.*
—John Muir, Our National Parks, 1901

THE FOOTPATHS ON THE WEST SIDE of the Sierra Nevada (Routes 12–15) originate in Sequoia and Kings Canyon National Parks. Sequoia National Park became the second of our national parks on September 25, 1890, after Yellowstone and just ahead of Yosemite, which was established six days later on October 1, 1890. Three weeks later Congress created General Grant National Park. These parks were established as wilderness sanctuaries to protect groves of giant sequoia trees from being methodically destroyed by loggers. Kings Canyon was established as a national park in 1940, absorbing Grant National Park. Together, Sequoia and Kings Canyon National Parks encompass much of California's High Sierra backcountry and contain thousands of acres of sequoia trees and some of the nation's wildest and most captivating alpine scenery.

There are untold miles of sweeping mountain vistas within Sequoia and Kings Canyon National Parks: rock upon rock, mountain upon mountain, snow-capped peak upon snow-capped peak as far as the eye can see. The parks are home to the highest peak in the Lower 48 (Mount Whitney), the largest living thing on earth (giant sequoia tree), and the deepest canyon in North America (Kings River Canyon).

Sequoia and Kings Canyon National Parks range from 2000 feet elevation on their western slopes all the way to the Sierra Nevada crest and the summit of Whitney rising to 14,491 feet on the park's eastern boundary. Mount Whitney is not visible from any road, only remote backcountry locations in the park.

The giant sequoia (*Sequoiadendron giganteum,* also called Sierra redwood or Big Trees) are the largest trees by weight and volume (but not the tallest) in the world and are the largest living organisms on earth. The world's seventy-five giant sequoia groves occupy moist, nonglaciated ridges on the

Sierra Nevada's west slope between 5000 and 7000 feet. Visually dominant by their massive size, sequoias grow in a mixed conifer forest of white fir, sugar pine, yellow pine, and incense cedar. Sixty million years ago these giant trees ranged more widely but shrank to their current range when the climate became drier. About 36,500 acres of sequoias remain and are under state and federal protection.

John Muir explored the Sequoia and Kings Canyon area before they were designated as national parks and named the Giant Forest, where four of the world's five largest trees stand. His writings and descriptions of the canyons, giant sequoia groves, and lofty summits were partially responsible for the area being designated a national park.

Kings Canyon reaches a depth of 8200 feet near the confluence of the middle and south forks of the Kings River. The depth of this canyon is without peer in North America. It is deeper than Hells Canyon in Idaho and the Grand Canyon in Arizona. At Roads End, the start of Routes 12 and 13, one can stand on the flat, glacial valley floor and peer up at canyon walls rising nearly a mile overhead. The Kern Canyon in Sequoia National Park (Routes 13 and 14) is 6000 feet deep, and several other prominent canyons, such as the Middle Fork of the Kaweah River Canyon, exceed 4000 feet.

About the magnificent canyons of the Kings River, John Muir penned an article in November 1891 for *The Century Illustrated Monthly Magazine* titled "The Cañon of the South Fork of Kings River: A Rival of the Yosemite," in which he wrote:

> *In the vast Sierra wilderness far to the southward of the famous Yosemite Valley, there is a yet grander valley of the same kind. It is situated on the south fork of Kings River, above the most extensive groves and forests of the giant sequoia, and beneath the shadows the highest mountains in the range, where the cañons are deepest and the snow-laden peaks are crowded most closely together. It is called the Big King's River Cañon, or King's River Yosemite. It appears that this new Yosemite is longer and deeper, and lies embedded in grander mountains, than the well-known Yosemite of the Merced. Their general characters, however, are wonderfully alike, and they bear the same relationship to the fountains of the ancient glaciers above them.*

To the east of the deep canyons and the majestic groves of giant sequoia are magnificent mountains, alpine meadows, glaciated cirques, and beautiful mountain lakes. This area is for exploring, hiking, fishing, mountain

Bailey Bridge spans the South Fork Kings River 2 miles from Roads End and the trailhead in Zumwalt Meadow.

climbing, ski mountaineering, and simply enjoying the superb scenery. All this and more are the destinations of the westside routes.

The four westside approaches to Mount Whitney (Routes 12–15) are long (53.9, 65, 73.5, and 72.2 miles, respectively). These trips require a five- to nine-day commitment and pass through breathtaking terrain for a rewarding and long-remembered wilderness experience. After summiting, descend the Mount Whitney Trail and exit at Whitney Portal on the eastside rather than retracing the long trail back to your starting point. This will save many miles of hiking and several days in the wilderness but necessitate a car shuttle (see Appendix 5).

Like the eastside routes, the westside trails also join the John Muir Trail (JMT) at various points before ascending to the summit of Whitney. The Bubbs Creek Trail (Route 12) reaches the JMT at Vidette Meadow, about 30 trail miles north of Whitney. The Avalanche Pass Trail (Route 13) and the High Sierra Trail (HST) (Route 14) join the JMT at Wallace Creek about 12 trail miles north of Whitney. The Farewell Gap Trail (Route 15) traverses to the south of Whitney and follows the JMT the last 8 miles.

Access to the westside trails is via three main roads from the towns of Fresno, Visalia, and Three Rivers. Fresno is located on Highway 99 near the geographic center of the state. It is about 220 miles north of Los Angeles and 170 miles south of Sacramento. Visalia is south of Fresno on Highway 198. Three Rivers is a small town about 40 miles east of Visalia on Highway 198. Highway 180 from Fresno, Highway 198 from Visalia, and the Mineral King Road from Three Rivers are the main roads to the westside trailheads. The following table summarizes the access roads to the various westside trailheads.

171

WESTSIDE ACCESS ROADS

Route Name	Trailhead, Elevation	Access Roads*	Nearest Town on US 395 From US 395 to Trailhead
12. Bubbs Creek Trail	Roads End, 5,035 ft	Highway 180	Squaw Valley/Fresno, Big Stump, 40 miles from park entrance
13. Avalanche Pass Trail	Roads End, 5,035 ft	Highway 180	Squaw Valley/Fresno, Big Stump, 40 miles from park entrance
14. High Sierra Trail	Crescent Meadow, 6,700 ft	Highway 198 to Crescent Meadow Road	Three Rivers/Visalia, Ash Mountain, 20 miles from park entrance
15. Farewell Gap Trail	Mineral King, 7,800 ft	Highway 198 to Mineral King	Three Rivers/Visalia, Mineral King, 25 miles from Highway 198

*All access roads are paved.

ROUTE 12: BUBBS CREEK TRAIL
(CHAPTER 7: MAPS, ROUTES 12-13)

Start............................Roads End, Kings Canyon National Park,
5035 feet
End...............................Whitney Portal, 8365 feet
Rating..........................Trail hiking (C-1)
Distance.......................53.9 miles
Elevation gain/loss......13,656/-10,326 feet
Trip duration...............5-8 days
Maps............................Tom Harrison Maps—Kings Canyon High
Country and Mount Whitney High Country
Access road/town........State Route 180 to Roads End/Fresno
Car shuttle...................Yes

TRAIL PROFILE

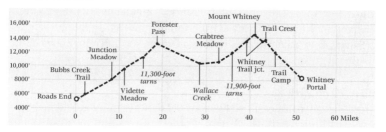

IN A NUTSHELL

This is the most direct route to Mount Whitney from any westside trailhead. At an elevation of 5035 feet, Roads End is the lowest starting point in this guidebook; consequently, you will ascend more than 13,000 feet over 43 miles to reach the summit.

The trail starts on the valley floor of Kings Canyon in beautiful Zumwalt Meadows. The meadows and the valley floor are surprisingly flat with the sheer granite walls of the spectacular South Fork Kings River Canyon towering more than 5000 feet overhead. Downstream, the Kings River Canyon deepens to more than 8000 feet, making it one of the deepest canyons in North America.

We are indeed fortunate today to be able to enjoy this magnificent canyon because it could have been dammed and inundated just like the Tuolumne River (Hetch Hetchy) canyon in Yosemite National Park. In the early 1900s water developers were considering damming the Kings River and flooding the canyon. As late as the 1950s, even though Kings Canyon was a national park, the thirsty city of Los Angeles harbored plans to build a 155-foot dam on the Kings River near Cedar Grove.

The sandy trail begins along the South Fork Kings River and then crosses the river to ascend Bubbs Creek to Junction Meadow. The trail continues up Bubbs Creek to Vidette Meadow, where it joins the JMT. From here follow Route 1 by ascending the beautiful glaciated valley to Forester Pass (the highest pass on the JMT). The trail crosses the Kings–Kern Divide at Forester Pass and the trail descends to the Shepherd Pass Trail junction and continues to Wallace Creek, Crabtree Meadow, Guitar Lake, and on to the summit.

There are two variations to this route—one that follows a trail the entire distance and another that requires expert cross-country skills and superior conditioning. Variation V12.1 ascends the South Fork Kings River and Woods Creek, passing through Paradise Valley before reaching the JMT at Woods Creek Crossing. Variation V12.2 is a rugged and difficult cross-country detour that explores seldom-visited regions of Sequoia and Kings Canyon National Parks; it is suitable only for the most energetic, fit, and experienced backcountry traveler.

Secure your wilderness permit in advance: the splendid Bubbs Creek Trailhead is popular.

HOW TO GET THERE

From Fresno, drive east on Highway 180 to Kings Canyon National Park at the Big Stump Entrance Station. Grant Grove Visitor Center is reached in a couple of miles. Cedar Grove and Roads End are 34 and 40 miles, respectively, from the park entrance. The road to Cedar Grove and Roads End is closed in the winter after the first major snowfall and usually is not opened again until the end of April. Call the National Park Service or Caltrans for road conditions (see Appendix 5).

TRAILHEAD FACILITIES

There are toilets and piped water near the trailhead at Roads End. At Cedar Grove (6 miles west) there is a visitor center, ranger station, market, restaurant, gift shop, books, and maps. Four campgrounds are nearby: Sentinel (83 sites), Sheep Creek (111 sites), Canyon View (23 sites), and Moraine (120 sites).

BEAR-PROOF WILDERNESS FOOD STORAGE BOX LOCATIONS

- Sphinx Creek: One box is above the Bubbs Creek Trail east of the crossing; a second box is across the creek on the Avalanche Pass Trail.

- Charlotte Creek: One box is below the Bubbs Creek Trail east of the crossing.
- Junction Meadow: One box is next to the Bubbs Creek Trail below Junction Meadow. Another box is on the west side of the East Lake Trail just south of Bubbs Creek.
- East Lake: One box is at the lower end and one is at the upper end of the lake.
- Vidette Meadow: Two boxes are in lower Vidette Meadow about 0.1 mile and 0.2 mile east of the Bubbs Creek Trail/JMT junction on the downhill side of the JMT. A third box is in upper Vidette Meadow about 1 mile southeast of the Bubbs Creek Trail/JMT junction above a series of switchbacks around 9800 feet.
- Center Basin Trail: One box is below the JMT approximately 150 yards south of the unmarked Center Basin trail junction (0.25 mile north of the Center Basin Creek crossing).
- Tyndall Creek Crossing: One box is west of the JMT about 350 feet north of the creek.
- Tyndall Creek Frog Ponds: One box is about 0.5 mile south of Tyndall Creek crossing on the east side of the trail.
- Wallace Creek Crossing: One box is west of the JMT about 100 feet south of the creek crossing.
- Crabtree Meadow: One box is about 100 yards southeast of the JMT and about 100 yards south of the Crabtree Patrol Cabin.

Bear Boxes for Variation V12.1
- Lower Paradise Valley: One box is above and another one below the trail.
- Middle Paradise Valley: One box is above the trail.
- Upper Paradise Valley: One box is below the South Fork crossing.

TRAIL PROFILE TABLE

Milepost	Distance (miles)	Cumulative (miles)	Elevation (feet)	Gain/Loss (feet)
Day 1				
Roads End	0.0	0.0	5,035	0/0
Bubbs Creek Trail	2.0	2.0	5,098	63/0
Junction Meadow	8.7	10.7	8,160	3,062/0

continued on next page

Milepost	Distance (miles)	Cumulative (miles)	Elevation (feet)	Gain/Loss (feet)
Day 2				
JMT/Vidette Meadow	2.9	13.6	9,600	1,440/0
11,300-foot tarns	4.4	18.0	11,300	1,700/0
Day 3				
Forester Pass	3.0	21.0	13,180	1,880/0
Shepherd Pass Trail	5.0	26.0	10,880	0/-2,300
Wallace Creek	4.7	30.7	10,400	680/-1,160
Day 4				
Crabtree Meadow R.S.	4.2	34.9	10,640	680/-440
11,900-foot tarns	3.0	37.9	11,900	1,380/-120
Day 5—Summit Day				
Mount Whitney Trail	3.0	40.9	13,480	1,580/0
Whitney Summit	2.0	42.9	14,491	1,011/0
Trail Camp	4.7	47.6	12,040	180/-2,631
Day 6				
Whitney Portal	6.3	53.9	8,365	0/-3,675
Totals	**53.9**	**53.9**	—	**13,656/-10,326**

ROUTE DESCRIPTION

Day 1—Roads End to Junction Meadow, 10.7 miles, 3125/0 feet

The sandy trail along the South Fork Kings River is nearly flat, gaining only 63 feet in 2 miles. Many large pine, cedar, and oak trees grow on the broad valley floor and have been scarred by fires over the years. As you hike along the river, the sheer granite walls of the canyon tower above. You will be constantly straining your neck to admire the towering rock faces. The South Fork is exceedingly powerful during the early season when the river is filled with snowmelt. The cascading falls are impressive sights, drawing many sightseers.

At the Bubbs Creek Trail junction, turn right and cross the steel Bailey Bridge that stretches across the river. (Variation V12.1 continues left along the South Fork.) Before flowing into the South Fork, Bubbs Creek fans out among the trees and across rock rubble deposited from previous floods. Cross these various channels on four wood plank and log bridges. After these crossings, the Bubbs Creek Trail climbs steeply, gaining about 1000 feet in a mile. After this initial climb, the trail continues its upstream ascent at a more leisurely rate. The views of Bubbs Creek and Sphinx Creek, as they cascade over the steep canyon walls, are spectacular. This is especially true when these creeks are overflowing with snowmelt and thundering down the canyons from the high mountains above.

After 1.9 miles pass the Avalanche Pass Trail (Route 13) junction. Just beyond this intersection and on the left are excellent campsites with a bear-proof food storage box and a pit toilet. Continue east on the Bubbs Creek Trail to Junction Meadow. Along this popular trail the National Park Service has placed bear-proof food storage boxes at Charlotte Creek, lower Junction Meadow, and East Creek in Junction Meadow.

Near each of these bear-proof boxes there are good spots to camp. At East Creek in Junction Meadow, a side trip to East Lake and Lake Reflection awaits (refer to Variation V12.2 for a description of a hike to these two lakes). The spectacular scenery is too good to pass up. An exceedingly strenuous but rewarding cross-country route over Thunder Pass also leaves the Bubbs Creek Trail at this same location (see Variation V12.2).

Day 2—Junction Meadow to 11,300-foot tarns, 7.3 miles, 3140/0 feet

Above Junction Meadow the Bubbs Creek Trail steepens as it climbs to Vidette Meadow. In the first mile the trail gains about 1000 feet and then levels off slightly for the rest of the way to the meadow. At Vidette Meadow the Bubbs Creek Trail joins the JMT. Head south on the JMT toward Forester Pass. Follow Route 1 the rest of the way to the summit of Whitney. There is an excellent opportunity for a side trip into Center Basin before reaching the 11,300-foot tarns. Refer to Route 1, Day 5, and Side Trip ST1.3 for details.

Along the John Muir Trail above Vidette Meadow looking toward Forester Pass (just out of view)

Day 3—11,300-foot tarns to Wallace Creek, 12.7 miles, 2560/-3460 feet
Refer to Route 1, Day 6, for a description of this trail segment. Refer to Peak Scramble PS5.1 for the route description to climb Mount Tyndall.

Day 4—Wallace Creek to 11,900-foot tarns, 7.2 miles, 2060/-560 feet
Refer to Route 1, Day 7, for a description of this trail segment.

Day 5—11,900-foot tarns to Whitney summit to Trail Camp, 9.7 miles, 2771/-2631 feet
Refer to Route 1, Day 8, for a description of this trail segment. If you plan to climb Mount Muir, refer to Peak Scramble PS1.3.

Day 6—Trail Camp to Whitney Portal, 6.3 miles, 0/-3675 feet
Refer to Route 8 for a description of the Mount Whitney Trail.

VARIATIONS, SIDE TRIPS, PEAK SCRAMBLES
Variation V12.1 (Woods Creek), trail hiking (C-1)
Start at Bubbs Creek/Woods Creek trailhead at Roads End and hike up the valley for 2 miles. At the Bubbs Creek Trail junction instead of turning right and crossing the river on the steel Bailey Bridge, stay left and continue up the South Fork Kings River toward Mist Falls and Paradise Valley. Reach Mist Falls in 1.8 miles and 1500 feet of climbing. The inspiring scenery towers more than 5000 feet overhead as you continue up one of the deeper canyons in the Sierra Nevada.

In another 2 miles and 900 feet of elevation gain you will reach lower Paradise Valley. Lower, middle, and upper Paradise Valley spans 3 miles spread out along the South Fork and below steep-sided canyon walls. As the name implies, this is a magnificent valley with large lush meadows and an abundance of colorful wildflowers. Mule deer are often seen in the mornings and evenings. Campsites, bear boxes, and pit toilets are located in each part of the valley.

Cross the South Fork at the upper end of Paradise Valley and hike alongside Woods Creek for 5.6 miles passing through Castle Domes Meadow and beneath Castle Domes on your way to Woods Creek crossing and the JMT. Join Route 1 for the rest of the way to Whitney (see Route 1, Days 4–9). Continue along the JMT past Rae Lakes, over Glen Pass, and down to Bubbs Creek at Vidette Meadow where you rejoin Route 12.

This variation is 14.6 miles longer and requires 2378 feet more climbing than Route 12, primarily because of the ascent of Glen Pass, but it provides an excellent opportunity to visit lovely Rae Lakes and the spectacular Sixty Lake Basin (Side Trip ST1.2)..

Variation V12.2 (Thunder Pass), 7.4 miles cross-country with one pass (C-2)

This route explores remote regions of Sequoia and Kings Canyon National Parks, crossing the Kings–Kern Divide at Thunder Pass. This may have been the pass Clarence King crossed on his attempt to climb Mount Whitney from a base camp near Mount Brewer in July 1864. This is a spectacular and rewarding detour for superbly fit and highly experienced cross-country travelers. I have been over much of this route on foot and on skis and it passes through some exceedingly wild yet picturesque topography.

From Junction Meadow, cross Bubbs Creek and follow the creekside trail to the upper end of East Lake (2.5 miles and 1285 feet). Continue up the canyon following the use trail to Lake Reflection (1.5 miles and 560 feet). There are excellent camping opportunities at both lakes. The trail is slightly overgrown in places and has not been maintained in years; nevertheless, it is not difficult to follow. Above East Lake, you will see the evidence and destruction caused by avalanches of yesteryear. Hundreds of trees are strewn across the valley having been snapped asunder or uprooted by the forces of numerous avalanches.

The Great Western Divide and the Kings–Kern Divide along with the formidable summits of Mount Jordan, Thunder Mountain, and Mount Brewer define the deep canyon in which Lake Reflection is nestled. The lake is in one of the most gorgeous settings of the High Sierra. Hike around the right side of the lake to its upper end and ascend alongside the main inlet stream in a southwesterly direction toward Longley Pass. At 10,400 feet follow the stream's right fork. (The left fork is the outlet stream for a tarn that you will be passing later on.) Continue the steep climb following the right fork to a cluster of tarns on a bench at 11,280 feet. These tarns are due east of Longley Pass and adjacent to a large unnamed lake at 11,480 feet.

From these tarns, angle southeast to a stream (the stream you bypassed at 10,400 feet) and a tarn at 11,600 feet. To partially avoid the large boulders in the area, head south for a distance before rejoining the stream at the next tarn (11,680 feet). Follow the stream, past a number of tarns, to the base of Thunder Mountain and Thunder Pass (0.2 mile east-southeast of Thunder Mountain). Climb up steep talus and snow to the pass. An ice ax may be needed.

Descend the south side of the pass, making your way to the large unnamed lake at 12,240 feet. There are a few large boulders, glaciated granite slabs, and small grassy benches near the lake's outlet. This magnificent spot, perched on the edge looking out over the basin below, would make an awesome campsite or rest stop to soak your tired and sore feet and legs.

From the lake's outlet, traverse left, away from the stream, crossing glaciated slabs and ledges. Work your way down to easier terrain. By making the sweep away from the creek, you will bypass the large talus blocks in the canyon near the lake at 11,880 feet. Rejoin the stream and hike through meadows, over granite slabs, and past an occasional conifer as you traverse gentle terrain to the large lake at 11,000 feet.

Hike around the left shore of the lake and turn south, following its bubbling outlet stream to a small lake just below 10,800 feet. Pick up a trail and follow it along the southeast shore of the lake. There are many camping opportunities along the streams or near the lakes in the area.

Hike south along the trail to a nearby pond (10,680 feet) and turn left (east) on the trail leading to the JMT. Follow this trial up, down, and around on its serpentine journey through meadows, over small rises, and across streams. Bypass the trail heading north to Lake South America and continue another 1.1 miles to the JMT. Turn right (south) and head toward the Shepherd Pass Trail junction and Tyndall Creek, where you rejoin Route 12.

Overall, this variation is the same distance as Route 12 but includes 7.4 miles of rugged cross-country travel plus 7.2 miles of trail hiking. It requires slightly less climbing because Thunder Pass is about 400 feet lower than Forester Pass, but the cross-country travel is much more demanding than trail hiking.

ROUTE 13: AVALANCHE PASS TRAIL
(CHAPTER 7: MAPS, ROUTES 12–13)

Start.............................Roads End, Kings Canyon National Park, 5035 feet
End..............................Whitney Portal, 8365 feet
Rating..........................Trail hiking (C-1)
Distance.......................65 miles
Elevation gain/loss......16,969/-13,639 feet
Trip duration...............5–8 days
Maps............................Tom Harrison Maps—Kings Canyon High Country and Mount Whitney High Country
Access road/town........State Route 180 to Roads End/Fresno
Car shuttle...................Yes

TRAIL PROFILE

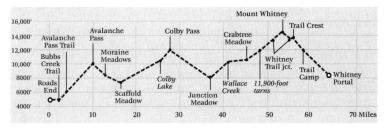

IN A NUTSHELL

Just like the Bubbs Creek Trail (Route 12), this lovely adventure starts on the valley floor of Kings Canyon in beautiful Zumwalt Meadows at Roads End. Because of the low-elevation trailhead, you will ascend nearly 17,000 feet over 54 miles to reach the summit of Whitney. The route stays on well-maintained trails the entire distance, but the hiking will be arduous with no "easy" days unless you plan a rest day to relax and enjoy the marvelous scenery.

Because of the lack of inspiring campsites between the trailhead and Colby Lake, the proposed itinerary for the first two days is strenuous—maybe too strenuous. You will hike about 13 miles each day with a 5000-foot climb over Avalanche Pass on the first day when your pack is the heaviest. This aggressive two-day start can be broken into thirds with a camp at Sphinx Creek, Scaffold Meadow, and then Colby Lake.

The route passes over Avalanche Pass (10,013 feet), ascends Cloud Canyon to Colby Pass (12,000 feet), and then plunges into the great Kern River Canyon at Junction Meadow (8040 feet). The canyon is nearly 5000 feet deep at this point. The trail quickly climbs out of the canyon following Wallace Creek to the JMT were it joins Route 1 to Whitney.

The ascent over Colby Pass and the descent down the Kern-Kaweah River to Junction Meadow has few rivals in terms of alpine grandeur. The remote trail passes through beautifully terraced terrain. These benches contain small meadows that are seemingly laid out like gardens carpeted with fresh spring grass and a multitude of colorful wildflowers. Small streams, flowing from the snowfields, dance over the granite as they cascade into the canyon. Glaciated granite walls ring the gorge. At the upper heights, formidable pinnacles reach for the sky. The panorama and the feeling of solitude are overpowering. It is as if an artist created a larger-than-life fantasy painting of majestic mountains, glacial valleys, and cascading waterfalls.

Variations V13.1 and V13.2 provide alternative starting points with each joining Route 13 at Scaffold Meadow and the Roaring River Ranger Station.

HOW TO GET THERE
From Fresno, drive east on Highway 180 to Kings Canyon National Park at the Big Stump Entrance Station. Arrive at Grant Grove Visitor Center in a couple of miles. Cedar Grove and Roads End are 34 and 40 miles, respectively, from the park entrance. The road to Cedar Grove is closed in the winter after the first major snowfall and usually is not opened again until the end of April. Call the National Park Service or Caltrans for road conditions (see Appendix 5).

TRAILHEAD FACILITIES
There are piped water and toilets near the trailhead at Roads End. At Cedar Grove (6 miles west of Roads End) there is a visitor center, ranger station, market, restaurant, gift shop, books, and maps. Four campgrounds are nearby: Sentinel (83 sites), Sheep Creek (111 sites), Canyon View (23 sites), and Moraine (120 sites).

BEAR-PROOF WILDERNESS FOOD STORAGE BOX LOCATIONS
- Sphinx Creek: One box is above the Bubbs Creek Trail east of the crossing. A second box is across the creek on the Avalanche Pass Trail.
- Roaring River Ranger Station: One box is on the west side of the bridge. A second box is 100 yards north of Lackey Cabin. A third box is 200 yards south of a cabin on the west side of the river.
- Junction Meadow (Kern River): One box is next to the High Sierra Trail near the southeast corner of Junction Meadow 230 yards north of the Wallace Creek stream crossing and 200 yards south of the junction with the Colby Pass Trail.
- Wallace Creek Crossing: One box is west of the JMT about 100 feet south of the creek crossing.
- Crabtree Meadow: One box is located about 100 yards southeast of the JMT and about 100 yards south of the Crabtree Patrol Cabin.

Bear Boxes for Variations V13.1 and V13.2
- Comanche Meadow: One box is next to a large camp toward the lower east end of the meadow.
- Sugarloaf Meadow: One box is at the camp area near the south end of the meadow near a hitching rail.

■ Ranger Lake: One box is on the eastside of the middle lake about 75 yards from the shore. Another box is at the north end of the lake about 80 yards from the shore.

TRAIL PROFILE TABLE

Milepost	Distance (miles)	Cumulative (miles)	Elevation (feet)	Gain/Loss (feet)
Day 1				
Roads End	0.0	0.0	5,035	0/0
Bubbs Creek Trail	2.0	2.0	5,098	63/0
Avalanche Pass Trail	1.9	3.9	6,240	1,142/0
Avalanche Pass	5.8	9.7	10,013	3,973/-200
Moraine Meadows	3.0	12.7	8,400	0/-1,613
Day 2				
Scaffold Meadow	3.4	16.1	7,400	0/-1,000
Colby Lake	9.5	25.6	10,584	3,184/0
Day 3				
Colby Pass	2.0	27.6	12,000	1,416/0
Junction Meadow	9.6	37.2	8,040	0/-3,960
Day 4				
Wallace Creek	4.6	41.8	10,400	2,360/0
Crabtree Meadow R.S.	4.2	46.0	10,640	680/-440
11,900-foot tarns	3.0	49.0	11,900	1,380/-120
Day 5—Summit Day				
Mount Whitney Trail	3.0	52.0	13,480	1,580/0
Whitney Summit	2.0	54.0	14,491	1,011/0
Trail Camp	4.7	58.7	12,040	180/-2,631
Day 6				
Whitney Portal	6.3	65.0	8,365	0/-3,675
Totals	**65.0**	**65.0**	—	**16,969/-13,639**

ROUTE DESCRIPTION

Day 1—Roads End to Moraine Meadow, 12.7 miles, 5178/-1813 feet

The sandy trail along the South Fork Kings River is nearly flat, gaining only 63 feet in 2 miles. Many large pine, cedar, and oak trees grow on the broad valley floor. The sheer granite walls of the canyon tower above. At the junction of the Bubbs Creek Trail, turn right, crossing the steel Bailey Bridge over the South Fork. Before flowing into the South Fork, Bubbs Creek fans out among the trees and rock rubble deposited from previous floods. After crossing these various water channels on four wood-planked log bridges, the Bubbs Creek Trail quickly ascends a series of switchbacks, gaining a 1000 feet in a mile. After this initial climb, the trail continues its upstream ascent but at a more leisurely rate.

In 1.9 miles of steady climbing, arrive at Avalanche Pass Trail junction. Just beyond this trail junction, on the left side of the Bubbs Creek Trail, there are excellent campsites, a bear box, and a pit toilet. Turn right and ascend the trail toward Avalanche Pass. The trail climbs steeply up closely spaced switchbacks that have been dynamited from the granite face. The trail crosses Sphinx Creek at a large meadow (8520 feet). There are campsites on the west side of the stream near the meadow.

The trail leaves the stream to make its final push to Avalanche Pass. Descend the south side of Avalanche Pass to Moraine Meadow and camp, or continue onto Scaffold Meadow at the Roaring River Ranger Station.

Day 2—Moraine Meadow to Colby Lake 12.9 miles, 3184/-1000 feet

From Moraine Meadow descend about 1000 feet to Scaffold Meadow. It is at the junction of several trails and streams, including the Roaring River, and the convergence of Cloud Canyon and Deadman Canyon. The Roaring River Ranger Station is ideally situated in this lovely setting of grasslands, meadows, and wildflowers. There are three bear boxes and good campsites near the meadow.

Leave the grasslands and head up Cloud Canyon toward Colby Lake and Colby Pass, a 4600-foot climb over 11.5 miles. Your goal for the day is Colby Lake, about 2 miles short of the pass. Hike past Cement Table Meadow and Big Wet Meadow. As the latter name implies, it is a long, swampy bog all too popular with mosquitoes. On a positive note, many colorful wildflowers thrive in the meadow.

Near the confluence (8800 feet) of the stream flowing from Cloud Canyon and the stream flowing from Colby Lake, the remains of an old cabin, Shorty's Cabin, are hidden from the trail. The cabin was a small structure tucked against a hill with rocks serving as one wall, the hillside as the back wall, and logs for the other two walls. Only the bare essentials of a small bed and table could fit inside.

On this stretch the trail crosses several streams. Depending on the amount of snowmelt, one or two of them may require wading.

Continue the climb to Colby Lake. There are campsites at the lower end and along the northeast shore. Beautiful wildflowers grow along the inlet stream.

Day 3—Colby Lake to Junction Meadow, 11.6 miles, 1416/-3960 feet

Above Colby Lake, the trail zigzags back and forth through boulder fields. Near the pass the trail becomes more rugged and steepens as it passes over and around steep granite cliffs.

Colby Pass (12,000 feet) is a small break in the Great Western Divide, a rugged wall of mountains stretching from Triple Divide Peak to Milestone Mountain. It is a continuous 9.6-mile descent from the pass to Junction Meadow following the Kern-Kaweah River. This seldom-used trail passes through gorgeous and remote wilderness terrain. The trail descends past a tarn and continues to the Kern-Kaweah River and a beautifully terraced valley at 10,300 feet. There are excellent spots to camp along this section of trail. The terraced benches contain small meadows that are seemingly laid out like manicured gardens carpeted with fresh spring grass and a multitude of colorful wildflowers. Streams flowing from the snowfields skip over the granite as they cascade into the canyon.

At Gallats Lake, glaciated granite walls ring the gorge. At the upper heights, formidable pinnacles reach for the sky much like the Aiguilles of Chamonix. The views are stunning and you cannot help but be struck with the feeling of just how far from civilization you are.

The trail continues along the river to Rockslide Lake where it drops steeply to Junction Meadow. Junction Meadow is the confluence of the Kern and Kern-Kaweah Rivers. The Kern River flows from the north out of the grand basin south of the Kings-Kern Divide. The Kern-Kaweah flows from the northwest out of the beautiful basin between Triple Divide Peak and Milestone Mountain. Do not confuse this Junction Meadow on the Kern River with the Junction Meadow along Bubbs Creek (Route 12), 12 miles to the north.

Although the Kern River divides into several smaller branches in the meadow, you may have to wade the river when crossing. Here the route joins the High Sierra Trail (Route 14).

Day 4—Junction Meadow to 11,900-foot tarns, 11.8 miles, 4420/-560 feet

At Junction Meadow (Kern River) turn north (left) following the Kern River for 1.2 miles climbing 800 feet. At 8800 feet turn right and leave the Kern River. Continue climbing and after about 1 mile the trail will come alongside Wallace Creek. The trail gains elevation, rapidly ascending from 8800 feet to 10,400 feet. Ascend along the stream's north shore to the JMT. Turn south (right) and follow the JMT and Route 1 to Crabtree Meadow, Guitar Lake, and the tarns at 11,900 feet. Refer to Route 1, Day 7, for a description of this trail segment.

Near the junction of the Mount Whitney Trail and the John Muir Trail

Day 5—11,900-foot tarns to Whitney summit to Trail Camp, 9.7 miles, 2771/-2631 feet

Refer to Route 1, Day 8, for a description of this trail segment. If you plan to climb Mount Muir, refer to Peak Scramble PS1.3.

Day 6—Trail Camp to Whitney Portal, 6.3 miles, 0/-3675 feet

Refer to Route 8 for a description of the Mount Whitney Trail.

VARIATIONS, SIDE TRIPS, PEAK SCRAMBLES
Variation V13.1 (Sugarloaf Trail), trail hiking (C-1)

This variation starts from Sunset Meadow (7840 feet) and heads east passing Rowell, Pond, Commanche, and Sugarloaf meadows before joining Route 13 at Scaffold Meadow and the Roaring River Ranger Station. It is 14.5 miles to Scaffold Meadow but there is only about 1600 feet of climbing.

From Fresno, drive east on Highway 180, and enter Kings Canyon National Park at the Big Stump Station. Proceed 1.6 miles and turn right toward Sequoia National Park. In 7 miles turn left to Big Meadow.

Continue past Big Meadow to Horse Coral and turn right on Sunset Meadow Road. Follow Sunset Meadow Road to the Sugarloaf trailhead.

Variation V13.2 (Silliman Pass), trail hiking (C-1)

This variation starts from Lodgepole (6800 feet) in Sequoia National Park. From Lodgepole, head north then east to Silliman Pass and descend to Ranger Lake. Pass Commanche and Sugarloaf meadows before joining Route 13 at Scaffold Meadow. It is 24.8 miles and about 4300 feet of elevation gain to reach Scaffold Meadow. This route variation is a bit longer than Variation V13.1 and Route 13 but this is offset by pleasant scenery at Silliman Pass and Ranger Lake.

Drive to Lodgepole in Sequoia National Park either via Highway 180 or Highway 198 and turn into the large Lodgepole Campground and proceed to the trailhead.

ROUTE 14: HIGH SIERRA TRAIL
(CHAPTER 7: MAPS, ROUTES 14–15)

Start...............................Crescent Meadow, Sequoia National Park,
6700 feet

End...............................Whitney Portal, 8365 feet

Rating..........................Trail hiking (C-1)

Distance.......................73.5 miles

Elevation gain/loss......15,531/-13,866 feet

Trip duration...............6–8 days

Maps............................Tom Harrison Maps—Mount Whitney High
Country Map

Access road/town........Highway 198 to Crescent Meadow Road in
Sequoia National Park/Three Rivers and
Visalia

Car shuttle...................Yes

TRAIL PROFILE

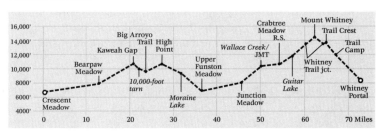

IN A NUTSHELL

The High Sierra Trail (HST) is one of the most breathtaking and scenic trails in California. The stunning scenery rivals that of any found in Yosemite and the Sierra Nevada. The trail begins at Crescent Meadow among the giant sequoia trees. It traverses high above the Middle Fork Kaweah River as it snakes its way up the rugged canyon to the High Sierra camp at Bearpaw Meadow, past countless glaciated domes, under the sheer face of Angel Wings, through the Valhalla, past beautiful Hamilton Lakes, and up to Precipice Lake. This extraordinary body of water, snow, and ebony black cliffs is the location of a famous Ansel Adams photograph.

Beyond Precipice Lake, you will cross the Great Western Divide at Kaweah Gap, pass Nine Lakes Basin, cross the Chagoopa Plateau, and drop into the Kern Canyon at Upper Funston Meadow. The trail then turns north up the Kern River, past the Kern Hot Springs to Junction Meadow (Kern River) to Wallace Creek, where the path joins the JMT. The remainder of the route follows the JMT and Route 1 to Whitney.

The trail is an engineering and construction marvel. In spots, the path has been blasted from solid granite rock and clings to the precipitous canyon walls. At other places the mountain is so steep and rugged that it overhangs the trail, and at another spot the trail passes through a short tunnel that has been blasted from the canyon wall.

HOW TO GET THERE

From Fresno, drive south on Highway 99 for 36 miles and turn east on Highway 198 to Visalia. Drive to the community of Three Rivers and continue into Sequoia National Park. From the park entrance, drive 17 miles over a narrow winding road to the Giant Forest and Museum. Turn right to Moro Rock and Crescent Meadow. Follow this secondary road as if forks to Crescent Meadow.

TRAILHEAD FACILITIES

The Lodgepole Visitor Center and Ranger Station are several miles beyond the turnoff to Crescent Meadow trailhead. Many activities and services are nearby including the Giant Forest Museum, a nature center, Crystal Cave, horseback riding, food, shops, market, showers, and laundry. There are also picnic areas and the Lodgepole (204 sites) and Dorst (201 sites) campgrounds.

BEAR-PROOF WILDERNESS FOOD STORAGE BOX LOCATIONS

- Mehrten Creek Crossing: A box is about 40 feet above the HST on the west side of the creek.

- Nine Mile Creek Crossing: One box is near the HST on the west side of the creek.
- Buck Creek Crossing: A box is on the west side of the creek.
- Bearpaw Meadow: Four boxes are in the main camp area.
- Upper Hamilton Lake: One box is in the open rocky area on the west side of the lake; a second box is 200 yards west of the lake on the south side of the outlet stream.
- Big Arroyo Crossing and Patrol Cabin: A box is on the east side of Big Arroyo Creek about 100 feet southeast of the Kaweah Gap–Little Five Lakes–Big Arroyo Creek trail junction.
- Moraine Lake: A box is adjacent to the trail along the east shore of the lake.
- Upper Funston Meadow: One box is southeast of the hitching rail at the northeast corner of the meadow near the river; the second box is near a campsite 60 yards farther south.
- Kern Hot Springs: One box is between the trail and the river; a second box is 50 yards east of the trail in a stand of Jeffrey pine.
- Junction Meadow (Kern River): A box is next to the HST near the southeast corner of Junction Meadow, 230 yards north of the Wallace Creek stream crossing and 200 yards south of the junction with the Colby Pass Trail.
- Wallace Creek Crossing: A box is west of the JMT about 100 feet south of the creek crossing.
- Crabtree Meadow: A box is about 0.1 mile south of the Crabtree Patrol Cabin southeast of the creek near the creek crossing.

TRAIL PROFILE TABLE

Milepost	Distance (miles)	Cumulative (miles)	Elevation (feet)	Gain/Loss (feet)
Day 1				
Crescent Meadow	0.0	0.0	6,700	0/0
Bearpaw Meadow	12.4	12.4	7,840	2,100/-960
Day 2				
Kaweah Gap	8.1	20.5	10,660	3,420/-600
10,000-foot tarn	1.2	21.7	10,000	0/-660
Day 3				
Big Arroyo Trail	1.8	23.5	9,600	0/-400
Moraine Lake	8.1	31.6	9,300	1,160/-1,460

continued on next page

Milepost	Distance (miles)	Cumulative (miles)	Elevation (feet)	Gain/Loss (feet)
Day 4				
Upper Funston Meadow	4.8	36.4	6,740	160/-2,720
Junction Meadow	9.3	45.7	8,040	1,500/-200
Day 5				
Wallace Creek	4.6	50.3	10,400	2,360/0
Crabtree Meadow R.S.	4.2	54.5	10,640	680/-440
11,900-foot tarns	3.0	57.5	11,900	1,380/-120
Day 6				
Mount Whitney Trail	3.0	60.5	13,480	1,580/0
Whitney Summit	2.0	62.5	14,491	1,011/0
Trail Camp	4.7	67.2	12,040	180/-2,631
Day 7				
Whitney Portal	6.3	73.5	8,365	0/-3,675
Totals	**73.5**	**73.5**	—	**15,531/-13,866**

ROUTE DESCRIPTION

Day 1—Crescent Meadow to Bearpaw Meadow,
12.4 miles, 2100/-960 feet

The trail begins in Crescent Meadow among the giant sequoia trees. It soon leaves the tranquil meadow protected by these majestic trees and begins a long traverse of the steep south-facing slopes high above the Middle Fork Kaweah River. Because of the southerly exposure the trail can be hot even in October. Consider an early morning start to avoid the heat.

Over the first 12 miles the canyon is covered with conifers offering limited vistas. However, these outlooks provide ample opportunities to view and enjoy the rugged canyon, sheer granite faces, and massive glaciated domes.

Although there are numerous undulations in the trail, the HST gradually gains elevation from 6700 feet at Crescent Meadow to 7840 feet at Bearpaw Meadow. The trail crosses Mehrten Creek at milepost 6.6 where there are three campsites, a fire pit, and a bear-proof food storage box above the trail. Other bear boxes are located on the west side of Nine Mile Creek and Buck Creek. Another bear box is located in a grove of trees near the trail before it crosses Buck Creek and climbs the final 400 feet to Bearpaw Meadow. Bearpaw High Sierra Camp and Ranger Station are located at Bearpaw Meadow. The designated camping area for backpackers is located before and below Bearpaw Meadow.

Opposite: Angel Wings from lovely Hamilton Lake along the High Sierra Trail

Day 2—Bearpaw Meadow to 10,000-foot tarn,
9.3 miles, 3420 feet/-1260 feet

Beyond Bearpaw Meadow the flora changes dramatically. Instead of dense timber offering limited views, the trees become smaller and more widely spaced, opening up grand vistas of the upper portions of the canyon with unobstructed views all the way to Kaweah Gap. At Lone Pine Creek the trail crosses a deep gorge on a spectacular 50-foot-long bridge. Beyond the bridge, the trail traverses beneath the impressive granite face of Angel Wings, passes through the Valhalla, ascends a series of switchbacks to Hamilton Lake, and passes through a tunnel below Precipice Lake. In places the narrow path is perched on overhanging ledges and, at other spots, cliffs and gigantic boulders overhang the trail.

In the first 1.7 miles, the trail loses elevation slightly, crosses the spectacular gorge of Lone Pine Creek, and passes the Elizabeth Pass Trail junction. In another 2.4 miles the trail passes upper Hamilton Lake. On its way to Hamilton Lake, the trail gains and then loses about 400 feet of elevation as it passes through the Valhalla and below the sheer granite face of the Angel Wings.

The scenery along this trail segment is as spectacular as any in the Sierra, and the camping environment at Hamilton Lake, situated in a magnificent amphitheater surrounded by the sheer granite walls of Eagle Scout Peak, Mount Stewart, and the Angel Wings, is second to none. One can fall asleep under the moonlit monolithic face of the Angel Wings and awaken in the morning to the red glow of sunrise on its sheer granite face.

From Hamilton Lake (8235 feet), climb 2000 feet over 4 miles to Precipice Lake (10,300 feet) and continue another 0.6 mile to Kaweah Gap (10,660 feet). There are limited camping opportunities at the lake made famous by a stunning photograph taken by Ansel Adams.

From Kaweah Gap you will have excellent views of Triple Divide Peak, Black Kaweah, the Kaweah Peaks, and Nine Lakes Basin. Black Kaweah is one of the great summits of the Sierra Nevada. Because of its remoteness and rugged slopes, this challenging peak is seldom climbed. When I climbed it in September 1990, the 1922 summit register was still in use and was only about one-quarter full. It appeared that fewer than 100 parties had reached this magnificent pinnacle. The summit register contained the names of many famous early climbers including Norman Clyde (twice) and Walter Starr, Jr. Evidently no pencil was available, so Starr signed his name in blood.

From Kaweah Gap, descend toward Nine Lakes Basin and turn south to the 10,000-foot tarn south of the Nine Lakes Basin. This lovely little lake, positioned at the base of Black Giant and Eagle Scout Peak, is an idyllic spot to camp (or continue to the Big Arroyo Trail junction ahead).

Day 3 10,000-foot tarn to Moraine Lake, 9.9 miles, 1160/-1860 feet

Continue down the HST following the Big Arroyo over gentle terrain to a three-way junction of the Big Arroyo Trail, the Little Five Lakes/Black Rock Pass Trail, and the HST. A bear-proof food storage box is located near this trail junction. Take the left fork toward the Chagoopa Plateau and Moraine Lake.

From this three-way junction, the HST gradually gains 1160 feet over the next 3.5 miles to 10,640 feet. The trail then starts a gradual descent. In 1.5 miles you will reach the trail junction to Moraine Lake. Leave the HST and follow the trail to beautiful Moraine Lake. This lovely spot, with a generous display of colorful wildflowers, is a bit of paradise among towering peaks, deep canyon gorges, and the lodgepole pines that define the border of the meadow. In the morning and evening you are likely to see deer grazing in the meadow.

Day 4—Moraine Lake to Junction Meadow (Kern River), 14.1 miles, 1660/-2920 feet

From Moraine Lake follow the trail around the edge of Sky Parlor Meadow and ford Funston Creek. You will soon rejoin the HST. Turn right and descend 3.8 miles into the canyon of the Kern River following the HST. Your path becomes steeper over the last 2 miles before arriving at Upper Funston Meadow. There are two bear-proof boxes and a pit toilet north of the meadow. An access trail leading to the campsites leaves the HST about 160 yards north of the meadow.

Seldom climbed, Black Kaweah is one of the great peaks of the Sierra.

You are now in as remote a location in the Sierra Nevada as you can possibly find. And, surprisingly, after more than 36 miles of hiking, you are no higher than your starting point in Crescent Meadow. At Upper Funston Meadow turn left and follow the trail as it heads north up the nearly flat canyon floor, following the Kern River toward Junction Meadow (Kern Meadow).

Pass Chagoopa Falls in the first mile and Kern Hot Springs in another 0.5 mile. The hot water springs are a favorite of many tired and sore-muscled backpackers. Two bear-proof food storage boxes are located near the hot springs and a pit toilet is located behind a clump of manzanita near the bear-proof box. In the next 7.5 miles the trail gains only 1200 feet to reach Junction Meadow.

Junction Meadow is at the confluence of the Kern and Kern-Kaweah Rivers. The Kern River flows from the north out of the great basin south of the Kings–Kern Divide. The Kern-Kaweah flows from the northwest out of the beautiful basin between Triple Divide Peak and Milestone Mountain.

To add a bit of confusion, there are two Junction Meadows in the Sierra Nevada, and they are not far apart. Routes 12 and 13 pass through Junction Meadow (Bubbs Creek) located about 12 miles due north of Junction Meadow (Kern River). Junction Meadow (Kern River) is a relaxing place to camp before climbing out of the canyon along Wallace Creek to the JMT. There is a bear-proof box near the southeast corner of the meadow near Wallace Creek.

Day 5—Junction Meadow to 11,900-foot tarns, 11.8 miles, 4420/-560 feet

At Junction Meadow the trail forks. The left fork descends from Colby Pass (Route 13). Take the right fork and continue up the HST following the Kern River for 1.2 miles. The trail steepens, gaining 800 feet. At the next trail junction, choose the right fork. The HST leaves the Kern River and ascends along the north shore of Wallace Creek. Over the next 3.4 miles the trail ascends rapidly from 8800 feet to 10,400 feet. Upon reaching the JMT, turn south (right) and follow the JMT and Route 1 to Crabtree Meadow, Guitar Lake, and the tarns at 11,900 feet. Refer to Route 1, Day 7, for a description of this trail segment.

Day 6—11,900-foot tarns to Whitney summit to Trail Camp, 9.7 miles, 2771/-2631 feet

Refer to Route 1, Day 8, for a description of this trail segment. If you plan to climb Mount Muir, refer to Peak Scramble PS1.3.

Day 7—Trail Camp to Whitney Portal, 6.3 miles, 0/-3675 feet
Refer to Route 8 for a description of the Mount Whitney Trail.

VARIATIONS, SIDE TRIPS, PEAK SCRAMBLES

Variation V14.1 (Whitney Creek cutoff), 3 miles cross-country (C-2)

About 7 miles north of Upper Funston Meadow, Whitney Creek flows into the Kern Canyon from the east. This cutoff leaves the HST at 9820 feet and heads cross-country up Whitney Creek for 3 miles to join Route 11 at Crabtree Meadow (10,360 feet). The crux of the shortcut is a 0.6-mile segment between the 8400- and 9200-foot level along Whitney Creek. This cutoff reduces the overall distance by 6.8 miles but includes 3 miles of steep cross-country travel without benefit of a trail. When you reach the Pacific Coast Trail at Crabtree Meadow, hike 1.3 miles to the Crabtree Meadow Ranger Station (10,640 feet). Continue to Guitar Lake and the 11,900-foot tarns to camp. Refer to Route 11, Days 4 and 5, for a description of the rest of the climb to Whitney.

ROUTE 15: FAREWELL GAP TRAIL
(CHAPTER 7: MAPS, ROUTES 14-15)

Start	Mineral King, Sequoia National Park, 7800 feet
End	Whitney Portal, 8365 feet
Rating	Trail hiking (C-1)
Distance	72.2 miles
Elevation gain/loss	16,268/-15,703 feet
Trip duration	6–9 days
Maps	USGS maps—Mineral King, Kern Peak, and Mount Whitney
Access road/town	Mineral King Road/Three Rivers
Car shuttle	yes

TRAIL PROFILE

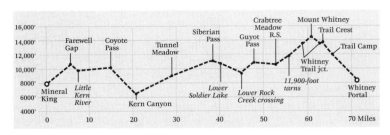

IN A NUTSHELL

In the 1870s, miners flooded into Mineral King valley on the wave of a silver rush. Several mines, including the Empire, White Chief, and Lady Franklin, were partially developed. However, by the end of the 1880s the silver rush and mining activity faded. One of the obvious results of the mining was the Mineral King Road, which was completed in August 1879. Someone has painstakingly counted the 698 curves in its 25-mile length. That's 28 curves per mile!

In the 1960s and 1970s, the Walt Disney Corporation attempted to construct a large alpine ski resort in the area. A long and complicated legal battle ensued. Finally on November 10, 1978, Congress transferred the management of the area from the Forest Service to the Sequoia National Park, ending any possibility of development.

Mineral King is a beautiful and isolated part of Sequoia National Park. Numerous peaks and high passes ring the valley, providing countless hiking, camping, and fishing opportunities. Alpine lakes, meadows, streams, and waterfalls abound. In the summer wildlife is abundant: deer, mountain lion, coyote, pine martens, wolverine, black bear, marmot, gray fox, and bobcat.

With the good comes the bad. Pesky and annoying marmots have been known to damage cars by climbing into the engine compartment and eating hoses and wires. If parking for any length of time, consider placing chicken wire completely around your car to keep the uninvited critters out. Also, check with the park ranger for suggestions.

This is the most southerly route included in this guidebook and it loops to the south of Sequoia National Park. The Farewell Gap Trail starts in Sequoia National Park at Mineral King and heads south over Farewell Gap, where it leaves the park. At the pass, the trail turns southeast to descend the Little Kern River to Shotgun Creek and Pistol Creek, where it then regains the lost elevation by ascending Coyote Pass. The trail reenters Sequoia National Park and turns east, descending Coyote Creek to the Kern River and the Kern Canyon Ranger Station. The trail leaves the park again at Kern River and enters the Inyo National Forest and the Golden Trout Wilderness Area, passing unique geologic features: a natural bridge, Tower Rock, Tunnel Meadow, Volcano Falls, and lava flows. The path reenters Sequoia National Park at Siberian Pass, traverses into the Rock Creek drainage following the Pacific Crest Trail (PCT) to Crabtree Meadow, and finally joins the JMT to the summit of Mount Whitney.

The Golden Trout Wilderness Area and the distant Golden Trout Creek are the birthplace of the golden trout, the official state fish of California.

Golden trout are a relative of the rainbow trout. About 20,000 years ago, tectonic movement combined with glacial and volcanic activity to isolate the Kern Plateau and create a barrier for the golden trout. Isolated, and no longer able to migrate to the ocean, the fish was forced to adapt to its permanent high-elevation habitat.

The waters at the high elevations where the golden trout are found are cold, clear, and often shallow. The golden trout's vibrant appearance has adapted to this unique environment. It has a yellow-gold to olive-green tint on its sides and belly. The fish also developed two brilliant red stripes. The gold and red, when viewed from above the water, make the trout virtually invisible in the shallow creeks. The fish's coloring is a type of camouflage making it difficult for predators to see them.

Golden trout are small, only about five to seven inches long, although up to ten inches has been recorded. Because of long cold winters and scarce food in their native high-elevation habitat, they are the least reproductive of the trout family (source: *www.fishingsociety.org*).

HOW TO GET THERE
From Visalia on Highway 198, proceed to the town of Three Rivers. Continue through Three Rivers and about 2 miles before the entrance to Sequoia National Park, turn right onto Mineral King Road, a long, narrow, winding road to Silver City Resort and Mineral King Valley. Allow at least ninety minutes to drive the 25 miles to the trailhead. The road is paved except for segments approaching Mineral King. The trailhead is located about 1.5 miles east of the of the ranger station near the pack station on the east side of the East Fork Kaweah River.

TRAILHEAD FACILITIES
The Mineral King Ranger Station and two campgrounds (no trailers or RVs) are located in Mineral King Valley: Atwell Mill (twenty-one sites) and Cold Springs (forty sites). Silver City Resort (privately owned), located about 7 miles from the trailhead, includes a store, restaurant, and lodging.

BEAR-PROOF WILDERNESS FOOD STORAGE BOX LOCATIONS
- Lower Rock Creek Crossing: One box is about 5 feet southwest of the PCT on the south side of the crossing.
- Lower Crabtree Meadow: A box is about 75 yards south of the Whitney Creek Crossing on the west side of the PCT.
- Crabtree Meadow: One box is southeast of the creek about 0.1 mile south of the Crabtree Patrol Cabin near the creek crossing.

TRAIL PROFILE TABLE

Milepost	Distance (miles)	Cumulative (miles)	Elevation (feet)	Gain/Loss (feet)
Day 1				
Mineral King	0.0	0.0	7,800	0/0
Farewell Gap	5.7	5.7	10,587	2,787/0
Little Kern River	1.5	7.2	9,700	0/-887
Day 2				
Coyote Pass	7.5	14.7	10,080	1,900/-1,520
Kern Canyon	5.9	20.6	6,400	300/-3,980
Day 3				
Tunnel Meadow	8.4	29.0	8,880	2,640/-160
Day 4				
Siberian Pass	8.6	37.6	10,960	2,240/-160
Lower Soldier Lake	2.7	40.3	10,760	200/-400
Day 5				
Lower Rock Creek rossing	4.8	45.1	9,520	160/-1,400
Day 6				
Guyot Pass	2.8	47.9	10,890	1,370/0
Crabtree Meadow R.S. and JMT	5.3	53.2	10,640	640/-890
11,900-foot tarns	3.0	56.2	11,900	1,260/0
Day 7				
Mount Whitney Trail	3.0	59.2	13,480	1,580/0
Whitney Summit	2.0	61.2	14,491	1,011/0
Trail Camp	4.7	65.9	12,040	180/-2,631
Day 8				
Whitney Portal	6.3	72.2	8,365	0/-3,675
Total	**72.2**	**72.2**	—	**16,268/-15,703**

ROUTE DESCRIPTION

Day 1—Mineral King to Little Kern River, 7.2 miles, 2787/-887 feet

The Franklin Pass and Farewell Gap Trail heads south from near the end of the Mineral King Road. Over the first 2 miles the gentle trail follows the East Fork Kaweah River as it ascends Farewell Canyon. Wildlife and wildflowers are abundant in this lush valley. Florence Peak, Vandever Mountain, White Chief Mountain, and other impressive summits ring Farewell Canyon. After 2 miles the trail steepens and over the next mile ascends several switchbacks to the junction with the Franklin Pass Trail.

Continue south up switchbacks to Farewell Gap where the trail leaves Sequoia National Park.

From the pass you will have expansive views in all directions. On the south side, the trail descends to the Little Kern River and passes the trail leading to Bullfrog Lakes. Continue descending past this junction to the river to camp.

Day 2—Little Kern River to Kern Canyon, 13.4 miles, 2200/-5500 feet

Continue your descent alongside the river to about 8900 feet and a trail junction. Take the left fork, the Farewell–Coyote Pass Trail, which leaves the Little Kern River and traverses Shotgun Creek and Pistol Creek before ascending to Coyote Pass. The trail crests about 0.5 mile to the west of Coyote Pass, at 10,350 feet, where it gradually descends 270 feet to the pass. The path reenters Sequoia National Park at the pass.

From Coyote Pass, the trail descends Coyote Creek, sometimes alongside the stream and at other times some distance away, to the Kern Canyon Ranger Station along the Kern River. The descent is continuous except for a short climb near 7800 feet. It is a moderate descent but steepens markedly as the trail nears the Kern Canyon. As you approach the canyon, Tower Rock comes into view, rising 2000 feet above the canyon floor. The trail descends to a low point 1400 feet below your start at Mineral King. At Kern Canyon, it is only 6 trail miles north to join Route 14; however, this route continues eastward, leaving Sequoia National Park and entering Golden Trout Wilderness Area.

Day 3—Kern Canyon to Tunnel Meadow, 8.4 miles, 2640/-160 feet

It is a long, continuous climb out of Kern Canyon following Golden Trout Creek. A small consolation to the climb is that the route traverses terrain unique for the granite-laden Sierra Nevada. You will pass through an area of ancient volcanic activity, including Volcano Falls, Natural Bridge, Little Whitney Meadow, Malpais lava fields, extinct volcanoes, and Groundhog Meadow, before reaching Tunnel Guard Station and Tunnel Meadow along the South Fork Kern River. (The word *malpais* is French for "bad country," an appropriate name for an extremely rough and jumbled lava flow about 3 miles long.)

Day 4—Tunnel Meadow to lower Soldier Lake, 11.3 miles, 2440/-560 feet

You have climbed out of Kern Canyon but there is still more elevation to be attained. From Tunnel Meadow and the guard station, hike northward

The stone hut on the summit of Whitney was built in 1909 for the Smithsonian Institution.

alongside Golden Trout Creek to Big Whitney Meadow and continue to Siberian Pass. You will climb about 2200 feet to reach the pass. At Siberian Pass, cross to its north side and hike across the upper portion of the Siberian Outpost. At the junction with the PCT continue north toward lower Soldier Lake. Lower Soldier Lake is in a lovely setting and the first opportunity on this trek to camp near a lake. It is worth the slight detour from the PCT junction to reach the lake. Refer to Route 11, Day 2, for details about camping opportunities.

Day 5—Lower Soldier Lake to Lower Rock Creek crossing, 4.8 miles, 160/-1400 feet

This is a leisurely day that allows for some much-needed rest or a side trip to beautiful Sky-Blue Lake. The lake is one of the true gems of the Sierra and a side trip to its azure waters would be a trip highlight. For details, refer to Side Trip ST11.1 and Route 10, Day 2.

For the hike from Lower Soldier Lake to Lower Rock Creek Crossing and up to Guyot Creek to camp, refer to Route 11, Day 3.

Day 6—Lower Rock Creek Crossing to 11,900-foot tarns, 11.1 miles, 3270/-890 feet

Refer to Route 11, Day 4, for a description of this trail segment.

Day 7—11,900-foot tarns to Whitney summit to Trail Camp, 9.7 miles, 2771/-2631 feet

Refer to Route 11, Day 5, and Route 8 for descriptions of this trail segment.

Day 8—Trail Camp to Whitney Portal, 6.3 miles, 0/-3675 feet

Refer to Route 8 for a description of the Mount Whitney Trail.

7 MAPS

KEY TO MAP AND GRAPH SYMBOLS

Described Routes

❶	Route number
ST	Side trip
PS	Peak scramble
V	Variation
━ ━ ━ ・	John Muir & Pacific Crest Trails
- - - - - - - ・	Other trail
• • • • • • • • • • •	Cross-country route

Symbols

⌂	Ranger station, patrol cabin, or visitor center
○	Trailhead
▲	Campground
) (	Pass
▲	Peak
～	River or stream
～	Waterfall
☁	Lake
○	Town
✪	State capital
═5═	Interstate highway
(395)	U.S. highway
(198)	State highway
──	Local road
— · — ·	National Park boundary
— — ·	National Forest boundary
— · · —	State border

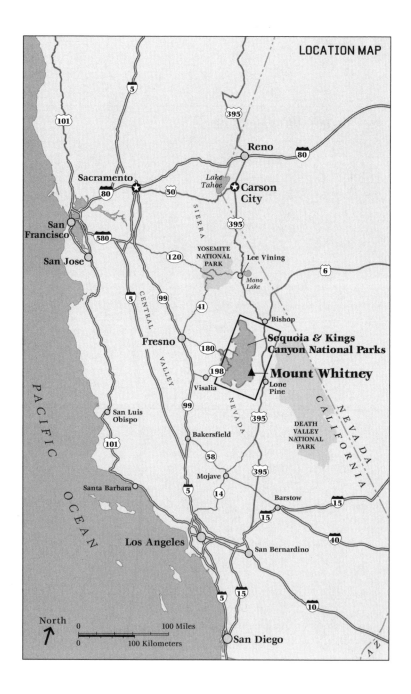

LOCATION MAP

101
5
395
Reno
80
Sacramento
Lake Tahoe
Carson City
80
50
395
San Francisco
580
SIERRA
YOSEMITE NATIONAL PARK
Lee Vining
San Jose
120
Mono Lake
5
CENTRAL
99
41
Fresno
Bishop
180
Sequoia & Kings Canyon National Parks
198
Mount Whitney
VALLEY
Visalia
Lone Pine
PACIFIC
San Luis Obispo
99
NEVADA
CALIFORNIA
Bakersfield
DEATH VALLEY NATIONAL PARK
58
Mojave
395
Santa Barbara
5
14
Barstow
15
OCEAN
15
40
Los Angeles
San Bernardino
5
15
10
North
0   100 Miles
0   100 Kilometers
San Diego
AZ

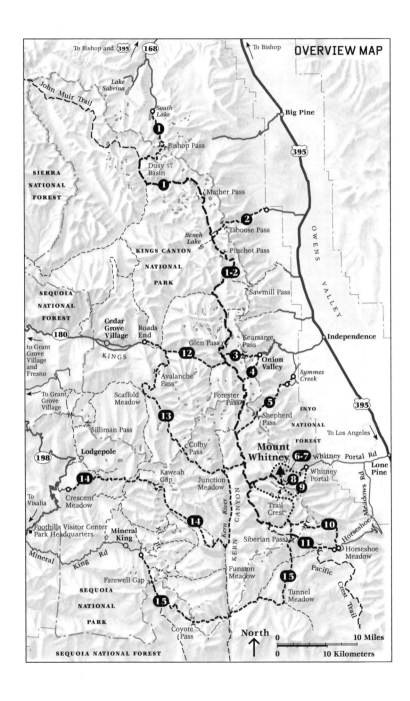

OVERVIEW MAP

To Bishop and (395) (168)

To Bishop

John Muir Trail

Lake Sabrina

South Lake

①

Bishop Pass

To Bishop

Big Pine

(395)

SIERRA NATIONAL FOREST

Dusy Basin

①

Mather Pass

②

Taboose Pass

Bench Lake

KINGS CANYON

Pinchot Pass

NATIONAL

1-2

PARK

Sawmill Pass

O W E N S   V A L L E Y

SEQUOIA NATIONAL FOREST

(180)

Cedar Grove Village

Roads End

Independence

to Grant Grove Village and Fresno

K I N G S

Glen Pass

12

Kearsarge Pass

③

④

Onion Valley

Symmes Creek

(395)

To Grant Grove Village

Scaffold Meadow

Avalanche Pass

Forester Pass

⑤

13

Shepherd Pass

INYO

Silliman Pass

Colby Pass

NATIONAL

To Los Angeles

Lodgepole

Kaweah Gap

FOREST

Mount Whitney

6-7

Whitney Portal Rd

(198)

14

Junction Meadow

Whitney Portal

⑧

⑨

Lone Pine

To Visalia

Crescent Meadow

Kern River

Trail Crest

KERN CANYON

⑩

Horseshoe Meadows Rd

Foothills Visitor Center Park Headquarters

Mineral King

14

Siberian Pass

⑪

Horseshoe Meadow

Mineral King Rd

Funston Meadow

Pacific

Farewell Gap

SEQUOIA

15

Tunnel Meadow

Crest Trail

NATIONAL

⑮

PARK

Coyote Pass

North

0   10 Miles

0   10 Kilometers

SEQUOIA NATIONAL FOREST

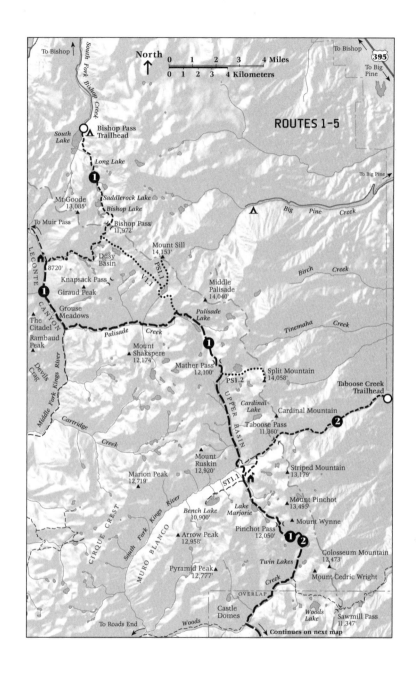

North ↑

0   1   2   3   4 Miles
0   1   2   3   4 Kilometers

ROUTES 1–5

To Bishop
To Big Pine
395
To Big Pine

South Fork Bishop Creek

Bishop Pass Trailhead
South Lake

Long Lake
1

Mt Goode 13,085'
Saddlerock Lake
Bishop Lake

To Muir Pass

Big   Pine   Creek

Bishop Pass 11,972'

Mount Sill 14,153'

Dusy Basin

8720'

LECONTE CANYON

Knapsack Pass
Giraud Peak
1

Middle Palisade 14,040'

Birch   Creek

PS1.1

V1.1

Grouse Meadows

The Citadel
Rambaud Peak

Palisade   Creek

Palisade Lake

Tinemaha   Creek

Devils Crag

Middle Fork Kings River

Mount Shakspere 12,174'

1

Mather Pass 12,100'

Split Mountain 14,058'
PS1.2

Taboose Creek Trailhead

Cartridge   Creek

Cardinal Lake
Cardinal Mountain
2

Taboose Pass 11,360'

UPPER   BASIN

Mount Ruskin 12,920'

Striped Mountain 13,179'

Marion Peak 12,719'

ST1.1

CIRQUE CREST

MURO BLANCO

South Fork Kings River

Bench Lake 10,900'
Lake Marjorie

Mount Pinchot 13,495'

Mount Wynne

Arrow Peak 12,958'

Pinchot Pass 12,050'
1 **2**

Colosseum Mountain 13,473'

Pyramid Peak 12,777'

Twin Lakes

Mount Cedric Wright

OVERLAP

Castle Domes

Woods Lake
Sawmill Pass 11,347'

To Roads End
Woods   Creek

➤ Continues on next map

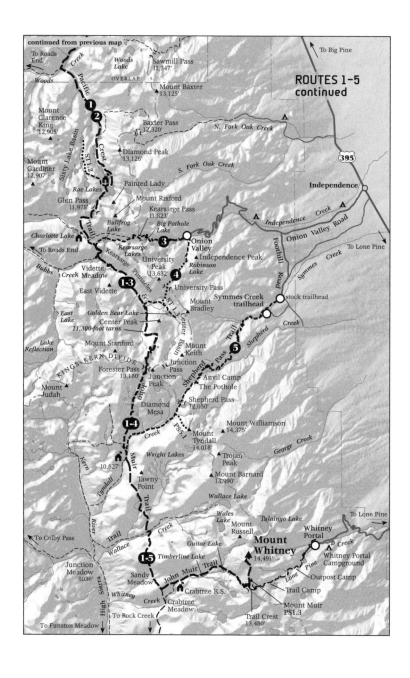

continued from previous map

To Roads End

Woods Creek

Woods Lake

Sawmill Pass 11,347'

To Big Pine

OVERLAP

Pacific

Crest

Mount Baxter 13,125'

ROUTES 1-5 continued

Mount Clarence King 12,905'

Baxter Pass 12,320'

N. Fork Oak Creek

Mount Gardiner 12,907'

Diamond Peak 13,126'

S. Fork Oak Creek

JST.2

Rae Lakes

Painted Lady

Mount Rixford

Kearsarge Pass 11,823'

Independence

395

Glen Pass 11,978'

Trail

Bullfrog Lake

Big Pothole Lake

Independence Creek

Charlotte Lake

Kearsarge Lakes

Onion Valley

To Roads End

To Lone Pine

Onion Valley Road

Kearsarge Pinnacles

University Peak 13,632'

Independence Peak

Bubbs Creek

Vidette Meadow

Robinson Lake

East Vidette

University Pass

Foothill

Symmes Creek trailhead

stock trailhead

East Lake

Golden Bear Lake

Center Peak

Mount Bradley

JST.3

Road

Symmes Creek

Center Basin

11,300-foot tarns

Lake Reflection

Mount Stanford

KINGS-KERN DIVIDE

Mount Keith

Creek

Forester Pass 13,180'

Junction Pass

Junction Peak

Shepherd Pass Trail

Mount Judah

Diamond Mesa

Shepherd Pass 12,050'

Anvil Camp

The Pothole

Mount Williamson 14,375'

PS1

Mount Tyndall 14,018'

George Creek

Kern

Muir

Wright Lakes

Trojan Peak

10,827'

Tawny Point

Mount Barnard 13,990'

Trail

Wallace Lake

Tyndall

River

Wales Lake

Wallace

Mount Russell

Tulainyo Lake

To Lone Pine

To Colby Pass

Creek

Guitar Lake

Whitney Portal

Creek

Junction Meadow 8036'

Timberline Lake

Mount Whitney 14,491'

Whitney Portal Campground

John Muir Trail

Sandy Meadow

Outpost Camp

Whitney

Creek

Crabtree R.S.

Lone Pine

Trail Camp

Crabtree Meadow

Mount Muir PS1.3

To Rock Creek

Trail Crest 13,480'

To Funston Meadow

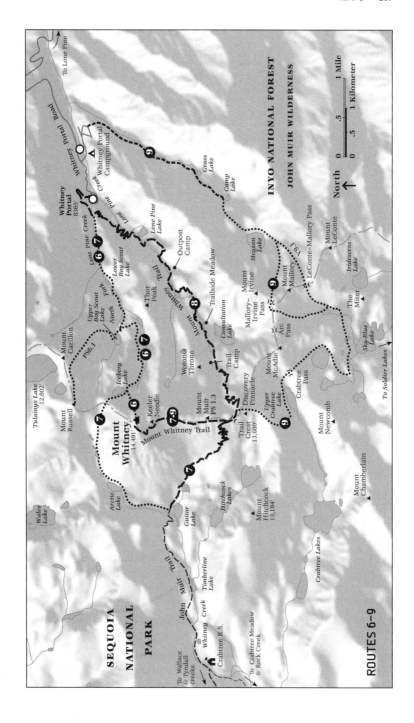

ROUTES 6-9

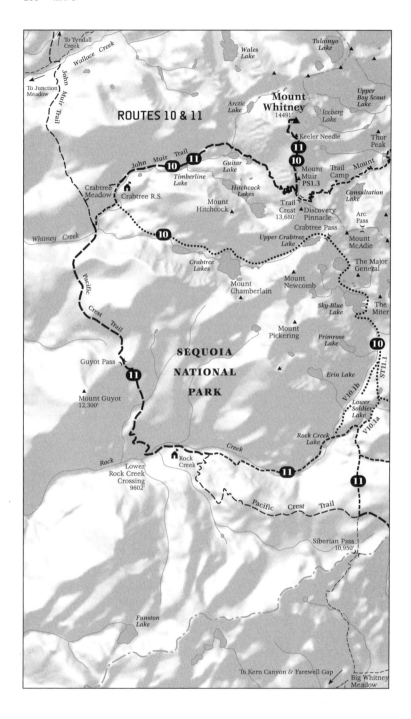

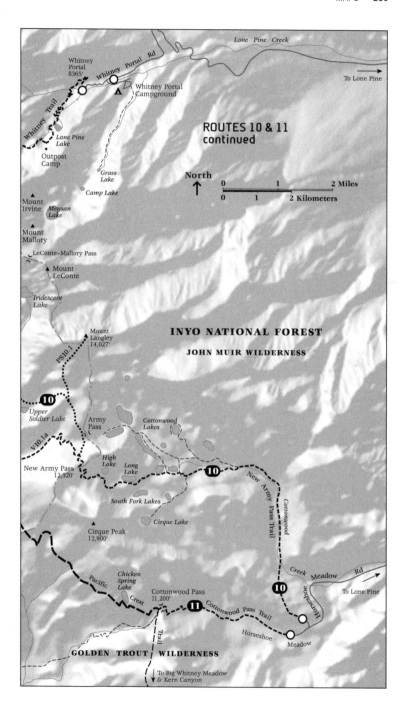

Lone Pine Creek

To Lone Pine

Whitney Portal 8365'

Whitney Portal Rd

Whitney Portal Campground

Whitney Trail

Lone Pine Lake

Outpost Camp

Grass Lake

Camp Lake

ROUTES 10 & 11 continued

North

0   1   2 Miles
0   1   2 Kilometers

Mount Irvine

Meysan Lake

Mount Mallory

LeConte-Mallory Pass

Mount LeConte

Iridescent Lake

Mount Langley 14,027'

INYO NATIONAL FOREST

JOHN MUIR WILDERNESS

PS10.1

Upper Soldier Lake

Army Pass

Cottonwood Lakes

V10.1a

New Army Pass 12,320'

High Lake

Long Lake

South Fork Lakes

New Army Pass Trail

Cottonwood

Cirque Lake

Cirque Peak 12,900'

Creek

Meadow Rd

To Lone Pine

Chicken Spring Lake

Pacific

Crest

Cottonwood Pass 11,200'

Cottonwood Pass Trail

Horseshoe

Horseshoe Meadow

Trail

GOLDEN TROUT | WILDERNESS

To Big Whitney Meadow & Kern Canyon

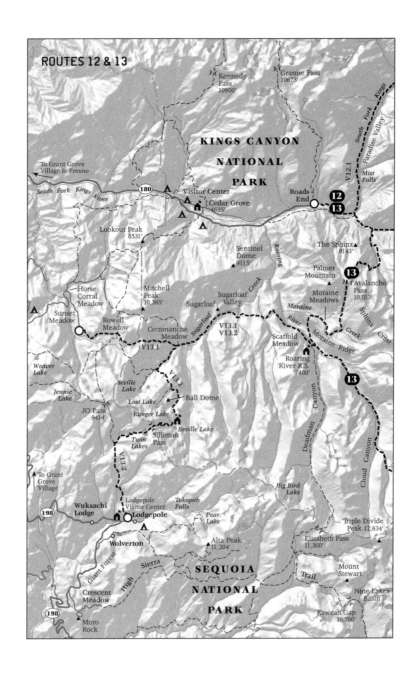

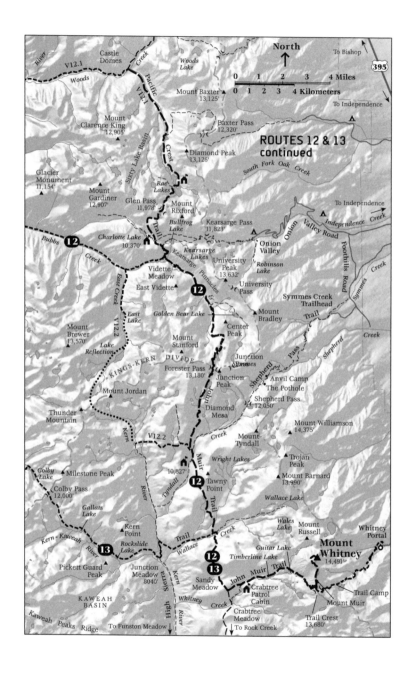

North

To Bishop
395
To Independence

Castle Domes
V12.1
Woods Creek
Woods Lake
Pacific
V12.1

0 1 2 3 4 Miles
0 1 2 3 4 Kilometers

Mount Baxter ▲
13,125'

Baxter Pass
12,320'

**ROUTES 12 & 13
continued**

South Fork Oak Creek

Mount Clarence King
12,905'

Diamond Peak
13,126'

Glacier Monument
11,154'

Crest

Mount Gardiner
12,907'

Rae Lakes

Glen Pass
11,978'

Sixty Lake Basin

Mount Rixford

To Independence

Independence Creek

Bullfrog Lake

Kearsarge Pass
11,823'

Bubbs
12

Charlotte Lake
10,370'

Kearsarge Lakes

Onion Valley

Onion Valley Road

Vidette Meadow
East Vidette
12

Kearsarge Pinnacles

University Peak
13,632'

Robinson Lake

Foothills Road

East Creek

University Pass

Symmes Creek Trailhead

Symmes Creek

East Lake

Golden Bear Lake

Center Peak

Mount Bradley

Trail

Mount Brewer
13,570'

Lake Reflection

V12.2

Mount Stanford

KINGS-KERN DIVIDE

Forester Pass
13,180'

Junction
Shannes

Shepherd Pass

Creek

Mount Jordan

Junction Peak

Anvil Camp
The Pothole

Shepherd Pass
12,050'

Thunder Mountain

Diamond Mesa

Kern

V12.2

Creek

Mount Tyndall

Mount Williamson
14,375'

Colby Lake

Milestone Peak

Wright Lakes

Trojan Peak

Colby Pass
12,000'

10,827'
12

Tawny Point

Mount Barnard
13,990'

Gallats Lake

River

Tyndall

Wallace Lake

Kern Point

Wales Lake

Mount Russell

Whitney Portal

Kern - Kaweah River

Rockslide Lake

13

Wallace Creek

Guitar Lake

Mount Whitney
14,491'

Pickett Guard Peak

Junction Meadow
8040'

Timberline Lake
12
13

Sandy Meadow

John Muir Trail

Mount Muir

Trail Camp

KAWEAH BASIN

Sierra High

Whitney Creek

Crabtree Patrol Cabin

Crabtree Meadow

Trail Crest
13,680'

Kaweah Peaks Ridge

To Funston Meadow

Kern River

To Rock Creek

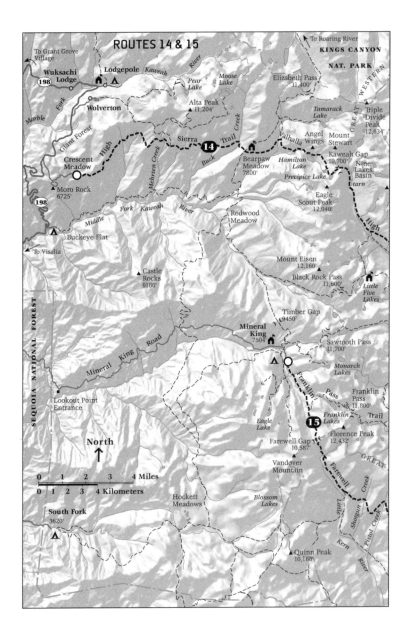

ROUTES 14 & 15

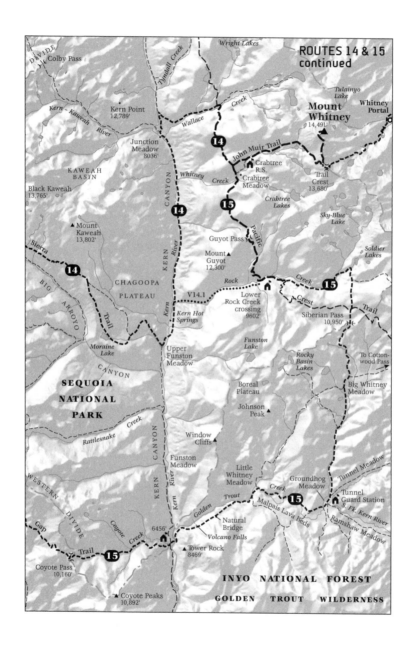

ROUTES 14 & 15
continued

Tarn along the John Muir Trail above Twin Lakes with Mount Clarence King in the background

APPENDIX 1: CALIFORNIA'S FOURTEENERS

This list was compiled from data contained in the photo-revised USGS 7.5-minute maps and R. J. Secor's *The High Sierra: Peaks, Passes and Trails.* The 7.5-minute maps adjust many elevations from the older 15-minute maps, based on more accurate mapping techniques.

Determining which peaks to include in a list of California fourteeners seems simple enough. However, it is not always readily apparent whether a given high point is a peak or merely a inconsequential subpeak on the ridge leading to the main summit. To minimize the amount of subjectivity, I used several general selection guidelines: it should have an elevation rise of at least 400 feet above the land bridge (col or pass) connecting it with its closest neighbor peak, and it should be at least 0.5 mile from its neighbor peak. These guidelines were not applied blindly but provided general parameters for selecting the 14,000-foot peaks.

The following list is arranged in descending order using the elevations

Two hikers at the lovely tarn below Iceberg Lake and the east face of Mount Whitney

of the 7.5-minute USGS maps. Peaks measured in meters have been converted to feet by multiplying by 3.2808 (39.3701 inches per meter divided by 12 inches). Example: 4416.9 meters (the height of Whitney) times 3.2808 equals 14,490.97 feet.

The California fourteeners listed here include the thirteen peaks in California exceeding 14,000 feet and eleven high points or subpeaks. These eleven subpeaks are noted in the list by an alphanumeric designation such as 1a or 2b.

The climbing routes of seven peaks and one subpeak highlighted by boldface type on the following list of California's fourteeners are described in this guidebook.

RANK	PEAK NAME	ELEVATION	SUBPEAK ELEVATION	REGION AND MOUNTAIN RANGE
1	**Mount Whitney**	**14,491**		**Mount Whitney, Sierra Nevada**
	1a. Keelers Needle	14,173 +	14,240 +	
	1b. Crooks Peak (Day Needle)			
	1c. Third Needle		14,107 +	
	1d. Aiguille Extra		14,042 +	
2	Mount Williamson	14,370 +		Mount Whitney, Sierra Nevada
	2a. West Horn		14,107 +	
	2b. East Horn		14,042 +	
3	White Mountain	14,246		White Mountain, White Mountains
4	North Palisade	14,242		Palisades, Sierra Nevada
	4a. Starlight Peak		14,180 +	
	4b. Polemonium		14,080 +	
5	Mount Shasta	14,162		Mount Shasta, Cascade
	5a. West Summit		14,040 +	
6	**Mount Sill**	**14,153**		**Palisades, Sierra Nevada**
7	**Mount Russell**	**14,088**		**Mount Whitney, Sierra Nevada**
	7a. East Summit		**14,042 +**	
8	**Split Mountain**	**14,042**		**Palisades, Sierra Nevada**
	8a. South Summit		14,000 +	
9	**Mount Langley**	**14,027**		**Mount Whitney, Sierra Nevada**
10	**Mount Tyndall**	**14,019**		**Mount Whitney, Sierra Nevada**
11	Middle Palisade	14,012		Palisades, Sierra Nevada
12	**Mount Muir**	**14,012**		**Mount Whitney, Sierra Nevada**
13	Thunderbolt Peak	14,003		Palisades, Sierra Nevada

APPENDIX 2:
SUMMARY OF ROUTES BY DIFFICULTY

CLASS 1 ROUTES (FROM THE SHORTEST TO THE LONGEST)

Route Number and Name	Rating/Class	Distance (miles)
8. Mount Whitney Trail	Trail hiking (C-1)	22.0
5. Shepherd Pass Trail*	Trail hiking (C-1)	41.8
11. Cottonwood Pass Trail	Trail hiking (C-1)	42.4
3. Kearsarge Pass Trail	Trail hiking (C-1)	50.6
12. Bubbs Creek Trail	Trail hiking (C-1)	53.9
V11.1. Return to Horseshoe Meadow	Trail hiking (C-1)	62.8
V13.1. Sugarloaf Trail	Trail hiking (C-1)	63.4
13. Avalanche Pass Trail	Trail hiking (C-1)	65.0
V12.1. Woods Creek	Trail hiking (C-1)	68.5
15. Farewell Gap Trail	Trail hiking (C-1)	72.2
14. High Sierra Trail	Trail hiking (C-1)	73.5
V13.2. Silliman Pass Trail	Trail hiking (C-1)	73.7
2. Taboose Pass Trail	Trail hiking (C-1)	75.4
1. Bishop Pass Trail	Trail hiking (C-1)	96.4

*Because of the low-elevation trailhead, the first 10 miles to Shepherd Pass are strenuous, I would rate this route more difficult than the Mount Whitney Trail, Cottonwood Pass Trail, Kearsarge Pass Trail, and Bubbs Creek Trail.

Elevation Gain (feet)	Trip Duration (days)	Car Shuttle	Nearest Town to Trailhead
6,486	1-3	No	Lone Pine
11,711	4-6	Yes	Independence
8,323	5-7	Yes	Lone Pine
11,651	4-7	Yes	Independence
13,656	5-8	Yes	Fresno
11,715	6-8	No	Lone Pine
13,391	5-8	Yes	Fresno
16,969	5-8	Yes	Fresno
16,034	6-8	Yes	Fresno
16,268	6-9	Yes	Three Rivers
15,531	6-8	Yes	Three Rivers
16,091	5-8	Yes	Fresno
20,279	5-8	Yes	Big Pine
20,911	7-10	Yes	Bishop

CLASS 2 AND CLASS 3 ROUTES (FROM THE SHORTEST TO THE LONGEST)

Route Number and Name	Rating/Class
6. Mountaineers Route**	10.8 miles x-c (C-2/2+/3)
7. Circumnavigation Route of Whitney	7.4 miles x-c w/1 pass (C-2)
V9.1. LeConte–Mallory Pass**	13.6 miles x-c w/6 passes (C-2/2+)
9. Meysan Lake Route**	14.6 miles x-c w/6 passes x-c (C-2/2+)
10. New Army Pass Route	7.5 miles x-c w/1 pass (C-2)
V10.1. Lower Solider Lake	5.7 miles x-c w/1 passes (C-2)
4. University Pass Route**	3.6 miles x-c w/1 pass (C-2)
V12.2. Thunder Pass Route**	7.4 miles x-c w/1 passes (C-2)
V14.1. Whitney Creek Cutoff	3.0 miles x-c/no passes (C-2)
V1.1. Palisades Basin**	7.9 miles x-c, w/3 passes (C-2/2+)

**These are the more strenuous and technically difficult routes described in the guidebook.

Distance (miles)	Elevation Gain (feet)	Trip Duration (days)	Car Shuttle	Nearest Town to Trailhead
12.4	6,126	1-3	No	Lone Pine
24.6	7,866	3-5	No	Lone Pine
27.8	11,866	4-6	No	Lone Pine
28.8	11,961	4-6	No	Lone Pine
36.9	9,051	4-7	Yes	Lone Pine
38.4	8,451	4-7	Yes	Lone Pine
43.0	11,631	4-6	Yes	Independence
53.9	13,256	5-8	Yes	Fresno
66.7	15,091	5-8	Yes	Three Rivers
92.2	19,938	7-10	Yes	Bishop

From the summit of Mount Russell looking at the north face of Mount Whitney. The Mountaineers Route is hidden behind the north ridge.

APPENDIX 3:
GOING-LIGHT EQUIPMENT CHECKLISTS

EQUIPMENT FOR MULTIDAY EXCURSIONS (SPRING–FALL)
Personal Items
✓Lightweight or medium-weight hiking boots
Backpack with removable pad
Sleeping bag rated to 20 degrees Fahrenheit
Three-quarter-length sleeping pad
✓Pair of lightweight gloves
✓Lightweight polypropylene long-sleeved zippered turtleneck
✓Lightweight polypropylene tee shirt
✓Lightweight fleece jacket
✓Lightweight waterproof nylon parka with hood
✓Lightweight polypropylene bottoms
✓Loose-fitting nylon shorts
✓Wind pants
✓Extra pair of wool socks
✓Hat with sun visor
✓Sunglasses
Plastic measuring cup (2 cup) and plastic fork/spoon
✓Water bottle (1 quart) and plastic water bag (2 quart)
Iodine tablets or chlorine dioxide drops
✓LED headlamp and extra batteries
Watch
Map and compass
✓Pocket knife
Personal toiletries: sunblock (SPF 50), lip balm, aloe vera gel, insect
    repellent, toilet paper, cleansing wipes, antibacterial waterless
    soap, toothbrush, toothpaste, bandana
Pack-out-your-poop kit

Group Equipment
Portable bear-resistant food storage containers
Single-burner backpack stove
6-quart cooking pot (cooking for two)
2 lighters
Fuel canisters
Free-standing (2- or 3-pole) tent

First-aid kit: ibuprofen, diamox, moleskin, antibiotic, codeine, decongestant, antacids, elastic bandage, 4-inch gauze pads, adhesive bandages, butterfly bandages, adhesive tape, antibiotic ointment, first-aid field manual

Optional Items
✓ Ski poles or walking sticks
Ice ax and crampons
✓ Camera and film
Altimeter
GPS receiver
Cellular phone
Walkie-talkie
Notebook and pen
Reading material
Light down jacket or down vest
✓ Cold-weather hat
Water filter or portable UV sterilizing light
Mosquito repellent
Tennis shoes or sandals for fording high-water streams

Food Items
See Appendix 4: Menu Planner.

EQUIPMENT FOR SINGLE-DAY HIKES
Personal Items
Trail hiking shoes or lightweight hiking boots
Day pack
Lightweight polypropylene long-sleeved zippered turtleneck
Lightweight polypropylene tee shirt
Lightweight fleece jacket
Lightweight waterproof nylon parka with hood
Lightweight polypropylene bottoms
Loose-fitting nylon shorts
Wind pants
Hat with sun visor
Sunglasses
Pair of lightweight gloves
Extra pair of wool socks
Water bottles (2 quarts)
Iodine tablets or chlorine dioxide drops

LED headlamp and extra batteries
Map and compass
Pocket knife
Watch
2 lighters
Personal toiletries: sunblock (SPF 50), lip balm, insect repellent,
   toilet paper, cleansing wipes, antibacterial waterless soap, bandana
Pack-out-your-poop kit

Group Equipment
First-aid kit: ibuprofen, diamox, moleskin, codeine, decongestant,
   antacids, elastic bandage, 4-inch gauze pads, adhesive bandages,
   butterfly bandages, adhesive tape, antibiotic ointment, first-aid
   field manual

Optional Items
Ski poles or walking sticks
Ice ax and crampons
Camera and film
Altimeter
GPS receiver
Walkie-talkie
Cellular phone
Water filter or portable UV sterilizing light
Mosquito repellent

Food Items
See Appendix 4 for lunch suggestions.

EQUIPMENT FOR A WINTER EXPEDITION
Personal Items
Skis or snowboard, climbing skins, and ski poles, or snowshoes and
   ski poles
Ski boots, snowboard boots, or boots for snowshoes
Ice ax and crampons
Avalanche transceiver/beacon
Snow shovel
Avalanche probes
Internal frame pack with removable pad
Sleeping bag rated to 0 degrees Fahrenheit
Three-quarter-length sleeping pad

Pair of lightweight gloves
Cold-weather gloves or mittens
Polypropylene long-sleeved zippered turtleneck
Polypropylene tee shirt
Powerstretch or microfleece vest
Softshell jacket with hood or fleece jacket with hood
Storm-proof nylon parka with hood
Polypropylene long-john bottoms
Softshell pants with built-in snow cuffs
Wind pants or Goretex pants with full-length zipper
Extra pair of wool socks
Hat with sun visor
Cold-weather hat
Sunglasses or glacier goggles
Plastic measuring cup (2 cup) and plastic fork/spoon
Water bottle (1 quart) and plastic water bag (2 quart)
Iodine tablets or chlorine dioxide drops
LED headlamp and extra batteries
Watch
Map and compass
Pocket knife
Personal toiletries: sunblock (SPF 50), lip balm, aloe vera gel, toilet
    paper, cleansing wipes, antibacterial waterless soap, toothbrush,
    toothpaste, bandana

Group Equipment
Hanging stove with 6-quart cooking pot
2 lighters
Fuel canisters
Four-season (3- or 4-pole) tent
First-aid kit: ibuprofen, diomax, moleskin, antibiotic, codeine, de-
    congestant, antacids, elastic bandage, 4-inch gauze pads, adhesive
    bandages, butterfly bandages, adhesive tape, antibiotic ointment,
    first-aid field manual

Optional Items
Gaiters
Camera and film
Altimeter
GPS receiver
Personal Locator Beacon

Walkie-talkie
Cellular phone
Notebook and pen
Reading material
Down jacket or vest
Water filter or portable sterilizing UV light
Snow saw
Heavy-duty rubber gloves

Food Items
See Appendix 4: Menu Planner.

APPENDIX 4: MENU PLANNER

The Menu Planner includes tasty meals that are inexpensive and easy-to-prepare. Most of the ingredients can be purchased at your local grocery store and are superior to costly freeze-dried backpacking meals. Remove as much packaging material as possible before leaving home. Adjust the portions based on the appetites of those in your party. Include a couple of extra packages of soup for emergency rations. If you cannot purchase freeze-dried vegetables or freeze-dried meat in your community, Just Tomatoes (*www.justtomatoes.com*) has a wonderful assortment of freeze-dried vegetables, and Mountain House (*www.mountainhouse.com*) has an assortment of freeze-dried meats.

As a general rule, plan 2 pounds of food per person per day. This can be shaved to 1.6 to 1.8 pounds per person per day with the weight-savings menus described below.

BREAKFAST (PER PERSON)

Weight	Food Item
1.5 ounces	instant oatmeal or cream of wheat
1.5 ounces	protein powder, powdered milk, raisins, freeze-dried fruit, sunflower seeds, pine nuts
2 ounces	nutritional bar that balances protein and carbohydrates
1 ounce	hot drink such as mocha, spiced cider, eggnog, coffee, or tea
6 ounces	breakfast subtotal

LUNCH (PER PERSON)

5 ounces	bagel with cheese or peanut butter
1.5 ounces	mixed nuts
1.5 ounces	candy bar or M&Ms
1.5 ounces	dried fruit, raisins
1.5 ounces*	sport drink (powder mix)
11 ounces	lunch subtotal

DINNER (SERVES TWO)

2.5 ounces	packaged instant soups; add freeze-dried vegetables
6 ounces	packaged dinners with pasta or rice (5–7 minutes cook time)
1.5 ounces**	freeze-dried chicken or beef, and olive oil
1.5 ounces*	sport drink (powder mix)
2 ounces	tea, coffee, mocha, spiced cider, or eggnog
3.5 ounces	two candy bars or cookies
17 ounces	dinner for two subtotal (8.5 ounces per person)

*To reduce the weight, mix a sugar-based sport drink with an artificially sweetened drink at 50/50% or 33/67%.

**Vacuum-sealed or canned chicken, tuna, or salmon will add 3–7 ounces to the total.

SNACKS (SELECT ONE)

2 ounces	potato chips packaged in a cardboard cylinder
2 ounces	beef/turkey jerky
2 ounces	string cheese and crackers
2 ounces	snack subtotal

27.5 ounces	grand total (per person, per day)

SIERRA GATORADE SLUSH

On a hot day, during or after a particularly hard climb, a Sierra Gatorade Slush is a tasty and refreshing treat. It is easy to make provided a snowbank is nearby. Drink slowly—too much of a good thing in one gulp can cause your esophagus, chest, lungs, and ribs to feel as if they are being instantaneously frozen. Make sure you bring plenty of powdered Gatorade mix. Below are the six easy steps to make this delightful and invigorating hot-weather drink.

1. Find a snowbank and clean off the dirty snow from the surface.
2. Fill a 1-liter water bottle with clean snow. Do not pack the snow into the water bottle. There must be adequate empty space in the water bottle for mixing of the snow, water, and Gatorade through shaking.
3. Add 1 cup of water.
4. Add enough powdered Gatorade mix (or your favorite powdered drink mix) to suit your taste.

5. Shake vigorously.
6. Drink slowly and enjoy. Shake again and drink.

DINNER FAVORITES

These three gourmet dishes are a special treat after a long day of hiking and are the creation of my sister, Judi Richins. The portions are ample for two hungry backpackers. To reduce the weight, use freeze-dried vegetables and meats.

1. Chicken/Top Ramen/Fresh Veggie Dinner

To 4.5 cups of cold water in a 2-quart saucepan, add:
- 1–2 small zucchini (thinly sliced)
- ½ carrot (thinly sliced)
- mushrooms (thinly sliced)

(Fresh vegetables will keep for a day or two, use 1-cup freeze-dried green beans or other freeze-dried veggies thereafter.)

Bring to a boil and add:
- 3 cubes "Herb Ox Garlic Chicken Bouillon"
- 3 teaspoons "very low sodium chicken bouillon granules"
- 2 shakes of garlic powder
- 1.5 packages Top Ramen noodles, crumbled (w/o flavor packets)
- 1 cup freeze-dried chicken (or 3–5 oz. canned/vacuum sealed packet of chicken

Simmer 3–4 minutes, stirring occasionally. Let it set a few minutes to fully hydrate the freeze-dried meats/veggies.

2. Tomato/Beef/Fettuccine Dinner

To 4 cups of cold water in a 2-quart saucepan, combine and stir:
- 1 package "Knorr Tomato with Basil Soup Mix"
- small portion of finely chopped fresh asparagus, broccoli tops, or green beans (or freeze-dried veggies)

When this boils, add:
- 6 ounces "al dente Garlic Parsley Fettuccine" (3-minute cooking time)
- 1 cup freeze-dried beef or chicken (or 3–5 oz. canned/vacuum packed chicken)

Simmer 3–5 minutes, stirring regularly. Let it set a few minutes to fully hydrate the freeze-dried meats/veggies.

3. Tuna/Rice/Corn Dinner

To 4 cups of cold water in a 2-quart saucepan, add ingredients from baggie #1:

- 1 cup uncooked instant rice
- 1 cup freeze-dried corn (or other vegetables)
- freeze-dried tomato pieces
- 2 bouillon cubes
- ½ teaspoon dried basil
- ¼ teaspoon dried oregano
- ½ teaspoon onion powder
- 4–6 ounces vacuum-packed tuna (or salmon/chicken)

Simmer for 5 minutes, stirring occasionally. Remove from heat and stir in ingredients from baggie #2:

- ½ cup instant potato buds
- ½ cup parmesan cheese

APPENDIX 5:
INFORMATION RESOURCES

MAPS, BOOKS, AND INFORMATION

Backcountry Resource Center—Information for hikers, climbers, backcountry skiers, snowshoers, and snowboarders wishing to explore the mountains of California and beyond.
  Website: *http://pweb.jps.net/~prichins/backcountry_resource_center.htm*
  Email: *prichins@jps.net*

Inyo National Forest
  Phone: 760-876-6200 and 873-2500
  Wilderness Permit Reservations: 760-873-2483
  Wilderness Information: 760-873-2485
  Website: *www.r5.fs.fed.us/inyo*

Sequoia and Kings Canyon National Parks
  Wilderness Office: 559-565-3766
  General information: 559-565-3341
  Website: *www.nps.gov/seki*

Sequoia Natural History Association
  Ash Mountain, Box 10
  Three Rivers, CA 93271
  Phone: 559-565-3759
  Website: *www.sequoiahistory.org*

Sierra Nevada Wilderness Education Project—devoted to providing the information needed to plan a backpacking trip into the Sierra Nevada wilderness. Sponsored by the Bureau of Land Management, U.S. Forest Service, and National Park Service.
  Website: *www.SierraNevadaWild.gov*

Tom Harrison Maps
  2 Falmouth Cove
  San Rafael, CA 94901
  Phone: 415-456-7940 or 800-265-9090
  Website: *www.tomharrisonmaps.com*

U.S. Geological Survey Maps
USGS Information Services
Box 25286, Federal Center
Denver, CO 80225
Phone: 800-HELP-MAP
Website: *www.nmd.usgs.gov*

Avalanche Center (CSAC)
Website: *www.avalanche-center.org/Bulletins/Calif/current/php*

Eastern Sierra Avalanche Center
Website: *www.esavalanche.org*

SPECIALITY STORES
Mammoth Mountaineering Supply—climbing and backpacking gear.
3189 Main Street
Mammoth Lakes, CA 93546
Phone: 760-934-4191
Website: *www.mammothgear.com*

Wilson's Eastside Sports—climbing and backpacking gear
232 North Main Street (US 395)
Bishop, CA 93514
Phone: 760-873-7520
Website: *www.eastsidesports.com*

Bear-proof Sacks
Website: *www.ursack.com*

Cold Cold World Packs
Lightweight packs
Phone: 603-383-9021
Website: *www.coldcoldworldpacks.com*

Vern Clevenger Gallery—superb outdoor photography
905 North Main Street
Bishop, CA 93514
Phone: 760-873-7803
Website: *www.VernClevenger.com*

Mountain Light Photography Gallery—exquisite photography by
Galen Rowell
106 South Main Street
Bishop, CA 93514
Phone: 760-873-7700
Website: *www.mountainlight.com*

SHUTTLE SERVICES
Sierra Express Transportation
  Phone: 760-937-8294

High Sierra Transportation
  Phone: 760-258-6060 or 760-872-1111

Inyo-Mono Transit
  Phone: 760-872-1901 or 800-922-1930

ROAD CONDITIONS
Caltrans (24-hour recorded message)
  Phone: 916-445-7623 (ROAD) or 800-427-7623 (ROAD)

MOUNT WHITNEY GUIDES
Some of the guides listed below lead backpacking trips while others focus
on more difficult routes such as the Mountaineers Route (Route 6—Class
2+/3) or technical rock-climbing routes such as the East Face and East
Buttress (Class 5.6 and 5.7). Currently, the Forest Service does not autho-
rize professionally guided trips on the Mount Whitney Trail (Route 8).

American Mountain Guides Association—The AMGA is a nonprofit
organization that seeks to represent the interests of American mountain
guides by providing support, education, and standards. They maintain a
complete list of AMGA-certified guides on their website, *www.amga.com.*

American Alpine Institute
  1515 12th Street
  Bellingham, WA 98225
  Phone: 360-671-1505
  Email: *info@aai.cc*
  Website: *www.aai.cc.com*
  (East Face, East Buttress, Mountaineers Route, and winter
  mountaineering)

Alpine Skills International
    11400 Donner Pass Road
    Truckee, CA 96161
    Phone: 530-582-9170
    Website: *www.alpineskills.com*
    (Avalanche education, East Face, East Buttress, and Mountaineers Route)

Mountain Adventure Seminars
    P.O. Box 5450
    Bear Valley, CA 95223
    Phone: 209-753-6556
    Email: *mail@mtadventure.com*
    Website: *www.mtadventure.com*
    (Avalanche education)

Recreational Equipment Inc.
    REI Adventures
    Phone: 800-622-2236
    Website: *www.rei.com/adventures*
    (Mountaineers Route)

Sierra Mountaineering International
    236 North Main Street
    Bishop, CA 93514
    Phone: 760-872-4929
    Email: *info@sierramountaineering.com*
    Website: *www.sierramountaineering.com*
    (Avalanche education, East Face, East Buttress, and Mountaineers Route)

Sierra Mountain Guides
    P.O. Box 446
    June Lake, CA
    Phone: 760-648-1122
    Website: *www.sierramtnguides.com*
    (Avalanche education, winter climbs of Whitney)

Sierra Wilderness Seminars
  P.O. Box 988, 210-East Lake Street
  Mt. Shasta, CA 96067
  Phone: 1-888-SWS MTNS (797-6867), 866-797-6867, 530-926-6003
  Email: *mail@swsmtns.com*
  Website: *www.swsmtns.com*
  (East Face, East Buttress, Mountaineers Route, and Winter
  Mountaineering Course)

Southern Yosemite Mountain Guides
  621 Highland Ave.
  Santa Cruz, CA 95060
  Phone: 800-231-4575
  Email: info@symg.com
  Website: *www.symg.com*
  (Multi-day backpack trips and horse/mule supported trips with an
  ascent of Whitney)

APPENDIX 6:
A LIST OF FACTS AND FIRSTS

July 2, 1864: Professor William Brewer of Yale University and Charles Hoffman of the California State Geologic Field Survey Party first spotted what appeared to be the highest peak in the land from Mount Brewer. Also part of the field party were James Gardiner, Yale; Clarence King, Yale; and Richard Cotter.

July 6, 1864: After several days of arduous cross-country travel over rugged terrain King and Cotter climbed Mount Tyndall (14,019 feet) and spotted the mountain of their desires still 6 miles away. From Tyndall, they named the peak Mount Whitney in honor of their boss, Josiah Dwight Whitney, professor of geology at Harvard and chief of the California State Geological Survey from 1860–1874.

August 18, 1873: Albert Johnson, John Lucas, and Charles Begole (three Lone Pine fishermen) made the first ascent.

August 20, 1873: William Crapo and Abe Leyda made their ascent. Crapo claimed a first ascent on August 15, 1873, but the evidence is not convincing. The likely date of the climb is August 20, 1873.

September 6, 1873: William Hunter, Carl Rabe, William Crapo, and Tom McDonough completed the third ascent.

September 19, 1873: Clarence King and Frank Knowles were the fourth party to climb the peak.

October 21, 1873: John Muir made the first ascent of the Mountaineers Route.

1875: John Muir made the first ascent of the north face above Arctic Lake.

1878: Mary Martin, Anna Mills, Hope Broughton, and Mrs. R. C. Redd were the first women to climb Whitney.

1881: Professor Samuel Langley, director of the Allegheny Observatory, made the first scientific expedition.

1904: G. P. Marsh of Lone Pine supervised construction of the Mount Whitney Trail. The residents of Lone Pine raised the funds for the trail project.

1909: G. P. Marsh supervised and completed the construction of the summit hut for the Smithsonian Institution.

January 10, 1929: Orland Bartholomew made the first winter ascent during his three-month solo south-to-north ski traverse of the Sierra Nevada.

February 22, 1956: Paul Arthur and Larry Yout made the first recorded ski descent following the Mount Whitney Trail.

August 16, 1931: Norman Clyde, Robert L. M. Underhill, Glen Dawson, and Jules Eichorn made the first technical climb on the east face.

September 5, 1937: Robert Brinton, Glen Dawson, Muir Dawson, Richard Jones, and Howard Koster first climbed the East Buttress.

1974: Galen Rowell was the first to complete a ski descent of the Mountaineers Route.

1983: Allan Bard and Tom Carter made the first ski descent of the north face.

NUMBER OF HIKERS/CLIMBERS REACHING THE SUMMIT

The popularity of the peak has been growing, as evidenced by those recording their names in the summit register. Many of the following summit register counts were provided by Ward Eldridge, Sequoia National Park, based on archived summit registers. The following are rough approximations as pages of the summit register can be misplaced, damaged by the weather, or lost in transport from the summit to Sequoia National Park headquarters. Also, many hikers/climbers do not sign the register. Therefore, the actual number reaching the summit will be greater than represented below.

Year	Number of Names in the Summit Register
1957	2658
1959	5490
1969	8869
1979	6560
1988	6200
1989	5800
1997	9760
1998	8100 *
1999	9520
2000	10,240
2001	12,160
2002	7300 **
2003	11,920
2004	13,200
2005	8800 *
2006	4230 ***

*The relatively low number of hikers reaching the summit in 1998 and 2005 may be attributed to the exceptionally heavy winter snow that blocked the high-elevation trails well into the summer.

**Many pages of the summit register are missing so the number count is understated.

***Includes only data from July 20, 2006, to the end of the year. The winter of 2006 was another heavy snow year so the summit register may not have been placed until July.

Source: Ward Eldridge, Sequoia National Park staff, reviewed archived summit registers for the number of climbers recording their accomplishment. His help is greatly appreciated.

APPENDIX 7: GLOSSARY

arête A sharp, narrow ridge.

aspect The exposure or direction a mountain slope faces.

cairn (rock cairn or rock duck) Three or more rocks placed on top of each other to mark a trail or cross-country route; a conical heap of stones built as a monument or landmark.

cirque A steep excavation high on a mountainside made by glacial erosion; a natural amphitheater.

climbers trail or use trail A route that has evolved over time by the use of many travelers heading toward a common objective such as a remote mountain pass, peak, or alpine lake.

col A gap or notch between high points or between two peaks along a ridge; a high mountain pass.

couloir A steep, deep mountain gash, gully, or chute, usually but not always leading to a col.

cross-country travel Travel in the backcountry without benefit of a maintained trail. Use of compass and map are necessary to keep on course.

edema An abnormal collection of fluid in some part of the body, as in pulmonary edema (an abnormal collection of fluid in the air sacs of the lungs) or cerebral edema (an abnormal collection of fluid in the skull cavity).

fourteener A peak higher than 14,000 feet in elevation. There are 13 such peaks in California (see Appendix 1).

Global Positioning System (GPS) A network of 24 orbiting satellites established by the Department of Defense. These satellites continually broadcast information to earth where GPS receivers use a combination of three or more satellite-transmitted information to triangulate the receiver's position on earth.

John Muir Trail (JMT) The JMT begins in Yosemite Valley and ends on the summit of Mount Whitney, about 220 trail miles later. The PCT and JMT are the same trail for much of the length of the JMT. In this guidebook, where the two trails share a common route, the trail is called the JMT.

High Sierra Trail (HST) The HST starts at Crescent Meadow in Sequoia National Park, crosses the Great Western Divide at Kaweah Gap, and descends to the Kern River before joining the JMT at Wallace Creek—a distance of about 50 miles.

light-emitting diode (LED) Headlamps using LED produce a bright light and require small amounts of battery power to operate.

moraine A mass of rocks, gravel, sand, and clay carried and deposited by a glacier, along its side (lateral moraine), at its lower end (terminal moraine), or beneath the ice and snow (ground moraine).

National Park Service (NPS) The National Park Service administers and manages four national parks in California (Lassen Volcanic, Yosemite, Sequoia, and Kings Canyon National Parks).

Pacific Crest Trail (PCT) The PCT stretches from the U.S.-Canadian border to Mexico. The PCT and the JMT are the same trail for much of the length of the JMT. In this guidebook, where they share a common route, the trail is called the JMT.

scree Small rocks and sand deposited below cliffs or steep mountain slopes, caused by erosion and decay of mountain slopes.

seasons (climbing season) The following arbitrary time segments are used to describe the four climbing seasons. "Early season" is May 16 to July 15, "midseason" is July 16 to September 15, "late season" ranges from September 16 to November 15, and "winter" is the remaining months, November 16 through May 15.

talus Large rock, boulders, and debris deposited at the base of a cliff; a mantle of rock fragments on a slope below a steep rock face.

tarn A small mountain lake or pond, especially one that fills a cirque.

traverse To move across a mountain slope in an oblique manner (slanting or contouring, diagonal to the slope).

United States Forest Service (USFS) The USFS manages the national forests and wilderness areas in California.

United States Geological Survey (USGS) The USGS is responsible for the National Mapping Program. Maps they publish and distribute include elevation (contour) lines.

use trail See climbers trails above.

universal transverse mercator (UTM) Under this coordinate grid system, the world is divided into 60 north–south zones each covering a strip of land 6 degrees wide in longitude. Ten zones cover the conterminous 48 states, from Zone 10 (West Coast) to Zone 19 (New England). Each zone is measured in meters. UTM grid coordinates are drawn on some maps with fine black or blue lines and on others by small blue tick marks in the margins spaced 1000 meters apart.

Mount Whitney and all locations described in this book are in Zone
11. Since most maps are based on North American Datum (NAD)
1927 that is what was used. For example, the UTM coordinates for
the summit of Whitney are 384490mE and 4048710mN. The first
UTM grid value represents the easterly coordinate in meters (mE)
and the second value the northerly coordinate in meters (mN).

APPENDIX 8:
SELECTED BIBLIOGRAPHY
AND REFERENCES

Beck, Charles S. *Trout-Fishing the John Muir Trail*. Portland, OR: Frank Amato Publications, Inc., 2000.

Cox, Steven M., and Kris Fulsaas, eds. *Mountaineering: The Freedom of the Hills*. 7th ed. Seattle: The Mountaineers Books, 2003.

Hellweg, Paul, and Scott McDonald. *Mount Whitney Guide for Hikers and Climbers*. Canoga Park, CA: Canyon Publishing Company, 1994.

Schaerer, Peter. *The Avalanche Handbook*. 3rd ed. Seattle: The Mountaineers Books, 2006.

Moynier, John. *Avalanche Aware: Safe Travel in Avalanche Country*. Helena, MT: Falcon Press, 1998.

Muir, John. "The Cañon of the South Fork of Kings River: A Rival of the Yosemite." *Century Illustrated Monthly Magazine,* 43 (November 1891): 77–97.

Muir, John. "Exhibit." Website maintained by Harold Wood. *www.sierraclub.org/john_muir_exhibit.*

Muir, John. *Our National Parks*. In *John Muir: The Eight Wilderness-Discovery Books*. Seattle: The Mountaineers Books, 1995.

Rébuffat, Gaston. *On Snow and Rock*. New York: Oxford University Press, 1968.

Richins, Jr., Paul. *50 Classic Backcountry Ski and Snowboard Summits in California: Mount Shasta to Mount Whitney*. Seattle: The Mountaineers Books, 1999.

Richins, Jr., Paul. *Trekking California*. Seattle: The Mountaineers Books, 2004.

Roper, Steve. *The Sierra High Route: Traversing Timberline Country*. Seattle: The Mountaineers Books, 1997.

Secor, R. J. *The High Sierra: Peaks, Passes and Trails*. 2nd ed. Seattle: The Mountaineers Books, 1999.

Twight, Mark F. *Extreme Alpinism: Climbing Light, Fast & High*. Seattle: The Mountaineers Books, 1999.

Wheelock, Walt, and Tom Condon. *Climbing Mount Whitney*. Rev. ed. Glendale, CA: La Siesta Press, 1970 (out of print).

INDEX

The author with camera and tripod at Iceberg Lake (Photo by Judi Richins)

ABOUT THE AUTHOR

Paul Richins was raised in Weaverville, California, and started hiking in the Trinity Alps at age twelve. He has more than forty years of wilderness experience backpacking, mountain climbing, and ski mountaineering.

As a longtime member of the American Alpine Club, he has participated in a number of major expeditions to Alaska (west ridge of Mount Hunter and the south ridge of Saint Elias), Canada (east ridge of Mount Logan), Argentina (Cerro Aconcagua), and Tibet (Cho Oyu, the sixth-highest peak in the world). Paul Richins and two climbing partners completed the first winter ascent of the southwest ridge of Stortind, a technically difficult peak in the Lyngen Alps of northern Norway.

He has hiked and climbed extensively throughout the western United States and has climbed hundreds of peaks in California and completed many first ski ascents/descents. He has climbed Mount Whitney numerous times by the various routes detailed in this guidebook, has skied Whitney's Mountaineers Route, and completed a ski circumnavigation of the peak.

Richins is author of three other popular guidebooks—*Trekking California, 50 Classic Backcountry Ski and Snowboard Summits in California,* and *Best Short Hikes in California's South Sierra.* He maintains the Backcountry Resource Center, a website of valuable information for the backcountry skier, climber, and hiker wishing to explore the mountains of California.

Professionally, Richins works for the California Energy Commission managing the work of air quality engineers, biologists, environmental scientists, engineering geologists, and public health specialists. He lives in the Sierra Nevada foothill community of El Dorado Hills, east of Sacramento, California.

Richins is interested in your feedback and encourages your comments and questions. His email address is prichins@jps.net, and his website is *http://pweb.jps.net/~prichins/backcountry_resource_center.htm.*

THE MOUNTAINEERS, founded in 1906, is a nonprofit outdoor activity and conservation club, whose mission is "to explore, study, preserve, and enjoy the natural beauty of the outdoors. . . . " Based in Seattle, Washington, the club is now the third-largest such organization in the United States, with seven branches throughout Washington State.

The Mountaineers sponsors both classes and year-round outdoor activities in the Pacific Northwest, which include hiking, mountain climbing, ski-touring, snowshoeing, bicycling, camping, kayaking, nature study, sailing, and adventure travel. The club's conservation division supports environmental causes through educational activities, sponsoring legislation, and presenting informational programs.

All club activities are led by skilled, experienced instructors, who are dedicated to promoting safe and responsible enjoyment and preservation of the outdoors.

If you would like to participate in these organized outdoor activities or the club's programs, consider a membership in The Mountaineers. For information and an application, write or call The Mountaineers, Club Headquarters, 300 Third Avenue West, Seattle, WA 98119; 206-284-6310. You can also visit the club's website at www.mountaineers.org or contact The Mountaineers via email at clubmail@mountaineers.org.

The Mountaineers Books, an active, nonprofit publishing program of the club, produces guidebooks, instructional texts, historical works, natural history guides, and works on environmental conservation. All books produced by The Mountaineers Books fulfill the club's mission.

Send or call for our catalog of more than 500 outdoor titles:

The Mountaineers Books
1001 SW Klickitat Way, Suite 201
Seattle, WA 98134
800-553-4453
mbooks@mountaineersbooks.org
www.mountaineersbooks.org

The Mountaineers Books is proud to be a corporate sponsor of The Leave No Trace Center for Outdoor Ethics, whose mission is to promote and inspire responsible outdoor recreation through education, research, and partnerships. The Leave No Trace program is focused specifically on human-powered (nonmotorized) recreation.

Leave No Trace strives to educate visitors about the nature of their recreational impacts, as well as offer techniques to prevent and minimize such impacts. Leave No Trace is best understood as an educational and ethical program, not as a set of rules and regulations.

For more information, visit *www.LNT.org*, or call 800-332-4100.

OTHER TITLES YOU MIGHT ENJOY FROM THE MOUNTAINEERS BOOKS

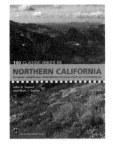

100 Classic Hikes Northern California, 3E
John Soares
The best hikes in a region of spectacular options!

Ice & Mixed Climbing
Will Gadd
"Offers tips and techniques from one of the best in the business . . ."
—*Blue Ridge Outdoors*

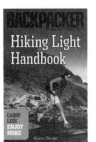

Best Hikes with Dogs: Central California
Linda Mullally and David Mullally
A wide scope of paw-friendly terrain is presented in this handy guide.

Trekking California
Paul Richins Jr.
Complete guide to 20 of California's finest treks

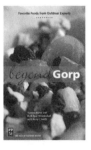

Hiking Light Handbook
Karen Berger
Lightweight strategies from *Backpacker* magazine!

Beyond Gorp
Yvonne Prater and Ruth Mendenhall
Tasty ideas for quick, healthy meals on the trail

The Mountaineers Books has more than 500 outdoor recreation titles in print.
Receive a free catalog at
www.mountaineersbooks.org.